Brecht and Post-1990s British Drama

Methuen Drama Engage offers original reflections about key practitioners, movements and genres in the fields of modern theatre and performance. Each volume in the series seeks to challenge mainstream critical thought through original and interdisciplinary perspectives on the body of work under examination. By questioning existing critical paradigms, it is hoped that each volume will open up fresh approaches and suggest avenues for further exploration.

Series Editors
Mark Taylor-Batty
University of Leeds, UK
Enoch Brater
University of Michigan, USA

Titles
Contemporary Drag Practices and Performers: Drag in a Changing Scene Volume 1
Edited by Mark Edward and Stephen Farrier
ISBN 978-1-3500-8294-6
Performing the Unstageable: Success, Imagination, Failure
Karen Quigley
ISBN 978-1-3500-5545-2
Drama and Digital Arts Cultures
David Cameron, Michael Anderson and Rebecca Wotzko
ISBN 978-1-472-59219-4
Social and Political Theatre in 21st-Century Britain: Staging Crisis
Vicky Angelaki
ISBN 978-1-474-21316-5
Watching War on the Twenty-First-Century Stage: Spectacles of Conflict
Clare Finburgh
ISBN 978-1-472-59866-0
Fiery Temporalities in Theatre and Performance: The Initiation of History
Maurya Wickstrom
ISBN 978-1-4742-8169-0
Ecologies of Precarity in Twenty-First Century Theatre: Politics, Affect, Responsibility
Marissia Fragkou
ISBN 978-1-4742-6714-4
Robert Lepage/Ex Machina: Revolutions in Theatrical Space
James Reynolds
ISBN 978-1-4742-7609-2
Social Housing in Performance: The English Council Estate on and off Stage
Katie Beswick
ISBN 978-1-4742-8521-6
Postdramatic Theatre and Form
Edited by Michael Shane Boyle, Matt Cornish and Brandon Woolf
ISBN 978-1-3500-4316-9

For a complete listing, please visit
https://www.bloomsbury.com/series/methuen-drama-engage/

Brecht and Post-1990s British Drama

Dialectical Theatre Today

Anja Hartl

Series Editors: Mark Taylor-Batty and Enoch Brater

methuen | drama
LONDON • NEW YORK • OXFORD • NEW DELHI • SYDNEY

METHUEN DRAMA
Bloomsbury Publishing Plc
50 Bedford Square, London, WC1B 3DP, UK
1385 Broadway, New York, NY 10018, USA
29 Earlsfort Terrace, Dublin 2, Ireland

BLOOMSBURY, METHUEN DRAMA and the Methuen Drama logo are trademarks of Bloomsbury Publishing Plc

First published in Great Britain 2021
Paperback edition published 2022

Copyright © Anja Hartl, 2021, 2022

Anja Hartl has asserted her right under the Copyright, Designs and Patents Act, 1988, to be identified as author of this work.

For legal purposes the Acknowledgements on pp. vi-vii constitute an extension of this copyright page.

Series design by Louise Dugdale
Cover image: Linda Bassett as Mrs. Jarrett in *Escaped Alone* by Caryl Churchill at the Royal Court Theatre, London (2016) (© Johan Persson / Arenapal)

All rights reserved. No part of this publication may be reproduced or transmitted in any form or by any means, electronic or mechanical, including photocopying, recording, or any information storage or retrieval system, without prior permission in writing from the publishers.

Bloomsbury Publishing Plc does not have any control over, or responsibility for, any third-party websites referred to or in this book. All internet addresses given in this book were correct at the time of going to press. The author and publisher regret any inconvenience caused if addresses have changed or sites have ceased to exist, but can accept no responsibility for any such changes.

A catalogue record for this book is available from the British Library.

A catalog record for this book is available from the Library of Congress.

ISBN: HB: 978-1-3501-7278-4
PB: 978-1-3502-0184-2
ePDF: 978-1-3501-7280-7
eBook: 978-1-3501-7279-1

Series: Engage

Typeset by Newgen KnowledgeWorks Pvt. Ltd., Chennai, India

To find out more about our authors and books visit www.bloomsbury.com and sign up for our newsletters.

Contents

Acknowledgements	vi
Introduction	1
Revisiting Brecht's Dialectical Theatre	4
Rethinking Dialectics via Adorno and Rancière	12
Towards a Post-Brechtian Theatre	18
1 'In-Yer-Face' Theatre and the Crisis of Dialectics: Mark Ravenhill's Post-Brechtian Drama in Anti-Dialectical Times	29
The Post-Brechtian Parable: *Some Explicit Polaroids*	31
Resisting the Banal Dialectic of (Counter-)Terrorism: *Shoot/Get Treasure/Repeat*	41
Conclusion	61
2 Reimagining Brecht: David Greig's Theatre of Dissensus	63
Appropriating the Imagination: *Dunsinane*	66
Interrupting Empathy: *The Events*	82
Conclusion	98
3 Strategic Naivety: The Dialectic of Sincerity in Andy Smith and Tim Crouch's Work	101
Post-Brechtian Meta-Theatre: *all that is solid melts into air*	104
The Limits of Sincerity: *The Author*	117
Conclusion	129
4 Political Theatre between Dialectics and Absurdity: Caryl Churchill's Twenty-First-Century Plays	131
Dystopian Negativity: *Escaped Alone*	136
Deconstructing the Dialectic: *Here We Go*	152
Conclusion	166
Conclusion	167
Bibliography	173
Index	189

Acknowledgements

Working on this interdisciplinary and intercultural project has involved a great deal of literal and metaphorical travelling over the past years between different places, cultures, disciplines and areas of research. This fascinating journey would soon have reached a dead end without the inspiring encounters with the many teachers, colleagues and friends who have so kindly engaged with my work on the way, helping me find new and exciting directions for my project. The idea for this book originated during a stay at the University of Edinburgh and I am grateful to Randall Stevenson for sparking my interest in Brecht and British theatre, which developed into a doctoral dissertation project at the University of Konstanz. I would like to express my immense gratitude to Christina Wald, my primary PhD supervisor, for her confidence and belief in me, for her diligent engagement with my work and for her ongoing support and advice over many years. My sincerest thanks go to my co-supervisor Martin Middeke for tirelessly supporting my project from its earliest stages at the University of Augsburg until its completion and beyond, for his thought-provoking criticism and for generously sharing his expertise. I would also like to thank Silvia Mergenthal who, together with Christina Wald and Martin Middeke, examined the thesis on 22 July 2019.

I have received generous help from the academic community at the Department of Literature, Art and Media Studies at the University of Konstanz. I would like to thank the participants of the research seminars for their valuable feedback; Juliane Vogel for her invitation to present my work in her colloquium; Michael Frank for his fruitful suggestions; and Julia Boll and Susanne Köller for their collegiality and friendship, without which the process of writing this book would not have been the same.

Over the past several years, I have been fortunate to have the support of the International Brecht Society, which has given me the opportunity to discuss and publish my work in multiple contexts. I am especially grateful to David Barnett, Tom Kuhn, Marc Silberman, Hans-Thies Lehmann, Steve Giles and Kris Imbrigotta for their constructive feedback and advice throughout; I am also indebted to Jürgen Hillesheim from the Bertolt-Brecht-Forschungsstelle Augsburg for his keen interest in my project.

I owe much to the members of the German Society for Contemporary Theatre and Drama in English (CDE) and the warm and enriching academic environment they have created. Special thanks go to Clare Wallace for her thorough and kind criticism of my work in the postgraduate forum

Acknowledgements vii

and beyond, as well as to Mireia Aragay, Cristina Delgado-García, Ariane de Waal, Clara Escoda, Jen Harvie, Heidi Liedke, Trish Reid, Verónica Rodríguez, Liz Tomlin, Enric Monforte, Graham Saunders, Aleks Sierz, Peter-Paul Schnierer and Eckart Voigts for their support and the stimulating discussions. I am also grateful to Martin Puchner for his insightful feedback, and would like to thank the German Shakespeare Society and Kirsten Sandrock, Lukas Lammers, Tobias Döring and Felix Sprang for their interest and support. Last but not least, I am grateful to Gordon McMullan for his early modern perspective on the contemporary and for providing food for thought whenever needed.

This project was funded by the German National Academic Foundation from 2016 to 2019 and I am thankful for the unique opportunity to participate in their academic programme. I have also benefited from several research trips which would have been impossible without the financial support of both the German Excellence Initiative and the mentoring programme of the Office of Equal Opportunities, Family Affairs and Diversity at the University of Konstanz. I especially wish to thank Vicky Angelaki for her mentorship before, during and after these research stays, and the staff and postgraduate students at the Department of Film, Theatre and Television at the University of Reading for welcoming me so warmly.

For kindly discussing their work with me, I wish to express my gratitude to playwrights Mark Ravenhill, David Greig and Tim Crouch and to Andy Smith, who very generously shared early drafts of his plays with me.

I am particularly grateful to Methuen Drama's Engage series editors Enoch Brater and Mark Taylor-Batty for their belief in this project and for their valuable feedback. The kind support, expertise and enthusiasm of Meredith Benson at Bloomsbury have turned the publication process of my first book into a swift, delightful and rewarding experience. I would also like to thank the Centre for Cultural Inquiry at the University of Konstanz for generously funding the editing process and Cecily Jones for her meticulous engagement with my work.

My most heartfelt thanks go to my family, my parents Sieglinde and Anton Haslinger and my grandparents Anna and Ernst Thiel for their loving and unwavering emotional support, their patience and their faith in me. For sharing the adventure of this project with me, for his unflagging positive spirit throughout and for gently reminding me that there is, in Brechtian spirit, *always* an alternative, the final and greatest thank you is reserved for my husband Michael.

Introduction

'It's that man again: Bertolt Brecht' – this is theatre critic Michael Billington's somewhat wry observation at the beginning of an article provocatively titled 'Bertolt Brecht: Irresistible Force or Forgotten Chapter in Theatrical History?', published in the *Guardian* in 2013. The question Billington raises is pertinent. A sense of crisis has pervaded both politics and the arts since the end of the twentieth century, with fundamental political, social and philosophical parameters shifting considerably under the impact of postmodernism, the demise of socialism and the global spread of neoliberalism. In this ambivalent, disorientating and unsettling environment – sometimes described as post-Marxist, post-ideological or even post-political – the forms and functions of political theatre have been radically interrogated (Kershaw 1999: 16). In Britain, these global trends have been reinforced by specific national developments in the political and cultural sectors, where the legacy of Margaret Thatcher's rule has arguably had a profoundly depoliticizing effect in the arts and in society (Kritzer 2008: 218). At the same time, however, a renewed interest in notions of political engagement and the possibility of resistance has become palpable in artistic practice and criticism alike since the turn of the millennium (Lavender 2016: 3). Crucially, as Billington's article correctly suggests, it is in particular Brecht who has played a significant role in this (re)turn to the political in Britain. His plays have not only enjoyed a conspicuous presence on the twenty-first-century British stage but have also represented an important touchstone for contemporary British playwrights such as David Harrower, Tanika Gupta, Mark Ravenhill and Simon Stephens, who have prolifically engaged with his works and have created new translations and adaptations of his texts. Given this genuine and ongoing commitment to Brecht's legacy on the part of British theatre practitioners, Brecht is far from being a 'forgotten chapter' in the history of British theatre – on the contrary, the contemporary moment seems to provide fertile ground for creative and stimulating encounters with Brecht and his oeuvre.

Crucially, Brecht's significance is reflected not only by the dramatists' rewritings of his plays but also, and most importantly, by some of their own theatrical works, which can, as I propose, be usefully described as post-Brechtian. As a wide range of examples discussed in this study will illustrate,

Brecht's concept of dialectical drama represents a privileged aesthetic mode in the broader context of political theatre at the turn of the millennium, and may therefore provide a valuable lens through which to approach and understand contemporary British drama. Investigating the forms and functions of Brecht's theoretical and aesthetic legacy in post-1990s British theatre, this book argues more specifically that the last decade of the twentieth century does not only represent a watershed moment in Britain from a political, social, economic and cultural perspective but also marks a turning point with regard to the role of the (post-)Brechtian in British drama. While the plays discussed in the following chapters substantiate the claim of an ongoing impact of Brecht's model as a salient – if by far not the only – method in the burgeoning field of political playwriting in Britain, they also offer a decidedly more critical approach to the German theatre practitioner's work. Even though Brecht's ongoing presence in contemporary British playwriting has been widely acknowledged, a comprehensive and systematic assessment of the challenges and implications of applying Brechtian principles of theatremaking in Britain today has not yet been undertaken. Only recently have scholars begun to recognize the importance of taking the complexity inherent in Brecht's concept into account as a prerequisite for unlocking its potential for the present moment. Taking up this renewed interest in a more thorough interrogation of Brechtian theatre, this study contends that Brecht's legacy in contemporary British drama must be understood as twofold, encompassing both a practical and, significantly, a theoretical level. What distinguishes Brecht's approach is his application of key principles of dialectical thought to playwriting and theatre-making to facilitate critical analysis and spectatorial engagement as a prerequisite for change and intervention – within as well as outside the theatre space. To the extent that the political fabric of Brecht's theatre model is fundamentally shaped by his engagement with dialectics, I argue that an acknowledgement of the significance of dialectical philosophy represents the key to understanding Brecht's role in contemporary drama, as it does not only enlighten the challenges of bringing Brecht into dialogue with the twenty-first-century moment but, paradoxically, also offers rich potential for applying his concept today. Interrogating the role of Brechtian dialectical theatre as a means of spurring resistance and ideological critique in the contemporary context, this book examines how the selected plays critically and self-consciously engage with Brecht's concept as a source of both inspiration and contestation for the purpose of developing a radical form of Brechtian-inspired political drama for the new millennium.

Significantly, the 'special relationship' between Brecht and British theatre which can be identified in the twenty-first century builds on a long history of creative exchange spanning the entire second half of the twentieth century.

Indeed, it is widely acknowledged that Brecht has represented a potent force on the British theatre landscape since the late 1950s. It is notably the visit of the Berliner Ensemble, Brecht's theatre company, to London in 1956 (only shortly after Brecht's death) which brought his works to the attention of theatre-makers and audiences in Britain, thereby initiating a significant turning point in the history of British theatre (Stevenson 2004: 29; Willett 1990: 79). The gradual evolution and growing significance of a distinctly Brechtian style of theatre-making in twentieth-century drama in Britain has been meticulously researched. Janelle Reinelt's seminal *After Brecht: British Epic Theatre* (1996) provides the most extensive account of British playwrights' engagement with Brecht between the 1960s and early 1990s. Focusing on the work of Howard Brenton, David Hare, Edward Bond, Trevor Griffiths, Caryl Churchill and John McGrath, Reinelt identifies the emergence of 'a hybrid British form of recognizably Brechtian theatre' (1996: 1). Applying a deliberately loose understanding of Brechtian theatre practice, Reinelt's emphasis on 'hybridity' does not only reflect the versatility of Brecht's model but also acknowledges the importance of other styles shaping the dramatists' works in conjunction with the Brechtian mode, foregrounding 'significant extensions, transformations, and even abandonments' (1996: 1) of Brecht's epic theatre in the playwrights' dramaturgies.

Speculating about the future of Brechtian drama, Reinelt rather pessimistically suggests that, in the light of the profound transformations of the late 1980s and early 1990s in the aftermath of the fall of the Berlin Wall and in the wake of Thatcher's uncompromisingly conservative rule in Britain, 'the "fittingness" of Brechtian dramaturgy has changed or slipped' (1996: 4). While this diagnosis has, as shown above, turned out to be unjustified, the continuous engagement with Brechtian theatre evident in contemporary British drama does indeed raise urgent questions which this book addresses: what implications do the radical changes of the past decades have for political theatre in general, and for Brecht's concept more specifically? How can Brechtian theatre be reimagined under these conditions as a radical device for theatre-making and as a useful tool for analysing contemporary drama? How does this implicit engagement with Brecht manifest itself in the playtexts? Which aspects have remained pertinent, and how do the plays perhaps also revise and go beyond Brecht's model? Crucially, acknowledging the possibility of Brecht's potential for the new millennium, Reinelt considers her book 'necessarily unfinished – that is, not tidy, not conclusive' (1996: 208). Taking up her implicit appeal to continue investigating the 'special relationship' between Brecht and Britain in spite of, or precisely because of, these difficulties, I situate my study to some extent in continuity with Reinelt's groundbreaking work. Critically examining how to bring Brecht into conversation with the twenty-first-century context, I suggest that Brechtian dialectics may still provide a useful methodology for understanding contemporary British theatre. Tracing the emergence of what I define as a post-Brechtian mode of theatre-making, I argue that it is above all the self-conscious interrogation of Brecht's model which reunites the plays discussed in this study. Here, however, my approach deliberately departs from Reinelt's loose treatment of the Brechtian paradigm. To offer a detailed and comprehensive analysis of Brecht's complex role on the contemporary British stage, I consider it indispensable to rigorously interrogate the philosophical premises underpinning Brecht's concept. For this purpose, the following sections will introduce and problematize this theoretical core, which can be located in Brecht's commitment to dialectics as a worldview, a method of analysis and a dramaturgical strategy, before considering possibilities of reimagining this dialectical model as a progressive tool for theatre-making for the twenty-first-century context.

Revisiting Brecht's Dialectical Theatre

'Brecht' is a label we frequently encounter in a variety of scholarly and non-academic contexts. Yet, which 'Brecht' are we in fact referring to when we ascribe a 'Brechtian' quality to playtexts or performances – the formal innovator of epic theatre, the Marxist, the director and practitioner, the dialectical theorist or even the poet? Despite the widespread usage of the term, this question usually remains unanswered, as the precise meaning and the implications of employing the category are only rarely accounted for. Instead, terms like 'Brecht' or 'Brechtian' are, in a majority of cases, used as supposedly self-explanatory 'shorthand[s] for ideas that are both specific and … complex' (Barnett 2015: 2). Challenging these tendencies which have produced reductive and misleading interpretations, David Barnett has offered an influential reconsideration of Brecht's method in his study *Brecht in Practice* (2015), in which he emphasizes that 'Brecht's contribution to theatre-making cannot be restricted to the innovations he introduced into theatre practice' and rather suggests that '[t]hey are a product of his method', which must above all be considered profoundly 'politicized' (2015: 5). As Barnett has argued, this political core of Brecht's model is key to understanding his theatrical experiments and is intricately connected to his interest in dialectical philosophy, which represents the 'non-negotiable prerequisite' (2015: 24) of Brechtian theatre. Indeed, it is through dialectics that the relation between the political fabric of his plays and his aesthetic innovations can be explained. In this vein, scholarship on both Brecht and contemporary applications of his theatre theory and practice has gradually begun to examine more closely and productively the role of dialectical thinking in Brechtian drama, initiating a shift in critical paradigm as well as in perceptions of Brecht and political theatre more broadly (Carney 2005; Stevens 2016). Without wanting to restate these insightful claims, I intend to expand on this groundbreaking work in this book by considering the dialectical legacy from a contemporary vantage point as a prerequisite for better understanding the forms and functions of Brecht's theatre model today. As I contend, it is precisely from Brecht's turn to dialectics that not only major obstacles but also a significant potential for Brechtian theatre may emerge for our times.

One of the reasons why dialectics constitutes such a highly contested – perhaps therefore to some extent neglected – field of enquiry, both within Brecht scholarship and beyond, is the fact that it has represented a central line of thought in Western philosophy ever since Antiquity, and has come to '[mean] quite different things in different contexts' (Ollman and Smith 2008: 2) as a result. Thus, over the centuries, the concept has considerably developed and has acquired a variety of meanings, which is complicated by the fact that it does not only describe a particular way of apprehending reality but also serves as a method of critical analysis and, in Brecht's case, functions as an aesthetic strategy. According to Lara Stevens, therefore, dialectics is 'both the means and tend[s] towards a desirable end point' (2016: 25). Critically engaging with this complex legacy, Brecht specifically draws on Karl Marx's dialectical theory, which is itself derived from Georg W. F. Hegel. What first and foremost attracted Brecht's attention to Marxist dialectics is its decidedly practical perspective, which is notably reflected in an emphasis on materialism. Applying dialectical principles to reality and taking into account the concrete conditions of life in society, Marx is convinced, as Stevens summarizes, that 'they can serve a real world function' (Stevens 2016: 25). This is above all evident in Marx's critique of capitalism and his 'desire to expose capitalist ideology and the socio-economic conditions that it generates' (Stevens 2016: 30) with the help of dialectical thinking. It is here that Stevens rightly identifies the ongoing significance of dialectical criticism for our times, since 'we continue to live under a powerful and ubiquitous capitalist system and struggle with its contradictions' (2016: 20). This subversive potential is taken up by Brecht and turned into the *raison d'être* of his dialectical theatre model. It is therefore crucial to acknowledge that it is these fundamental theoretical and philosophical considerations which have spurred Brecht's aesthetic innovations (rather than the other way around). To reflect the significance of these premises, Brecht's terminology also shifted in later years from 'epic' to 'dialectical' theatre. In a self-critical move, Brecht himself rejected the original label as 'entirely general and indefinite, almost formalistic' (2015a: 284) to the extent that it has invited fundamental misunderstandings about his intentions. Indeed, what distinguishes Brecht's concept is precisely not its epic, that is, formal elements (which he had himself borrowed from a variety of sources in the first place, ranging from the Ancient Greeks to Shakespeare to Asian theatre traditions), but the dialectical uses they were put to.

Essentially, a dialectical approach analyses social reality in terms of contradictions, which constitute a powerful motor for transformation: a thesis and a dichotomously opposed antithesis are brought into tension, with the aim of negotiating and resolving the contradiction through a process of synthesization, out of which a new thesis develops, and so on. This process is vividly illustrated by Brecht's poem 'In Praise of Dialectics', which is recited by the character Pelagea Vlassova at the end of the play *The Mother* and which reads like an agenda for Brecht's artistic project:

> Those still alive can't say 'never'.
> No certainty can be certain
> If it cannot stay as it is.
> When the rulers have already spoken
> That is when the ruled start speaking.
> Who dares to talk of 'never'?
> Whose fault is it if oppression still remains? It's ours.
> Whose job will it be to get rid of it? Just ours.
> Whoever's been beaten down must get to his feet.
> He who is lost must give battle.
> He who is aware where he stands – how can anyone stop him moving on?
> Those who were losers today will be triumphant tomorrow
> And from never will come today.
>
> Brecht (1997: 151)

With dialectical contradictions determining its structure and line of argumentation, this poem represents a passionate defence of dialectical thinking – both as an epistemological strategy for apprehending reality and as an aesthetic method. The belief in change and the resulting possibility of intervention in the supposedly natural, fixed order of society and politics it articulates constitute the heart of dialectics, which posits an essentially dynamic, flexible and fluid understanding of historical development. Rather than aiming to re-establish identity, totality and harmony – concepts dialectical thinking has often been reduced to – dialecticians emphasize that 'real change is both possible and evident' (Barnett 2017: 246). It is through this focus on the potentially transformable quality of history, society and politics that the dialectic acquires its progressive and radical significance. Rather than presenting the social and political order as intrinsic, dialectical thinking makes it possible to perceive the process of historical development as subject to decisions for one and against another option, from which a fundamental agency and a possibility of intervention in the course of things can be derived, as Stevens explains: 'the dynamic nature of the dialectic enables humans to view themselves as both victims and potential agents of change, both objects and subjects simultaneously' (2016: 24). This is reflected in the poem's forceful call for action ('No certainty will be certain / If it cannot stay as it is'), the extent to which it raises awareness of the individual's agency ('Whose job will it be to get rid of it? Just ours.') and its optimistic attitude towards the emancipatory quality of art. Hence, dialectics aims to challenge any unquestioning approach to reality by offering a critical perspective that makes it possible to look underneath the surface of social and political ideology, thereby empowering individuals to identify a potential for change – core convictions which have defined Brecht's approach to political art in his theoretical writings, his prose and poetry and, above all, his theatrical undertakings.

Applying dialectics as a dramaturgical method to the theatre, Brecht aims to stage a dialectical view of reality which reveals the contradictions underlying social relations and, on this basis, to encourage dialectical thinking in the audience as a prerequisite for critique and intervention. Brecht's theatre is therefore characterized first and foremost by its prioritization of the principle of contradiction, which shapes the plays on the level of content and form, and determines the interaction between stage and auditorium. Thus, as Fredric Jameson stresses, 'we may honor Brecht for his insistence on this requirement, and for his lesson, in a great variety of contexts and forms, that dialectical thinking begins with the contradiction, that it means finding the inevitable contradiction at the heart of things and seeing and reconstructing them in terms of contradictions' (2008: 120). This eminent dialectical concern is most notably encapsulated in the concept of *Verfremdung*, which represents '[t]he cornerstone of Brecht's theory' (Diamond 1997: 45). Despite its central importance, however, *Verfremdung* is also one of the most fiercely contested notions in Brecht's theory, as it has invited a considerable degree of terminological confusion – both in German and in English (Silberman, Giles and Kuhn 2015: 5). According to Brecht, *Verfremdung* is 'supposed to remove only from those incidents that can be influenced socially the stamp of familiarity that protects them against intervention today' (2015a: 242). Hence, the process of making the familiar strange aims to facilitate a fresh perspective on reality – one which, ideally, reflects an awareness of potential alternative scenarios and the fundamental changeability at the heart of society and politics. To achieve this, *Verfremdung* serves to encourage thinking in contradictions and thereby creates a dynamic understanding of social reality: 'for anything that has not been altered for a long time seems to be unalterable' (Brecht 2015a: 242). This critique of what is presented as the ostensibly natural order by challenging common patterns of perception is enabled by a certain instability and liminality inherent in dialectical representation, as it oscillates between the familiar and the unfamiliar, the ordinary and the extraordinary, as Brecht writes: 'A representation producing *Verfremdung* is one that allows us to recognize an object, but at the same time makes it appear strange' (2015a: 241). Consequently, offering a fundamentally estranged representation of reality on stage serves to transform spectatorial viewing habits with the aim not just of gaining insight into the functioning of society but also of fostering critique and spurring intervention. As Bruce McConachie succinctly explains, *Verfremdung* is 'a triadic operation for audiences – from contentment with the normal, to bewilderment about its strangeness, to the insight that the normal must be transformed' (2012: 155). What is fruitfully combined in *Verfremdung* is thus a metatheatrical endeavour with a political investment. Essentially, it is a self-reflexive strategy that undermines and 'reboots' (Silberman, Giles and Kuhn 2015: 5) conventional approaches to performance and spectatorship by self-consciously drawing attention to the artificiality of the theatre and by de-automating spectators' patterns of interpretation, thereby generating curiosity and amazement about otherwise ordinary events. Ideally, these metatheatrical experiments and insights are subsequently applied to an analysis of society: 'If the audience can recognize the stage as an artificial configuration then it is Brecht's (perhaps overly optimistic) hope that they can equally notice the ideologically constructed elements in the real-world systems outside the theatre' (Stevens 2016: 37).

This intricate relation between theatre and reality hinges on a fundamentally revised understanding of realism, which Brecht reinterprets in dialectical terms. Rejecting conventional realist modes which aim for an accurate representation of reality, Brecht's approach seeks to convey a particular 'stance, a positioning of oneself towards reality' (Barnett 2015: 104). Thus, in dialectical theatre, it is crucial 'to make reality talk' (Brecht 2015a: 53): 'The problem is that making reality recognizable in the theatre is just one of the tasks of true realism. You still need to be able to see through this reality, though. The laws that determine how the processes of life develop must be made visible' (Brecht 2015b: 98). This effect hinges on an oscillatory movement between typicality, on the one hand, and abstraction and stylization, on the other. Thus, while making situations and characters recognizable to expose the social constraints within which they are forced to operate, dialectical realism also adopts a certain distance, which makes it possible to lay bare the fundamentally (ideologically) constructed nature of reality and to identify the power relations and interests shaping common perceptions of society and politics. It is thus a question of establishing a precarious balance between authenticity and artificiality, between identification and critical analysis and hence between 'retaining the surface of reality' to make it familiar, on the one hand, and 'distrusting reality's surfaces' and 'probing the ways in which it is constructed' (Barnett 2015: 106), on the other. It is this dialectical core of Brecht's realist method that encapsulates the essence of his theatrical project, in which theory and practice, fiction and reality as well as society and theatre coalesce and fruitfully intersect to form a radical model of political drama.

Representing the pillar of his approach to theatre-making, *Verfremdung* and dialectical realism set the frame for the specific formal characteristics of Brecht's plays. In scholarly accounts of epic theatre, these aesthetic features have often been prioritized over a consideration of the political motivations behind Brecht's innovations and therefore represent a well-rehearsed formula, almost a stereotype. However, it is crucial to emphasize that these familiar traits of epic theatre must be considered, in line with Brecht's dialectical way of thinking, as historically specific themselves and thus as open to change and adaptation. In this spirit, Brecht self-consciously acknowledges that '[m]ethods become exhausted; stimuli no longer work. New problems appear and demand new methods. Reality changes; in order to represent it, modes of representation must also change' (Brecht 1977: 82). The concrete strategies employed in contemporary drama to realize a dialectical dramaturgy will therefore necessarily have to differ from Brecht's if they are to unfold a progressive impetus on stage. As Duška Radosavljević asserts, 'it is the understanding of the principles of his philosophy of theatre, rather than any prescriptive rules distilled from it, that help us to recognize Brecht's influence in certain twenty-first-century theatre trends' (2013: 125). Hence, I will limit myself at this stage to introducing two fundamental principles of *Verfremdung* underlying Brecht's dialectical stagecraft which will be of particular relevance for the analyses in this book – interruption and emphasis on the social dimension – before providing concrete examples of how they are realized dramaturgically in contemporary British playwriting and performance in the following chapters.

Putting the idea of *Verfremdung* into practice, interruption can be described as a key strategy in Brechtian epic theatre because it serves to foster an attitude of analysis and critique in the audience. It is in particular Walter Benjamin who has foregrounded the significant role of interruptions in

Brecht's theatre model: 'The interrupting of the action is one of the principal concerns of epic theatre' (1998: 24). For this purpose, Brechtian theatre aims for 'disunity' (Brecht 2015a: 242) created by a 'radical *separation of the elements*' (Brecht 2015a: 65) as its guiding aesthetic principle. This is first and foremost achieved through the integration of epic elements of narrative mediation, as they disrupt the play on the level of both dramatic plot and form to allow spectators to 'interpose [their] judgement' (Brecht 2015a: 251). As Lindsay B. Cummings explains, interruption has a fundamental impact on the audience's experience of a performance, as it 'call[s] attention to the spectator's role as interpreter and offering the audience alternatives to the action on stage' (2016: 42). It is through this self-reflexivity enhanced by Brecht's interruptive aesthetics that analysis and critique are facilitated in the relation between stage and auditorium.

This emphasis on interruption is intricately tied to Brecht's interest in the social rather than individual dimension of characters, actions and events. This is paradoxically realized through an emphasis on showing rather than telling, which effectively blurs dramatic and epic paradigms in performance. Crucially, a dialectical perspective considers individuals in terms of their wider social context, acknowledging the conflicts, contradictions and dissonances that exist in society as well as their impact on individual lives. As a result, Brecht's plays aim to foreground the conditions under which decisions are made by the characters, underlining social factors and suggesting potential alternatives. This principle is encapsulated most comprehensively by the concept of gestus, which represents a 'notion that connects theatre event, society and audience by making actions observable, pointing to the structurally defining causes behind them and enabling social critique' (Silberman, Giles and Kuhn 2015: 6). Combining 'sensual activities (gestures) and ideas or social meanings (gists)' (Mumford 2009: 55), gestus goes beyond the gestural to also inform a play's use of music and language: it is 'a matter ... of overall attitudes' (Brecht 2015a: 167) and thereby determines the relationship between theatre and social reality to the extent that it 'exceeds the play, opening it to the social and discursive ideologies that inform its production' (Diamond 1997: 53). Significantly, Benjamin foregrounds gestus as Brecht's most important technique – '[e]pic theatre is gestural' – and in fact, gestus and interruption, presented here as the two fundamental principles of Brechtian theatre, are intimately connected in Benjamin's understanding: 'the more frequently we interrupt someone engaged in an action, the more gestures we obtain' (1998: 3). Together, these two strategies thus help realize a dialectical dramaturgy by uncovering the contradictions underlying a dramatic situation to make them available for analysis and critique.

What distinguishes Brecht's dialectical dramaturgy most strikingly from other models of theatre of his time is the centrality it attributes to the audience. Thus, the key principles underpinning Brechtian theatre are, ultimately, all designed to foreground the spectators and to redefine the relationship between stage and auditorium. In this sense, the success of Brecht's project hinges above all on the audience's engagement with the performance. Given the responsibility the audience is charged with in the process of interpretation, Brecht's model has also been described as a 'theatre of the spectator' (Fischer-Lichte 2004: 324). To emphasize their fundamental importance, Brecht himself goes so far as to say that spectators become 'theatricalized' (2015a: 58). Hence, in Brecht's understanding, '[i]ndividuals are not just consumers any more – they have to produce. The event is only a half-event without them as participants' (Brecht 2015a: 58). Importantly, this emphasis on the participatory quality of Brecht's concept as a prerequisite for active engagement to some extent challenges the stereotypical view of Brechtian theatre as based on reason and distance, as opposed to feelings and proximity. This widespread orthodoxy overlooks, however, that the dialectical way of thinking Brecht aims to encourage in the audience has never been a question of the intellect alone. Rather, as Brecht himself states, his theatre 'by no means renounces emotions …; it is so far from renouncing these that it … tries to arouse or reinforce them. The "critical attitude" that it tries to awaken in its audience cannot be passionate enough for it' (2015a: 264). While characteristic of Brecht's provocative way of theorizing, this recognition makes a more nuanced treatment of the relationship between reason and emotion in Brechtian theatre indispensable, as feelings may, after all, perform a decisive role for the political impetus of his plays. What is crucial about the use of emotions for Brecht is that, rather than inviting the spectators to unquestioningly imitate the characters' emotional reactions, dialectical theatre needs to facilitate 'a critical approach to the spectator's emotions' (2015a: 163), which makes it possible to analyse not only the play itself but, in a self-reflexive turn, also the spectators' own (affective and rational) engagement with the performance. The significance Brecht attributes to the audience members can therefore be understood as an implicit acknowledgement of the essentially unpredictable nature of the process of interpretation. Consequently, it is important to recognize that Brecht's concept is not, as often assumed, characterized by its didactic quality, but rather by a fundamental openness. Instead of dictating a specific lesson, dialectical theatre is designed to make a variety of options available to its spectators; it is emancipating to the extent that it seeks to turn them into dialecticians. In this sense, Brechtian theatre must be understood as situated in a liminal space, where it reunites conflicting poles within its framework. Oscillating between epic and dramatic, tradition and avant-garde, aesthetics and politics as well as reason and emotion, Brecht's concept reflects an inherent instability, and it is this ambiguity which lends itself to adaptation in the contemporary context, opening up a considerable potential for reimagining Brecht in the twenty-first century.

Rethinking Dialectics via Adorno and Rancière

As the previous section has outlined, my reading challenges received understandings of Brechtian theatre by foregrounding the essentially undogmatic nature of Brecht's politics, and by emphasizing a fundamental openness at the heart of his conceptualization of dialectics. This approach has revealed an 'other Brecht', one who prefigures twenty-first-century concerns and artistic practices, particularly regarding questions of spectatorship and participation, thereby paving the way for a productive dialogue between Brecht and the new millennium. This dialogue is, however, highly controversial, fraught with conflicts and subject to tensions; it is, in a way, dialectical in itself, since it is shaped by the paradoxes involved in reconciling Brecht's early- to mid-twentieth-century framework with contemporary lived experience. Notably, the demise of socialism and the triumph of capitalist globalization seem to have created obstacles for applying conventional forms of dialectical thought based on notions of dichotomy and harmonization to a critical analysis of social reality. In this respect, the impact of neoliberal ideology has been particularly pervasive. Successfully imposing itself as the seemingly only viable economic system, it has subjected everything – not only in the economic but also in the social, cultural and, most importantly, private spheres – to the laws of the market, turning citizens into consumers, and attributing commercial value to material as well as immaterial goods (Solga 2016: 9; Brown 2017; Harvey 2005: 2). Through this mechanism, it has ostensibly paralyzed our capacity to think dialectically, to imagine alternatives and to intervene in social reality; instead of stimulating debate, it has promoted consensus, thereby obstructing dialectical criticism based on notions of difference and contradiction. As Sean Carney concludes, 'we increasingly lose the ability to think dialectically' under these circumstances as 'the negation of capitalism's mythic universal becomes increasingly impossible' (2005: 185).

Intimately connected to the anti-dialectical impulses of neoliberalism is the impact of postmodernism, which Jameson has described as the 'cultural logic of late capitalism' in the title of his influential study (1991). Postmodernist ideology is often presented as having had a similarly destructive effect on dialectical processes, as its characteristic suspicion towards all forms of totality is thought to have destabilized dialectical notions of teleology and clarity, as well as processes of synthesization based on binary structures and absolute values. Particularly in response to Jean-François Lyotard's definition of 'the postmodern condition' as the 'incredulity toward metanarratives' (1986: xxiv), Marxist thinkers like Jameson have rejected what they have perceived as postmodernism's 'sheer heterogeneity' and 'random difference' (1991: 6), which interrogate notions of progress, utopia and truth at the heart of Marxist philosophy (Belsey 2008: 26–8; Stevens 2016: 46). In this context, Brechtian theatre seems to occupy a particularly problematic position. Despite its undogmatic quality as well as its proto-postmodernist openness and ambivalence, it is undeniable that Brecht's idea of dialectical criticism is fundamentally grounded in his conviction of the possibility of control; Brecht pursues the aim of 'put[ting] reality in the hands of people in such a way that it can be *mastered*' (Brecht 2015a: 202; my emphasis). This insistence on objectivity, agency and progress radically clashes with postmodernism's central tenets, which have invalidated any such claims to absolute truth. Moreover, Brecht's belief in hierarchy is ideologically informed. Thus, however idiosyncratic, Brecht's 'theatre of knowledge' (Barnett 2017: 248) is still determined by his interest in the Marxist narrative of dialectical materialism, and it is this 'ideological straitjacket' (Barnett 2013b: 52) which may be considered limiting in the light of postmodernist notions of ideological relativism.

Under the impression of neoliberalism and postmodernism, therefore, an anti-dialectical environment seems to have established itself, in which fundamental dialectical mechanisms have been undermined, raising serious questions about the validity of dialectics as an apt epistemological and dramaturgical method for the twenty-first century. At the same time, however, a renewed interest in dialectics and its radical impetus has manifested itself among post-Marxist thinkers, who have asserted that, far from futile or irrelevant, dialectics seems 'more indispensable now than ever before' (Ollman 2008: 11). Instead of rejecting dialectics *per se*, therefore, critics have become invested in reimagining dialectical concepts and processes as progressive tools for the contemporary moment. In this sense, while certain principles may have been undermined, this does not imply that any form of dialectical critique has been rendered moot. The implications of postmodernist relativism do precisely *not* 'negate the possibility of dialectical debate' as such, as Liz Tomlin (2008: 357) seems to suggest in line with Jameson and other Marxist critics' analyses. Indeed, these pessimistic interpretations to some extent mistake postmodernism as 'a single, unitary, undifferentiated, non-contradictory phenomenon' (Belsey 2008: 30). On the contrary, a more nuanced understanding of the postmodernist legacy based on a recognition of its inherent contradictions can in fact open up a considerable potential for rethinking dialectics today. It is not 'the absence of truth' (Tomlin 2013: 30) *tout court* but rather the absence of *absolute* truth which is at the heart of postmodernism's critique, giving rise to a potentially 'healthy' (Lavender 2016: 19) and 'democratising' (Kershaw 1999: 18) scepticism towards ideological structures, which can be made productive for the purposes of contemporary political theatre. Thus, while postmodernist relativism 'tends not to ascribe absolute value', it does, crucially and in decidedly dialectical spirit, '[acknowledge] difference' (Barnett 2015: 210). In this sense, Catherine Belsey insightfully draws attention to 'another postmodernism, this time of the left, which emphasizes dissension, difference as opposition, and a possible consequent historicity which tells of the *resistance* that continues to challenge power from the position of its inevitably, differentiating other' (2008: 30). It is thus from this paradox in the encounter between postmodernism and dialectics that an impetus to innovation may arise. This decidedly pluralist, open and indeterminate understanding of difference does not only challenge conventional dialectical notions but also creates an opportunity for developing a new form of dialectical analysis, which is based on notions of uncertainty, multiplicity and openness and may therefore be better suited to respond to the radically transformed and supposedly anti-dialectical twenty-first-century moment. Given that the dialectical challenge has shifted from the question of how to achieve synthesis and reconciliation to the issue of how to counter the very suppression of difference in the first place, and of how to reintroduce the principle of contradiction as a prerequisite for dialectical critique, postmodernism's emphasis on the value of difference offers a useful impulse for reimagining dialectics as a progressive tool for analysis and critique.

Yet, what concrete implications do these observations have for the premises of dialectical criticism? How can postmodernism's plurality and dissolution of categories effectively be reconciled with a dialectical system of thought based on fixed stances and clear structures? How effective is dialectical thinking under these conditions? In an attempt to answer these questions, scholars have notably turned to Theodor W. Adorno's concept of negative dialectics, which has served as a central point of reference in reconsiderations of dialectics and dialectical theatre, particularly in Carney's rereading of Brecht in *Brecht and Critical Theory: Dialectics and Contemporary Aesthetics* (2005). While Adorno's significance for contemporary usages of Brechtian drama has been widely acknowledged – for example in Barnett's definition of the 'post-Brechtian' to which I will turn below – questions regarding the modes, conditions and implications of applying Adorno's concept in a post-Brechtian context have so far not been addressed in detail. Drawing on Carney's significant observations, I suggest that it is worth dwelling a little longer on the tenets of Adorno's dialectical philosophy, as it may help to identify more precisely the challenges of rethinking dialectics from a contemporary perspective. Crucially, Adorno takes the complex intersections between dialectics and capitalism as a point of departure for his critique of conventional dialectical mechanisms, which, he argues, have been co-opted and appropriated by capitalist ideology. Hence, a new approach is indispensable if dialectics is to function as a progressive critical method. As Carney summarizes, Adorno is particularly suspicious of the fact that traditional dialectics 'always presupposes a teleology, a totalizing identity' (2005: 160). Dismissing this approach as positivist and affirmative to the extent that it defines synthesis as its ultimate aim, Adorno probes the idea of a 'non-totalizing' (Carney 2005: 160) or negative dialectic instead. This emphasis on negativity is central, as it underscores Adorno's core premise that '[d]ialectics is the consistent sense of non-identity. It does not begin by taking a standpoint' (Adorno 1973: 5). Breaking away from conventional forms which prioritize dichotomous structures as a means of negotiating a reconciliation of the underlying tensions, Adorno's theory offers an 'assertion of the negative, the non-identical and unique' (Carney 2005: 161) to underscore the essentially conflict-laden, paradoxical and open-ended quality he considers essential in dialectical criticism. It is thus through negativity that the dialectic may, according to Adorno, reassert its radical charge by effectively countering 'capitalism's attempts to conceal and falsely resolve the antagonisms, internal conflicts and tensions prevalent in modern society' (Gritzner 2015: 36). It is therefore in the very 'space of contradiction' (Carney 2005: 166) itself, rather than through synthesization, that dialectics may unfold its progressive thrust.

While this sets the frame for a new form of dialectical critique based on the principle of negativity, Adorno's approach also entails complex implications for art and the relations between politics and aesthetics more broadly. Importantly, as Karoline Gritzner explains, Adorno insists 'that art must not eschew its critical potential' even though '[s]uccessful critique, protest and negation seem impossible today' (2015: 34). Convinced of the ongoing necessity of dialectical thinking, Adorno seeks to relocate art in relation to reality and thereby takes above all issue with notions of 'engaged' and 'autonomous' art forms in his essay 'Commitment' (1977). In his critique of engaged literature, Adorno is particularly sceptical of Brecht and arguably rejects fundamental processes of epic theatre, which is why Adorno and Brecht have often been presented as dichotomously opposed to each other (Ray 2010; Buck-Morss 1977). Yet, scholarly criticism has recently offered more nuanced readings of their relationship, focusing notably on the productive intersections that can be identified between their respective philosophical approaches (Rothe 2018: 1047; Carney 2005: 152–7; Ray 2010: 4–5). Expanding on these debates, what I consider crucial about Adorno's essay is not first and foremost its polemical rejection of Brecht, but rather its intention to dismiss and go beyond the very distinction between commitment and autonomy in the first place. This is evident in his assertion that 'an emphasis on autonomous works is itself socio-political in nature' (Adorno 1977: 194). This dissolution of categories, which is expressed throughout his writings, represents the core of Adorno's critique of art more broadly. Hence, he attributes a decidedly more indeterminate and precarious position to art, and it is in this liminal space that its progressive potential may be reactivated. Inscribing contradiction and paradox at the very heart of aesthetics itself, Adorno conceptualizes art as both 'social fact (fait social) and autonomous negativity' (Gritzner 2015: 17–18). Art is thus situated on the threshold between autonomy and engagement, aestheticism and didacticism, and it is by virtue of this liminality that it may eschew the danger of appropriation through late capitalism, and instead re-emerge as a critical force. Crucially, Adorno relocates this radical impetus on an aesthetic rather than thematic level, as 'the negation of synthesis becomes a principle of form' (1997: 155). As I will further explore in the following chapters, Adorno's insistence on negativity and liminality provides a productive methodology through which to approach the question of the forms and functions of dialectical thought and art in the new millennium.

Similar considerations on the relation between politics and aesthetics can be found in the writings of French philosopher Jacques Rancière, whose work has been widely applied in the context of theatre studies and literary criticism in the twenty-first century. Despite Rancière's critique of Adorno's understanding of aesthetic autonomy – which must, however, as shown above, be considered much less absolute than Rancière assumes (2004: 40) – it is instructive to examine the parallels between both philosophers more closely. As I suggest, Rancière's ideas offer a particularly apt lens through which to critically examine dialectical theatre, because it can be usefully connected to Adornian theory, and may thereby pave the way for a new understanding of Brecht in the contemporary moment. Rancière's approach is rooted in the observation that politics has been co-opted by neoliberalism, resulting in an 'absolute identification of politics with the management of capital' (1999: 113). In this state of 'post-democracy' (Rancière 1999: 95), he identifies conformism to the status quo as well as a lack of opposition and critique as fundamental obstacles to genuine political engagement. To reclaim its emancipatory potential, it is therefore indispensable to rethink democratic politics and to redefine the political as such. For this purpose, Rancière approaches politics from an essentially aesthetic perspective. Departing from traditional conceptualizations which posit a qualitative relation between politics and art, Rancière stipulates instead that politics and aesthetics must be understood as always already inherently intertwined with each other: the political is aesthetic and vice versa. The reason for this is that both domains are concerned with what he calls the 'distribution of the sensible', which describes 'the system of self-evident facts of sense-perception that simultaneously discloses the existence of something in common and the delimitations that define the respective parts and positions within it' (Rancière 2004: 7). This notion represents the cornerstone of Rancière's theory. What he is first and foremost interested in is the question of who, within a political system, is integrated, represented and therefore hearable and perceivable and who, by contrast, is disenfranchised, not granted a voice and thus forced to play 'the part of those who have no part' (Rancière 1999: 29). In this sense, Rancière offers a significant repositioning of politics, which he distinguishes from the 'police', 'the set of procedures whereby the aggregation and consent of collectivities is achieved, the organization of powers, the distribution of places and roles, and the systems for legitimizing this distribution' (1999: 28). By contrast, politics is defined as an aesthetic practice to the extent that it represents a process of disruption through which common schemes of perception are interrogated; it is, in Davide Panagia's words, 'an event of appearance' with the 'capacity to disrupt conventional forms of looking, of hearing, of perceiving' (2010: 103). This means that, vice versa, aesthetics, too, emerges as an inherently political practice. It is through aesthetics that politics can be apprehended and, taking this argument further, it could be said that it is in particular through the theatre, the *theatron* as the paradigmatic 'seeing place', that politics can be explored – and indeed sensuously experienced.

Rancière refers to this core political mechanism of disrupting the established order as 'dissensus', which describes the fact that 'every situation can be cracked open from the inside, reconfigured in a different regime of perception and signification' (2011: 49). Going beyond simple notions of disagreement or discord, the concept of dissensus is, as Adam Alston summarizes, 'an aesthetic intervention: a reordering of appearance and of what can or cannot be said, done and/or understood by others' (2016: 195). Rather than denoting a systematic political agenda, dissensus initiates a fundamentally open-ended process of destabilization which creates 'a moment of change or new awareness' (Lavender 2016: 139). It is in this notion of dissensus that the dialectical potential of Rancièrean thought emerges most clearly, as it derives its political charge from its insistence on tensions and contradictions in opposition to an environment shaped by conformism and consensus. Positing the essential contingency of any order, Rancière is not interested in a potential synthesis of the tensions shaping the relations between politics and police; rather, the emancipatory quality of his project resides in a constant awareness of difference and opposition. In this sense, Rancière's understanding of dissensus can be fruitfully connected to Adorno's negative dialectics, as both philosophers emphasize the value of contradiction and paradox as a prerequisite for disrupting the commonsensical, and thus for reclaiming the progressive potential of dialectical critique. This shift in emphasis must be understood as an active rather than passive endeavour, a process rather than a fixed state of tension, which considers contradiction as an act, carried out by political subjects, and is therefore constantly in flux, dynamic and provisional through its ongoing negotiation of the tensions between the visible and sayable, on the one hand, and the invisible and unsayable, on the other. Challenging preconceived notions of politics, political art, commitment and, indeed, dialectical thinking itself, this emphasis on ambivalence and liminality evident in Adorno and Rancière's approaches shapes a new understanding of dialectics which may accommodate the complex challenges of contemporary lived experience in a profoundly anti-dialectical context.

Towards a Post-Brechtian Theatre

At the heart of a revised understanding of dialectics as a paradoxical, open and flexible method is, as both Rancière and Adorno's approaches reflect, a redefinition of the relationship between politics, on the one hand, and aesthetics as a medium for critical reflection and an arena for (dialectical) debate, on the other. While both philosophers continue to attribute a fundamental significance to the nexus between political and artistic practices, they are also acutely alert to its decidedly more precarious nature in the contemporary moment. Above all, this requires a new approach to the theatre, for which the connection between stage and auditorium – understood as the intersection between the real and the fictional and, by implication, between the political and the aesthetic – represents the *sine qua non*. Indeed, the very notion of 'political theatre' seems to have come under considerable pressure in the light of the radical transformations of the past decades. Given the impact of postmodernist and neoliberal ideologies, the theatre has to some extent itself become complicit with the very structures it sets out to interrogate, which poses major obstacles to politically progressive theatrical art, and particularly raises the question of the forms and functions of resistance and critique in the contemporary context. Rather than dismissing the possibility of political theatre altogether, however, the challenge is, as Simon Malpas concludes with reference to Jameson and Jean Baudrillard, to imagine 'a form of critique that attempts to work through the injustices of contemporary capitalism ... without resorting to an oppositional grand narrative or positing the idea of an exterior and operative reality that lies behind some sort of contemporary false consciousness' (Malpas 2005: 128). This requires 'modes of resistance that are immanent to capitalism itself rather than a politics that derives from a straightforwardly oppositional grand narrative that is based on alternative foundations' (Malpas 2005: 128). Therefore, it is essential for contemporary political theatre to acknowledge the complications resulting from its own embeddedness within these hegemonic structures – not, however, in terms of a recognition of its impossibility, but precisely as a prerequisite for unlocking its potential for resistance from within the system itself. As Philip Auslander eloquently summarizes Hal Foster's argument for a postmodernist political theatre, it is thus a question of 'offering strategies of counterhegemonic resistance by exposing processes of cultural control and emphasizing the traces of nonhegemonic discourses within the dominant without claiming to transcend its terms' (Auslander 1987: 23). In this sense, self-reflexivity may function precisely as such a politicizing strategy. It is through a self-conscious recognition of the theatre's potential entanglement with the dominant order that the ideological processes underlying its own artistic practice can be laid bare, as a first step towards awareness and, eventually, change.

Under these circumstances, the connection between theatre and political reality can no longer be considered (and perhaps never has been in the first place) direct and straightforward, an observation which is at the heart of Rancière and Adorno's shared call for an increasingly disrupted, indeterminate and ambiguous understanding of politics and aesthetics. In this sense, Hans-Thies Lehmann locates contemporary theatre's progressive impetus precisely in an interruption of this relation (2012: 23). It is here that a vital connection with Brechtian drama can be established, as interruption represents one of its key principles, thereby underscoring Brecht's significance as a source for current reinterpretations of political theatre more broadly. In this vein, rejecting '"simple," "unmediated" conjunctions of theatre and politics, of real and representation', contemporary theatre practice has, as Brandon Woolf argues with reference to Lehmann, 'turned toward more nuanced, more dialectical readings of these relations', foregrounding 'theatre's (negative) political potential as much more indirect, much more unpredictable' (Woolf 2013: 44). While forcefully attesting to the progressive potential of this decidedly more ambivalent notion of political theatre, it nevertheless raises urgent questions, in particular regarding Brecht's dialectical legacy: what implications do these diagnoses have for dialectical theatre in the twenty-first century, both theoretically and practically speaking? How can the Brechtian model be reimagined as a progressive tool in the light of the theatre's own potential complicity? Which forms do dialectical aesthetics take, and which functions can they fulfil under these conditions?

In scholarly discourse, attempts to reconcile Brecht's model with the context of the late twentieth and early twenty-first centuries – both regarding adaptations of his own plays and applications of his theoretical premises and dramaturgical techniques – have usually been categorized as 'post-Brechtian'. While certainly widespread, the use of this label is not altogether unproblematic. Like the term 'Brechtian' itself, it is often employed uncritically, as a shorthand to loosely describe 'theatre after Brecht': 'It *is* unusual … to find it defined in anything but broad terms, if at all' and it is frequently 'merely [dropped] … into an argument in the hope that its implicit meaning will be clear' (Barnett 2011: 333). Even if it is clearly defined, a wide range of different understandings of the post-Brechtian compete, and, to make matters worse, it is not only applied to plays which can, in one way or another, be considered to have been inspired by Brecht, but, problematically, it is also used to refer to theatre practice which seeks to consciously reject and transcend the Brechtian tradition. Given this lack of agreement, it is indispensable to critically reflect on the term's implications if it is to serve as a meaningful framework for analysing the role, forms and functions of Brecht's legacy on the contemporary (British) stage.

That the category has nevertheless remained a powerful and useful tool is most notably reflected by Barnett's seminal work on the post-Brechtian, which he considers a paradigm or 'method and not an aggregation of devices' (Barnett 2013b: 48). Offering the most comprehensive definition of the concept so far, Barnett's approach is distinct because it foregrounds Brechtian theatre's dialectical core. Interrogating more specifically the implications of postmodernist thought for these dialectical premises, Barnett loosely and with certain simplifications draws on Adorno to argue 'that the dialectic in postmodernity is a site of uncertainty' (2013b: 52). This epistemological uncertainty gives rise to 'a refreshed dialectic' (Barnett 2017: 262) in which contradictions are merely 'identif[ied] rather than account[ed] for' (Barnett 2015: 213), as Barnett shows with reference to contemporary productions of Brecht's own and other classical texts. Lacking explanation and orientation, the post-Brechtian dialectic can therefore 'no longer be articulated with the minutiae of knowable details; its elements are complex and do not submit themselves to harmonising hierarchical structures' (Barnett 2013b: 52). As a result, post-Brechtian theatre must be understood as decidedly more open and ambivalent, which is, however, perceived as an enriching rather than limiting factor because it arguably makes dialectical theatre more compatible with, and amenable to, the complex conditions of the contemporary context. Aesthetically speaking, Barnett identifies five key principles which underpin this post-Brechtian mode: (1) acknowledgement of epistemological uncertainty; (2) preservation of Brechtian dialectics and stagecraft; (3) Brechtian emphasis on showing; (4) criticism of Brecht's interpretive system; and (5) focus on association instead of interpretation on stage (Barnett 2011).

Barnett's focus on the nexus between dialectical thinking, Brechtian aesthetics and the twenty-first-century context has undeniably facilitated invaluable fresh perspectives on Brecht, and has broken new ground for rethinking Brechtian theatre in the contemporary context. At the same time, however, the insistence on dichotomies and neat categorizations detectable in Barnett's argument – between the 'Brechtian' and the 'post-Brechtian', the dramatic and the epic as well as the 'post-Brechtian' and the 'postdramatic' – seems somewhat counter-intuitive, especially given his explicit foregrounding of openness and pluralism as key elements of post-Brechtian aesthetics (2013b: 52). Thus, while the characteristics identified by Barnett may provide a useful point of reference for bringing Brecht's model into dialogue with the contemporary moment, I agree with Delgado-García that 'circumscribing post-Brechtian performance to these five points might generate strict dichotomies that are not necessarily representative of Brecht's legacy' (Delgado-García 2015: 150–1). In this respect, while demonstrating that Barnett's framework can be fruitfully applied to an examination of Brecht's influence on contemporary drama, Stevens's excellent monograph *Anti-War Theatre after Brecht: Dialectical Aesthetics in the Twenty-First Century* (2016) is to some extent limited in its approach. Even though Stevens acknowledges the risk of 'turning the Brecht model' yet again 'into dogma' and compellingly argues for 'the need for ... flexible interpretations of Brechtian "dialectical theatre"' (2016: 47), she nevertheless applies Barnett's five principles and focuses primarily on formal manifestations of dialectical aesthetics, which may, while certainly delivering important insights, ultimately not do justice to the actual potential – and limits – of Brecht's concept on the twenty-first-century stage.

Taking these issues into consideration, my understanding of the post-Brechtian aims to go beyond the perceived rigidity of previous models to develop a comprehensive methodology for interpreting late-twentieth- and early-twenty-first-century British drama, which, beginning with the so-called 'in-yer-face' generation, marks a significant turning point in the history of contemporary political drama in Britain more generally, and of Brechtian-inspired theatre more specifically. Indeed, some current British political playwriting might usefully be described as post-Brechtian. In dialogue with Barnett, this book pursues a nuanced and open approach by situating the analysis firmly within the wider context of the political, social and aesthetic implications of Brechtian dialectical theory in the new millennium in order to identify the challenges and contradictions of applying Brecht's model today, and to determine the role, forms and functions of the post-Brechtian method in post-1990s British drama. Taking Rancière and Adorno's observations on the intersections between politics and aesthetics as its point of departure, my discussion of post-Brechtian dialectics thus attempts to respond to the broader question of the relationship between politics and art in the present moment, critically interrogating the ongoing potential of Brechtian-inspired theatre to spur resistance and ideological critique in a decidedly anti-dialectical age.

Therefore, rather than trying to pin down specific aesthetic characteristics of the post-Brechtian method, my approach focuses on the theoretical core of Brechtian theatre to examine how the plays discussed in the following chapters might be understood to engage with Brecht's dialectical drama – not only as a source of inspiration but also and above all of contestation. For this purpose, I will investigate Brecht's dialectical legacy on two levels: as a means of apprehending and analysing the contemporary world, on the one hand, and as an aesthetic strategy in the context of political drama, on the other. What I argue reunites the plays selected for this study is the extent to which they express, in Barnett's words, 'a dissatisfaction with the narrowness' (2013b: 66) of conventional dialectical thought, in particular with regard to its rigid, bifurcating structures, its ideological framework as well as its preference for rationality, synthesis and harmony. Hence, critically interrogating traditional dialectical mechanisms and concepts, the plays collectively diagnose the inadequacy and dysfunctionality of these structures, a critique which materializes on the level of both content and form. At the same time, however, by virtue of their critical interrogations, the plays can also be said to reflect a firm belief in the ongoing value of dialectical thought and aesthetics. What they stage is, as I propose, an implicit struggle with the question of how to reimagine dialectics as a progressive theatrical device. Searching for new forms of Brechtian-inspired dialectical theatre-making, the pieces attempt to transcend the perceived shortcomings of conventional approaches by foregrounding, in an Adornian vein, an experience of ambivalence, paradox and indeterminacy on the stage itself and, by implication, also in the relationship with the audience. In this context, they probe a variety of aesthetic strategies and modes of spectatorship and, significantly, offer not only different forms of critical engagement with Brecht's legacy but also diverging diagnoses as to the future of the (post-)Brechtian on the contemporary British stage in-between potentiality and failure. Hence, my analyses pursue a double interest – metatheatrically speaking, in the question of how the plays position themselves with regard to Brecht's dialectical method and, aesthetically speaking, in how their respective approach to dialectical theatre is realized formally. My focus is thus not primarily and exclusively on 'Brechtian dialectical aesthetics … as dramaturgical techniques' (Stevens 2016: 47), as Stevens proposes, but rather on how the plays can be understood to negotiate the challenges of dialectics today, how they engage creatively and critically with Brecht's model, how they transform, adapt and reimagine dialectics aesthetically and how, in the process, they possibly also go beyond (post-)Brechtian drama.

What underpins this mechanism is, crucially, and in line with the argument on the forms and functions of contemporary political theatre presented above, a particular emphasis on self-reflexivity. For this purpose, the post-Brechtian mode can be shown to exploit and radicalize the metatheatricality intrinsic to Brecht's own model. Brecht considered an awareness of the theatre apparatus and thus of the artificiality of the performance situation indispensable for establishing distance between stage and audience and for facilitating critical analysis. In post-Brechtian drama, self-reflexivity is itself turned into a strategic (meta-)dialectical device for interrogating the usefulness of Brecht's legacy. Thus, serving specific purposes which are political in nature, self-reflexivity is decidedly not employed in postmodernist spirit as an end in itself, but as a means of critical interrogation. As a result, it is the very undecidability and ambivalence resulting from the plays' self-reflexive engagement with Brecht which emerge as important sources for their diverse reconceptualizations of the dialectical model in the contemporary moment, as the case studies will demonstrate. By virtue of its self-reflexivity, the post-Brechtian must hence be understood as an indeterminate and open project which is created performatively and thereby emerges as radically ephemeral and provisional, continuously in the process of making and, most decisively, always subject to revision.

This revaluation of self-reflexivity as a dialectical strategy notably enhances the role of the spectators in post-Brechtian theatre. Indeed, presenting dialectical contradictions without providing any interpretive orientation, it is in the relationship with the audience – rather than on the stage itself – that the dialectical mechanism has to be completed. Hence, through its strategic indeterminacy, the post-Brechtian radicalizes the privileged position of the spectator evident in Brecht's own model. While Brecht, too, stresses the importance of the audience members as participants and agents, they do not only perform a more central but also a more uncertain role in the post-Brechtian mode. To the extent that no 'particular interpretive directions' (Barnett 2017: 21) are given and that 'the material on stage is not packaged in a way that elicits a particular response from an audience' (Barnett 2016: 14), post-Brechtian drama privileges a decidedly more open approach in which the spectators' individual interpretations and associations may be accommodated, thereby to some extent rewriting the theatrical contract by destabilizing the interpretive hierarchy between stage and auditorium.

In this context, Stevens has highlighted the significance of Rancière's conceptualization of spectatorship, which can, despite Rancière's fierce criticism of what he dismissed as Brecht's didacticism, be brought into fruitful dialogue with Brechtian ideas (Stevens 2016: 12–16). Thus, critical of the notion of spectatorial passivity and rejecting any form of hierarchy in the theatrical event, Rancière envisions a 'theatre without spectators … where the passive optical relationship implied by the very term is subjected to a different relationship' (2011: 3) – namely, one in which '[t]he separation of stage and auditorium is … transcended' (2011: 15). This erosion of boundaries gives rise to what Rancière defines as 'emancipated spectatorship', which 'challenge[s] the opposition between viewing and acting', turning audience members into 'both distant spectators and active interpreters of the spectacle offered to them' (2011: 13) as a vital prerequisite for inciting dissensus. Crucially, the ideal of equality between all participants involved in the theatrical exchange underpinning this model is defined by Rancière as a fundamentally inherent quality. Equality can, as Delgado-García summarizes, 'never be gained or bestowed on others – it can only be confirmed, verified' (2014: 74), as any spectator is always already equal and emancipated. It is for this reason that Rancière rejects any deliberate form of spectatorial 'activation', which he identifies for example in the Brechtian model. Crucially, however, such a reading of Brechtian theatre as overly didactic is, as shown above, certainly reductive, overlooking, as it does, the essentially open and dynamic dimension of Brecht's concept. More to the point, Rancière's approach heavily draws on pedagogic theory itself and is in fact a far cry from the ideal of absolute equality, neutrality and disinterestedness he may have had in mind. Given these reservations, therefore, a more nuanced understanding of both Rancière and Brecht's ideas is necessary. Thus, as Stevens has insightfully argued, the value of Brecht's dialectical theory for reconsidering Rancièrean emancipation resides in the fact that the Brechtian framework 'provide[s] a vantage point from which to view the bigger picture of social relations' at which Rancière's project is directed, but which are ultimately not accounted for by his model: 'it is the dynamic, dialectical core of Brecht's theory that holds the possibility for moving the spectator between the poles of viewing and acting' (Stevens 2016: 14).

Building on this argument, I propose that these intersections between Rancièrean and Brechtian theories represent a particularly useful lens for investigating spectatorship in contemporary experiments with dialectical drama. Radicalizing, as shown above, the premises underpinning Brecht's 'theatre of the spectator' by explicitly conceptualizing audience members as agents and participants in the performance, the post-Brechtian mode increasingly dissolves essential distinctions between stage and auditorium in the spirit of Rancière's 'theatre without spectators'. Rather than on the stage itself, therefore, it is what happens in the auditorium which is to some extent turned into the core of the plays, blurring the boundaries between performers and spectators, action and interpretation as well as theatre and reality. Significantly, Rancière's definition of emancipated spectatorship is based on a fundamental process of oscillation between 'acting' and 'looking' – which can also be understood as an oscillation between reason and emotion, as Stevens proposes: 'An "emancipated spectator" is one who moves back and forth between a Brechtian-style critical specular relation to the stage and a more Artaudian immersive, experiential connection to the performance' (2016: 13). This crucial observation offers an insightful perspective on post-Brechtian spectatorship, which radicalizes the juxtaposition between the rational and the emotional, between distance and involvement identified above as key to Brecht's own model by shifting attention more decisively to the spectators' individual and, above all, emotional experiences of the performance. Thus, as Barnett explains – like Stevens, however, without pursuing this argument any further – it is through the confrontation with ambivalence and indeterminacy in post-Brechtian drama that a different process of interpretation is initiated: 'the audience is involved in a more sensuous experience of dialectical theatre. Because interpretation takes place in the auditorium rather than on the stage, the audience is not so busy decoding information; instead it *experiences* it' (2015: 216). Hence, it is the audience's affective investment which is itself turned into a dialectical instrument. The case studies will pay particular attention to the plays' reconfigurations of spectatorship to critically interrogate the ostensibly progressive and emancipatory potential emerging from the various forms of interaction shaping the relationship between stage and auditorium: to what extent can the plays actually spur critical engagement on the basis of an experience of ambivalence? Is this radical emphasis on indeterminacy not rather an impediment to interpretation? How complicit do spectators become in the process? Where are the limits of this specifically experiential form of dialectical thinking in-between reason and emotion?

To answer these questions, the following chapters will critically examine the emergence of this post-Brechtian paradigm and its implications for spectatorship in contemporary British theatre. Building on Reinelt's emphasis on the 'hybridity' of pre-1990s Brechtian epic theatre in Britain, I will offer a comprehensive account of the role of Brecht's legacy on the twenty-first-century British stage by situating the post-Brechtian in dialogue with a thriving and rich variety of theatrical styles, foregrounding its multiple intersections with the heterogeneous trends shaping the energetic field of playwriting in Britain, from the 'in-yer-face' sensibility to amateur theatre to the theatre of the absurd. To illustrate the productivity and diversity of applications of Brechtian dialectical drama today, the chapters will focus on the works of Mark Ravenhill, David Greig, Andy Smith, Tim Crouch and Caryl Churchill. While other dramatists – notably debbie tucker green, Zinnie Harris, Lucy Prebble or Edward Bond – may come to mind, the playwrights collected in this study stand out because they have enjoyed a continuous and influential presence on the British stage for several decades, and because their distinct approaches to theatre-making have left an important mark on British drama. More to the point, their oeuvre reflects a consistent engagement with Brechtian methodologies – an engagement which can be explicit, marked and acknowledged, but also more implicit, unmarked and unacknowledged. To reflect this broad spectrum of manifestations of the post-Brechtian, the case studies will offer detailed readings of the plays, ranging from more classical, more readily identifiable examples to less obvious cases of Brechtian-inspired drama which, crucially, also makes it possible to identify the limits of applying the dialectical paradigm in the present moment.

To trace what I consider the origins of this post-Brechtian turn in contemporary British drama, Chapter 1 offers a fresh examination of the contested political quality of 'in-yer-face' theatre by examining Mark Ravenhill's *Some Explicit Polaroids* (1999) and *Shoot/Get Treasure/Repeat* (2007) from a (post-)Brechtian perspective. Identifying a dialectical dimension at the core of his plays, the chapter identifies productive intersections between the 'in-yer-face' sensibility and Brechtian dramaturgy so far overlooked in scholarly criticism. Thus, I will argue that the 'in-yer-face' style can be understood as participating in a reinvigoration of Brecht's legacy, as provocation is employed as a dialectical tool to identify a crisis of dialectics as an epistemological and aesthetic device at the turn of the millennium.

Chapter 2 explores the political and ethical implications of theatrical acts of imagining in David Greig's works from a post-Brechtian perspective. Characteristically, these plays employ and appeal to the imagination of the playwright, the characters and the audience in a way which can be understood in terms of Adorno's concept of irrationality. In Greig's use, the imagination functions as a dialectical strategy for identifying, staging and experiencing the contradictions shaping life under the impression of neoliberal globalization and as a prerequisite for speculating about alternative possibilities and realities. While *Dunsinane* (2010) achieves this through a post-Brechtian form of appropriation of William Shakespeare's *Macbeth*, *The Events* (2013) experiments with interruptions of empathy. Staging dissensus, the plays introduce a profound impression of ambivalence and openness which appeals to the spectators' imaginative capacities as a means of engaging with the paradoxes presented on stage.

Chapter 3 offers a new perspective on Andy Smith and Tim Crouch's work by interpreting the theatre-makers' use of metatheatricality as a device of post-Brechtian *Verfremdung*. Arguing that self-reflexivity is employed as a means of dialectical interrogation, I propose that Smith's *all that is solid melts into air* (2011) and Crouch's *The Author* (2009) search for a new form of Brechtian-inspired political theatre after postmodernism by interrogating notions of change and engagement. For this purpose, they foreground the role of the spectators as co-creators of the performance and negotiate a new, critical and dialectical form of sincerity in the interaction with the audience. Based on a precarious oscillation between genuine dialogue and ironic destabilization, they probe the possibility of moving beyond postmodernist relativism towards a new form of engagement.

In an effort to look both back and forward, Chapter 4 concludes the study with a focus on the work of Caryl Churchill, one of the most influential playwrights – and certainly the defining female dramatist – in Britain. For the purpose of creating politically progressive theatre, Churchill has, throughout her long career, fruitfully combined an interest in Brechtian methodology with her unique creative imagination to develop an original and highly experimental form of post-Brechtian aesthetics. Taking into account these artistic developments in Churchill's oeuvre ever since the 1960s, I will focus on her twenty-first-century plays *Escaped Alone* (2016) and *Here We Go* (2015) to argue that her works have exhibited an increasingly critical stance towards Brechtian dialectics, self-reflexively problematizing and moving beyond Brecht, while still implicitly maintaining a dialectical framework and actively searching for ways of reinventing Brechtian-inspired drama. Diagnosing a crisis of conventional dialectical forms, Churchill most characteristically employs tools of Samuel Beckett's theatre of the absurd and paradoxically juxtaposes them with Brechtian strategies. Reconsidering, via Adorno, the relationship between Brecht and Beckett, conventionally presented as dichotomously opposed in accounts of theatre history, this chapter shows that both playwrights' approaches in fact fruitfully intersect, paving the way for a negative dialectic in the Adornian sense of the term. Creating an experience of confusion and disorientation for the audience, Churchill's plays combine absurd and dialectical strategies as a means of reinvigorating dialectical critique which, however, also pushes at the boundaries of dialectics as an epistemological and dramaturgical tool.

As both the most radical interrogation and the most innovative reconceptualization of dialectical theatre, therefore, Churchill's oeuvre offers an apt conclusion to this study. Situated between potentiality and failure, optimism and pessimism as well as hope and negativity, the plays leave the question of Brecht's future on the contemporary stage radically unanswered – handing it over to dramatists, theatre-makers, audiences and critics alike to consider and experiment with. Yet, as Brecht forcefully asserts, '[t]he contradictions are the hopes' (1992: 448; my translation). In this spirit, contemporary British drama demonstrates that it is paradoxically from this very openness and indeterminacy that the most powerful creative potential for the post-Brechtian paradigm may arise.

1

'In-Yer-Face' Theatre and the Crisis of Dialectics: Mark Ravenhill's Post-Brechtian Drama in Anti-Dialectical Times

While the 'in-yer-face' wave has inarguably initiated 'a new golden age in British theatre' (Saunders 2008: 1), the political quality of these groundbreaking works has remained fiercely contested. Coined by Aleks Sierz to describe a visceral theatrical style based on the use of shock aesthetics and provocation through explicit representations of violence and sex designed to '[take] the audience by the scruff of the neck and [shake] it until it gets the message' (2001: 4), the term has invited a wide range of responses which have, however, obscured rather than enlightened the potentially critical and progressive value of the plays subsumed under this label. With reception focusing almost exclusively on their use of intense emotions, explicit language and shocking imagery, the sensationalism which initially emerged in the 1990s in reaction to this new sensibility has somewhat overshadowed the intricate connections between form and content shaping the political fabric of plays by Mark Ravenhill, Sarah Kane and Anthony Neilson, among others. In this vein, scholars have raised concerns about 'in-yer-face' theatre's ostensible voyeurism, its perceived glamorization of violence as well as its potential complicity with the very form of neoliberal consumerism it seeks to critique (Gottlieb 2003; Müller 2002; Wallace 2005). Sierz himself remains ambiguous in his assessment of the political quality of these plays, locating them 'on the extreme left' (2015b: 26) while elsewhere more tentatively attributing an 'implicit politics' and 'an unstable mixture of traditional leftwing beliefs' (2004: 54) to them. Without providing a definite answer, he perspicaciously asks: 'But if the term really is political, what do its politics imply?' (2008: 25).

Taking up this central question, this chapter looks at the politics of 'in-yer-face' drama through a (post-)Brechtian lens to examine its radical impetus in terms of its dialectical qualities, highlighting the productive intersections that can be established between the 'in-yer-face' style and Brechtian dramaturgy for rethinking dialectical drama on the contemporary stage. Contending that the 'in-yer-face' sensibility can be understood as a reinvigoration of dialectical theatre in a period of political disengagement, I suggest that the mid-1990s not only mark a moment of rupture and aesthetic renewal but are also characterized by a certain continuity of traditions. I will substantiate this argument by focusing on the plays of Mark Ravenhill, which reflect both the challenges and the potential of a Brechtian mode of theatre-making at the turn of the millennium. At the root of what I identify as a post-Brechtian turn in British drama during this period, Ravenhill's dramatic works therefore represent a crucial point of departure for this book.

Passionately defending Brecht in an article entitled 'Don't Bash Brecht' published in the *Guardian* in 2008, Ravenhill shows a profound and continuous interest in Brecht as an important source of inspiration and, crucially, also as a considerable point of contestation. Interrogating the role of the theatre as a radical force in an environment which seems increasingly hostile to cultural expression and political commitment, Ravenhill calls not for 'a theatre of relativism and consensus but a genuinely dialectical theatre where opposing ideas, forces, energies can be fully experienced, embodied and examined and the most difficult, even insoluble problems can be witnessed and confronted' (2016). Crucially, this statement does not only echo Brecht by taking up central categories of his model – notably the pivotal role of contradiction as a driving force of dialectical dramaturgy – but also paves the way for a critique of Brecht's concept for the purposes of the contemporary context. This is most evident in the notions of 'experience', 'embodiment' and 'confrontation' Ravenhill embraces to underscore the central role of an experiential mode of reception and thus of the audience for his reconceptualization of dialectical drama. Hence, as the case studies will show, the visceral and provocative style of his plays is not so much irreconcilable with, as indicative of, a new approach to Brecht's enduring legacy which can be identified at the turn of the twenty-first century.

In this sense, rather than focusing on language and stage imagery, what I suggest is most provocative about Ravenhill's dramaturgy from a Brechtian perspective is its distinct interrogation of dialectical form. While 'in-yer-face' drama's potential for provocation has previously been identified on a formal level in terms of its deliberate disruption of aesthetic conventions (Sierz 2001: 6; Boll 2013: 44), my reading goes beyond these approaches to suggest that provocation is specifically employed as a dialectical tool in Ravenhill's post-Brechtian drama to stage the crisis of Brechtian dialectics as an epistemological and aesthetic means in the light of the profoundly transformed political, social and economic context. In fact, this questioning of dialectical mechanisms represents a broader, but often overlooked concern of 'in-yer-face' theatre, which, as Sierz valuably argues, 'challenges the distinctions we use to define who we are … These binary oppositions are central to our worldview; questioning them can be unsettling' (2001: 6). Crucially, this dysfunctionality of traditional dialectics based on concepts of clarity, teleology and dichotomy is not only exposed in terms of content and plot, as Sierz suggests, but also, and most importantly, with regard to the plays' aesthetics, as traditional dialectical approaches are exposed as obsolete. As I propose in the following, it is by provocatively confronting the audience with such a form of 'aesthetic shock' (Boll 2013: 44) that Ravenhill's 'in-yer-face' theatre seeks to engage its spectators in a search for new forms of dialectical drama and criticism as progressive and emancipating devices for the contemporary moment.

The Post-Brechtian Parable: *Some Explicit Polaroids*

Cool Britannia and the Manipulation of Dialectics

Ravenhill's preoccupation with dialectics as both a system of critical thought and a theatrical strategy is most clearly reflected in *Some Explicit Polaroids* (1999), which explores the challenges of political theatre in general and of Brecht's legacy in particular on the threshold of the new millennium. Featuring central thematic and aesthetic characteristics of Ravenhill's previous plays such as *Shopping and Fucking* (1996), while foreshadowing key developments in his twenty-first-century works – notably a return to a more 'explicit' engagement with political matters – *Polaroids* can also be considered a turning point in Ravenhill's career; the play represents 'a study not only of a society in turmoil but also ... of an artist at a crossroads' (Svich 2003: 90). In this respect, *Polaroids* stands out as it offers a significant metatheatrical perspective which facilitates wider conclusions regarding Ravenhill's oeuvre and, through this lens, also regarding his generation of playwrights as well as the question of political drama at this decisive moment in history. It is in this sense that I propose to read *Polaroids* as a self-reflexive post-Brechtian parable. It offers a critical and self-conscious perspective on political engagement and the forms and functions of political art at the turn of the millennium – observations which, I argue, decidedly transcend the *fin-de-siècle* moment of the play to exemplify trends which were to shape the future development of Brechtian-inspired engaged drama in Britain.

The parable represents a privileged form in Brechtian theatre. As plays like *The Good Person of Szechwan* and *The Resistible Rise of Arturo Ui* demonstrate, it is ideally suited to realize a dialectical dramaturgy. Combining principles of aesthetic condensation and abstraction, the parable breaks down complex realities to reveal their essential mechanisms, thereby making them available for analysis and critique. In *Polaroids*, Ravenhill applies these ideas and turns the parable into a meta-dialectical device. Thus, the microcosm constructed around Nick and the other characters functions as a prism through which the play's broader interrogations into political commitment in general and dialectical theatre more specifically at the turn of the millennium are refracted. In this sense, he opts for a self-reflexive approach which focuses attention on the dialectical processes at the heart of the play. Employing a dialectical methodology on the level of content and form, *Polaroids* is based on the principle of contradiction as well as on notions of agency and change. Crucially, however, this meticulous dialectical structure is a strategic device that paradoxically serves to diagnose the very dysfunctionality of these conventional forms as progressive tools for social analysis and theatre-making in the contemporary context. Aiming to encourage a critical examination of the political and social conditions in which the play is embedded, Ravenhill's parabolic strategy is also indebted to Brecht's specific understanding of realism, which stages 'no longer a reflection of a situation, but an interrogation of it' (Barnett 2016: 8). It is in a Brechtian vein that Patrice Pavis describes *Polaroids*'s realism as 'critical', as it 'models its fictional and dramatic world in order to make it available to political interpretation' (2004: 8). In a post-Brechtian turn, the fundamental role of the spectators, who are to establish these analogies between fiction and reality and to draw practical conclusions from the parable, is experientially enhanced in Ravenhill's play through the specific use of provocation, as this chapter argues.

Set in the heyday of the Cool Britannia era, *Polaroids* exposes the challenges faced by the characters of living in an unsettlingly ambiguous historical moment. This is expressed through a series of seemingly clear-cut, dichotomously structured confrontations between different historical contexts, generations, political beliefs and personal motivations. These contradictory dynamics are triggered by Nick, who functions as a key (meta-)dialectical device for *Polaroids*'s parabolic mechanism. At the beginning of the play, Nick suddenly reappears after his release from prison, where he has served a fifteen-year-long sentence for assaulting Jonathan, his nemesis and capitalist entrepreneur. Nick's incarceration in 1984 signifies a notorious date in British political history – the year of the last Miners' Strike, and thus a turning point for leftist politics. This is exemplified by Nick's trajectory. As a militant activist and staunch socialist, he now returns to a world which has become unrecognizable to him, forcing him to gradually realize that the political ideals he still resolutely clings to seem to have lost all relevance in a world now characterized by a profound sense of uncertainty and disorientation. Notably, his conflict-laden encounters with Helen are deeply alienating for Nick, as his former girlfriend and fellow activist has, in his opinion, betrayed their former commitment and instead opted for a career in the political establishment, managing the status quo rather than working towards real change. Instead of pursuing 'the big targets' (Ravenhill 2001b: 8), Helen is content with 'rearranging the same old shit backwards and forwards ... And you call it politics' (Ravenhill 2001b: 52), as Nick disparagingly remarks. In Rancièrean terms, Helen has made herself complicit with the hegemonic system – the police – and embodies the very demise of politics, understood as an emancipating project based on conflict and opposition. At the same time, however, Helen's compromises also reveal the failure of their erstwhile socialist convictions. Asking '[w]hat did we ever do? Sure talk, talk, talk, march, march, protest. Ban this, overthrow that, but what did we ever do?' (Ravenhill 2001b: 8), Helen exposes the naivety of their one-time political ambitions. Unsettling both his own and the other characters' belief and value systems, Nick's reappearance creates a distinct interruption which brings the sweeping changes of the past decades and the resulting contradictions of contemporary lived experience into sharp focus.

This sense of disconnection, both personal and political, is reinforced when Nick begins to mingle with the representatives of the younger generation, who have grown up in the ostensibly anti-ideological, neoliberal era of post-Thatcher Britain. Under these conditions, the play suggests, Nadia, Tim and Victor have developed dichotomously opposed ideas about life, meaning and responsibility as a result of a profound lack of orientation and, indeed, intention. What separates Nick and the youths most radically is their respective attitudes towards political engagement, as Nick's emphasis on shared values, collectivity and commitment has, to them, turned out to be a '[b]ig fucking lie' (Ravenhill 2001b: 41) and has motivated their isolation and retreat into the private sphere. Instead of 'grand' political narratives, it is a selfish pursuit of 'happiness' which guides the younger characters, manifesting itself most vividly in their hedonistic, purely individualistic search for pleasure and gratification. This is exemplified by the relationship between Tim and Victor. In a scenario reminiscent of Ravenhill's previous play *Shopping and Fucking*, Tim has bought Victor like a commodity; all that counts for them is 'trash' (Ravenhill 2001b: 11) – material rather than immaterial or 'spiritual' (Ravenhill 2001b: 13) values; they 'just want to have fun, just want to enjoy' (Ravenhill 2001b: 12). Any binding, sincere form of personal or, indeed, political commitment is thereby deliberately ruled out. Their understanding of 'happiness' thus runs counter to any genuine expression of feelings; instead, the characters withdraw into an exclusively self-centred life.

This diagnosis can be aligned with the wider cultural context of the time, which was marked by a revitalization of Britain's cultural scene, turning British identity itself into the market commodity of 'Cool Britannia' by propagating a 'consensus of happiness' (Fragkou 2018: 18). With reference to Lauren Berlant's influential study *Cruel Optimism*, Marissia Fragkou argues that 1990s British drama is preoccupied with the 'fantasies for the good life' (Berlant 2011: 3) promulgated by the Cool Britannia ideology, which it exposes as highly 'dubious' and 'precarious' (Fragkou 2018: 17–18). Hence, in *Polaroids*, the younger characters' adherence to this ideological optimism can be understood as 'cruel' to the extent that what they 'desire is actually an obstacle to [their] flourishing' (Berlant 2011: 1). Rather than searching for sincere connections with others, they content themselves with assuring their own 'happiness' – an altogether artificial, inauthentic experience, however, based exclusively on values of consumption and ownership. Thus, for the members of the new generation, happiness is a solipsistic, selfish and isolating rather than shared experience.

Associated with a 'libertarian attitude of "Whatever"' (Urban 2004: 358) and a deeply rooted individualism, the ideology of Cool Britannia has therefore had a profound impact on the political sphere, notably by devaluing political commitment as 'uncool'. This shift in ideals was complemented by a new direction in British politics. Concomitant with the cultural revival of the decade, Tony Blair's 'New Labour' associated itself with this movement of 'coolness' in the arts to profit from its popularity and to underscore its distinctiveness from previous political styles, increasingly exploiting culture for ideological ends (Urban 2004: 356). However, while suggesting a supposedly rigid binary between Left and Right, New and 'old' Labour as well as Labour and Tory, the label successfully concealed the fact that Blair's agenda was, in fact, deeply conservative itself, thereby collapsing and rendering meaningless the very differences it evoked (Pountain and Robins 2000: 172). Thus, discursively exploiting what can be effectively described as characteristic dialectical concepts while deliberately dissolving the very distinctions from which critical analysis can emerge, the political rhetoric of the time strategically instrumentalized these conventional dialectical mechanisms for its own purposes. More to the point, the resulting indeterminacy has created a profoundly anti-dialectical environment in which thinking in dynamic contradictions as a pillar of dialectical critique was rendered inefficient. Instead, committed to perpetuating rather than interrogating neoliberal principles, politics is thus turned into a Rancièrean form of consensus, 'the art of living with [global capitalism], not a vocation to overcome it' (Panitch and Leys 2001: 248).

In this sense, *Polaroids* reflects how any form of political (dis-)engagement evidenced by the characters is ultimately co-opted by the logic of Cool Britannia, complicating any genuine form of political alliance. While Helen's turn to realpolitik is partly, at least, also motivated by her desire for a profitable career, the younger characters' retreat marks the selfishness of their existence, regardless of any wider social and political implications, thereby 'happily' contributing to maintaining the neoliberal status quo: they are 'content with what [they]'ve got' and 'take responsibility for [them] selves' (Ravenhill 2001b: 43). Nick, who at first seems to offer a sincere counterexample and source of critique, is himself incapable of providing an efficient model of resistance, recognizing the irrelevance of his socialist ideals while failing to define a new political identity for himself (Ravenhill 2001b: 80–1). To the extent that Nick's reappearance unsettles the values and attitudes of all characters, the distinctions and categories on which they rely are shown to collapse, thereby reinforcing their fundamental disconnection. It is here that the play's parabolic and meta-dialectical conceit takes shape. Just as the characters' interactions are based on misunderstandings and a seemingly unbridgeable difference, the dialectical contradictions employed as a key dramaturgical method are revealed as distorting rather than orientating tools which spur indeterminacy, stifle critique and can thus, in their conventional form, no longer foster a progressive form of political theatre, thereby underscoring the play's diagnosis of a crisis of dialectical thought and aesthetics.

Staging the conflicts between two generations and thus between two radically different historical moments, *Polaroids* stresses that the crisis of dialectics must first and foremost be understood as a crisis of historical consciousness. In dialectical thought, a diachronic perspective is vital for identifying historically specific, and thus unique, contexts and factors which have brought about events and decisions in the past and which have an impact on the present. Instead of 'treat[ing] the past as if it were the same as the present', dialectics therefore encourages us to understand that 'actions and behaviours are relative rather than absolute' (Barnett 2015: 75) and, importantly, that historical processes are influenced by our intervention. Breaking with the traditions of conventional 'bourgeois theatre', which tends to '[emphasize] the timelessness of its objects' and presents '"universal" situations' as well as characters who are 'bound by the alleged "eternally human"' (Brecht 2015a: 156), Brecht proposes a technique of historicization which facilitates a dialectical, analytical approach to what is represented on stage: 'The actor must play the incidents as historical ones. Historical incidents are unique, transitory incidents associated with particular periods' (Brecht 2015a: 187–8). While the past needs to be presented as different from the present to underscore the potential for change, it must also be possible to productively relate history to the contemporary moment to make it relevant for the spectators. Designed 'to expose what we perceive to be natural and show how it has been constructed' (Barnett 2015: 74), Brecht employed history as a means of *Verfremdung* and turned it into a central device of dialectical theatre.

This form of Brechtian historicization as a means of critical analysis, however, seems to have become fundamentally compromised by the end of the twentieth century. With no fixed political (or other) stances left as an anchor, the crucial link between past and present seems to have been lost. Thus, Ravenhill describes his generation of playwrights as 'disconnected from history' and as 'locat[ing] everything in the now' (Ravenhill 2015: 160). Referring to his plays of the 1990s, he explains that 'it was almost impossible to make the present talk to the past ... We seemed to be inmates that are trapped in an eternal present, only existing in the now without a contact' (Ravenhill 2015: 161). This diagnosis is reflected in *Polaroids*, where the characters' lack of productive engagement with their own past is presented as a major impediment to their critical engagement with the wider social and political context. While Nick is both stuck in his obsolete political ideals and incapable of 'fac[ing] up to [his] past' (Ravenhill 2001b: 51) by coming to terms with his crime, the past represents a source of pain for Jonathan, who is intent on finding closure by taking revenge on Nick (Ravenhill 2001b: 37). When they finally meet, however, they indulge in nostalgia rather than succeeding to reconcile their dissonant experiences of past and present. By contrast, Helen has opted for denial, pretending that her former socialist self 'was another person' (Ravenhill 2001b: 33). While the older generation reflects a certain degree of commitment to history – unproductive because shaped by denial or sentimentalism though it may be – Nadia, Tim and Victor are completely deprived of any sense of the past. All that counts for them is the present; they 'see each day as a new day' (Ravenhill 2001b: 48) and as unrelated to either yesterday or tomorrow. Regarding these corrupted forms of historical awareness, none of the characters manages to engage fruitfully and sincerely with the past and its complex challenges for the present.

Preoccupied with the question of the role and function of the past in the characters' lives, *Polaroids* can be said to employ history in post-Brechtian spirit as a medium for its political and meta-dialectical investigations. Rather than facilitating an interrogation of the contemporary moment from a temporal distance, *Polaroids*'s use of history serves to dramatize and exacerbate the fundamental rupture between past and present, as the characters' paralysis reflects. Therefore, while the play appears, on the surface, as an example of conventional dialectical theatre – based, as it is, on antithetical structures and key notions of political engagement and resistance – its construction is decidedly more complex, blurring distinctions and emphasizing disconnection. In this sense, the play acquires a significant parabolic and meta-dialectical dimension, as the characters' microcosm seems to be symptomatic of the play's wider investigations into political theatre today. Thus, the specific dramaturgical and epistemological mechanisms identified above are self-reflexively employed to expose their inadequacy as a means of engaging with social reality, in a context in which fundamental dialectical methods have become manipulated by political rhetoric, and thereby deprived of their resistant thrust.

Dialectical Emotions

Rather than rejecting dialectics as a potentially empowering framework, however, *Polaroids* is committed to a search for a new form of dialectical theatre which may respond to contemporary social reality and its ambivalent, disorientating political terrain. Staging a paradox between the crisis of dialectical criticism, on the one hand, and an affirmation of the ongoing value of thinking in dialectical categories, on the other, the play explores the potential of the emotions as a means of reconnecting with each other and with the wider context. Focussing on the microcosm of the characters' conflict-laden relationships, a clear shift can be identified. It is not as a result of their heated, inconclusive discussions, which merely result in increasing their disconnection from each other and their surroundings, but through their specific emotional experiences that the characters can be said to undergo a decisive development. In a post-Brechtian vein, therefore, the play reflects Ravenhill's overarching interest in 'dialectics, not necessarily a dialectic [sic] argument, but a dialectic emotion or mood, dialectic in the sense of contradiction' (Ravenhill qtd. in Monforte 2007: 103). Hence, Ravenhill's works indicate a broader trend in 1990s British drama as 'politics in the theatre shifted from an explicitly socialist agenda to a focus on the experiential and the intimate' (Fragkou 2018: 22), noticeable first and foremost in an emphasis on the private rather than public sphere, and on personal rather than collective issues. In this sense, Fragkou identifies an '*intimate politics* or *politics of intimacy*' in these plays which 'is driven by an investment in affective engagement' (2018: 23). As I will argue in the remainder of this chapter, this political impetus can be described in terms of the dialectical functions *Polaroids* attributes to the characters' and, by extension, the audience's emotional experiences.

As the younger generation illustrates, however, the form of authentic emotional expression the play seeks has become increasingly problematic. As Tim and Victor repeatedly assert, emotions represent a sign of weakness for them and hence supposedly play no role in their lives. They reject Nick's passionate commitment as well as any emotional attachment to each other: 'Loving, spiritual, vulnerable, ill. Fuck this. ... Means? Means?

Fuck this "means." Nothing means anything, ok?' (Ravenhill 2001b: 12). In line with Stjepan G. Meštrović's diagnosis of contemporary society as 'postemotional', *Polaroids* reflects that genuine feelings have been replaced by 'carefully crafted', 'synthetic quasi-emotions' (1997: xi) under the impact of neoliberalism – a development which Eva Illouz usefully describes as '[e]motional capitalism' (2007: 5). Crucially, it is this commodified, instrumentalized and thus inauthentic quality of emotional engagement which spurs indifference and prevents any meaningful political action (Meštrović 1997: xi). In this vein, Tim, Victor and Nadia remain paralyzed in their self-centred pursuit of 'happiness'.

Rather, *Polaroid*'s emotional centre can again be found in Nick, whose passionate and rebellious nature introduces 'an emotional thaw' (Carney 2013: 254) into the play: he 'serves as the return of the repressed, not socialism, or activism, or even a politicized sensibility, but emotions' (Carney 2013: 254). While Nick's anger alienates the other characters, his appearance nevertheless marks a moment of Brechtian interruption which encourages them to revisit their own emotions and, eventually, brings about a certain degree of change. The characters not only realize that it is impossible for them to run away from their feelings, but the confrontation with Nick also enables them to acknowledge their profound unhappiness. Thus, Victor is finally able to express his love for Tim: 'I wish I knew what to do. I think maybe inside us, if we were allowed feelings we would know what to do' (Ravenhill 2001b: 64). Yet, this turning point only occurs at the very moment when he is about to lose Tim, who suffers from AIDS and refuses to continue to take his life-prolonging medicine, and thus comes too late for any real connections to be established and for any substantial consequences to emerge from this experience. In a surreal scene set after his death, (the ghost of) Tim connects his unhappiness with the new experience of a seemingly infinite life and the sheer endless range of opportunities made available to him by medication, which has resulted in his profound disorientation and aimlessness: 'My life was a tragedy. ... But I knew where I was going. ... I used to know everything and that's what those fucking pills have taken away from me' (Ravenhill 2001b: 58–9). Tim's deep yearning for teleology and 'choice' (Ravenhill 2001b: 57) finally lead him, in a fatal gesture that represents both a radical assertion and an outright denial of agency, to commit suicide. As a metaphor for the wider context explored by the play, this omnipresent form of violence in the younger generation's lives can therefore be understood as a symbol of their 'perverse attempt at connection' (Rebellato 2008: 204). Thus, the destructive quality of their relationships reflects how '[t]he political anger once voiced explicitly ... through protest and immediate social action is now displaced through acts of physical and psychological violence' (Svich

2003: 41). In this sense, the play foregrounds the importance of the body as a site of meaning and connection. This emphasis on corporeality can be fruitfully linked to Brecht, in whose plays, too, 'the body stands clarified as a nexus of social gestures and relationships' (Garner 1990: 149). Thus, as a form of Brechtian gestus, the body as the characters' most intimate dimension acquires a wider social and political significance in these instances. Crucially, however, while Tim's death represents a turning point for Victor and Nadia, who are finally able to reconnect with their feelings in the face of loss, their isolation and disconnection emerges as even more pronounced; after this scene, the young characters completely disappear from the stage.

Looking backwards rather than forward, *Polaroids* thus finishes with a focus on the older generation and seems to reinforce this pessimistic gesture by foregrounding the problematic nature of the characters' emotional investments. Realizing that his politically spurred anger can no longer be brought in tune with the contemporary conditions, Nick begins to openly embrace the Cool Britannia generation's 'happiness' mantra. As the only one to move flexibly in-between the opposing groups, Nick's indecisive back and forth reflects an inability 'to commit himself to either, feeling divided between neoliberal reformism and alienated nihilism' (Pavis 2004: 11). Whereas he gradually distances himself from his former anger, Helen develops in a different direction. Her rational, calculating spirit is challenged by Nick's strong emotions, forcing her to confront her rebellious past. The final scene, which stages a reunion between Helen and Nick, has therefore often been interpreted as a resolution – in dialectical terms, as a synthesis – of their conflict between reason and emotion (Kritzer 2008: 47; Svich 2003: 92). Far from an authentic expression of love, however, the renewal of their relationship is based on Helen's selfish need for Nick's anger as an antidote to her rationality: 'I want you to be angry. ... I want to make you into what you used to be' (Ravenhill 2001b: 84). This attempt is, however, doomed to fail, since Nick's rebellious nature can no longer provide an adequate form of commitment at the turn of the millennium, as has been made clear throughout. In this sense, Helen's nostalgia represents neither a genuine engagement with her past nor a solid basis for their relationship – a lesson Nick has had to learn in the course of the play. Consequently, while 'Nick's return ... provokes those around him out of their stasis' (Carney 2013: 256), the conflicts triggered by his disruptive appearance remain unresolved and Helen and Nick's prospects are highly uncertain.

Hence, *Polaroids* ends on a decidedly ambivalent note; rather than offering, as Amelia Howe Kritzer has suggested, 'a fully formed narrative that creates a tentative paradigm for political action' (2008: 45), it refuses to indicate a clear direction. Both socialism and neoliberalism are exposed, in the play's wording, as 'big fucking lies', and the characters are presented as stuck in a dead-end street, since none of the options available to them seem valid. Yet, from the meta-dialectical and parabolic perspective inscribed into the play, this lack of alternatives is not synonymous with a rejection of political commitment in the form of dialectical critique as such. Instead, it is precisely by denying clarity and orientation that *Polaroids* foregrounds the ongoing value of dialectical thought, privileging concepts of opposition, conflict and debate over harmony and closure. Thus, by withholding a reconciliation of the paradoxes shaping the play – between past and present, socialist and capitalist ideals, reason and emotion – the play embraces Adornian and Rancièrean notions of negativity and dissensus as sources of a new understanding of dialectical theatre. While Sean Carney suggests in his Adornian reading that this sense of negativity is realized in *Polaroids* itself through the figure of Nick as the parable's driving force (2013: 253), this assessment overlooks the fact that the dialectical processes spurred by Nick's return are based on conventional strategies, which the play ultimately rejects as inefficient.

Rather than embodied by Nick, I therefore propose that the negativity essential for reinitiating dialectical dissensus must be located in the relationship between stage and auditorium. The play's open-endedness has a profound impact on the audience's interpretation and the prevailing indeterminacy at the end can be understood as an implicit appeal to the spectators to negotiate the paradoxes on stage. Instead of clearly outlining a way towards synthesis, *Polaroids* hands over the challenge of articulating a new politics to the spectators. Consequently, in a post-Brechtian vein, the dialectical dynamics are reinvigorated not so much within the play itself as through the audience's interpretive efforts. Just as the characters discover the importance of emotional engagement as a means of reconnection, the play's formal provocation or 'aesthetic shock', which manifests itself in the crisis of conventional dialectics and its emphasis on ambivalence, facilitates a decidedly more tentative and subjective process of interpretation based on a shift from argument, reason and analysis to emotion and experience. In post-Brechtian spirit, Ravenhill's meta-dialectical parable thus suggests that it is 'at the level of feeling and metaphor' (Rebellato 2008: 202) that a new form of dialectical critique can be initiated in the interaction between stage and spectators. In this sense, *Polaroids* emerges as a turning point in the British reception of Brecht's legacy, heralding a new approach to Brechtian dialectical drama and prefiguring major developments in twenty-first-century political theatre in Britain. As the remainder of this book will argue, it is this emphasis on experience, ambivalence and self-reflexivity which is indicative of a wider trend in contemporary forms of dialectical theatre which critically examine and innovate Brechtian dialectics as a progressive theatrical model for the new millennium.

Resisting the Banal Dialectic of (Counter-)Terrorism: *Shoot/Get Treasure/Repeat*

Taking up and revising central strands of the lively scholarly discussions of Ravenhill's dramatic texts, the previous section has offered a fresh perspective on the politics of his works by examining their characteristic 'in-yer-face' sensibility in terms of its crucial intersections with a Brechtian dialectical mode of theatre-making. As a prime example of Ravenhill's commitment to dialectics as a means of critical dramaturgy and social analysis, *Polaroids* has thereby emerged as a cornerstone of his oeuvre. Written on the cusp between two millennia and at a creative crossroads for the playwright, the play can be attributed a wider significance, as it reunites central thematic and aesthetic interests predominating Ravenhill's work as a whole. Most notably, this is reflected in how the play parabolically and self-reflexively exposes a fundamental crisis of conventional dialectical mechanisms while initiating a new form of Brechtian-inspired dialectical theatre and critique on the basis of notions of ambivalence, negativity and emotional experience. Building on these observations, I will argue in the following that these tendencies are precisely not a phenomenon exclusive to the 1990s Cool Britannia era; on the contrary, Ravenhill's twenty-first-century plays have continued to explore similar questions with the help of an experiential approach to dialectics for the purpose of creating a progressive form of contemporary political drama.

It is the ambitious play cycle *Shoot/Get Treasure/Repeat* (2007) which most impressively attests to Ravenhill's enduring engagement with Brecht's legacy. Its seventeen short, twenty-minute playlets offer kaleidoscopic, aesthetically diverse perspectives on the social, political and economic challenges of terrorism and war in the neoliberal age by uncomfortably blurring the boundaries between here and there, home and front, us and them, victims and perpetrators as well as private and public. In this sense, *Shoot*'s Brechtian dimension emerges most explicitly on an intertextual level, as significant thematic and dramaturgical parallels can be established with Brecht's twenty-four-scene play *Fear and Misery of the Third Reich*, a complex montage of scenes on everyday life in Nazi Germany. Yet, whereas the political situation and alliances in Brecht's *Fear and Misery* are comparatively straightforward, *Shoot*'s post-9/11 world is characterized by a profound indeterminacy, as fundamental distinctions have been eroded. As a result, *Shoot* refuses to present 'political alternatives or role models' – a sharp contrast with Brecht's 'impulse of resistance against the Third Reich and the hope for an alternative political system' (Wessendorf 2011: 339). It is this shift from ideological clarity to uncertainty which points towards a post-Brechtian dimension in Ravenhill's approach, as I will demonstrate in the following.

While comparative readings of this kind are insightful to the extent that they bring a post-Brechtian perspective into focus, what I suggest is most pertinent about *Shoot*'s commitment to Brecht is of a more theoretical nature. As I contend, the play cycle engages in a critical examination of dialectics as both a form of critical thought and a dramaturgical tool. Situating its interrogations in the context of twenty-first-century terrorist warfare, the play focuses on the distinctive discursive practices that have developed in response to atrocious terrorist acts and exposes them as profoundly anti-dialectical. Crucially, even though the discourse of (counter-)terrorism has been prolifically analysed (Jackson 2005; Zulaika and Douglass 1996; Hodges 2011), its fundamental dialectical dimension, which I posit as central to understanding its ideological impact, has so far remained underexplored. While Ariane de Waal proposes a compelling reading of Ravenhill's cycle through the lens of the discourses of war and terrorism, her analysis does not foreground the role of Brechtian dramaturgy and does not explore the discursive practices from the point of view of dialectical theatre (2017b). Vice versa, Lara Stevens examines the intersections between anti-war theatre and Brecht's dialectical legacy, but neither focuses on the discursive practices of (counter-)terrorism nor on Ravenhill's work (2016). Even though I am not denying the materialist manifestations of (counter-)terrorism – indeed, the play cycle itself does not shy away from confronting its spectators with gruesome forms of terrorist violence – it is nevertheless useful for an analysis of *Shoot* to examine (counter-)terrorism from the perspective of political discourse to identify its strategic manipulation of dialectical mechanisms and its deeply paralyzing implications for both public and private life. Exposing this radical instrumentalization, Ravenhill's cycle is invested in a search for a way of resisting these exploitative processes. As the remainder of this chapter will show, this is above all achieved by reimagining dialectical dramaturgy on the basis of a strategic provocation.

(Counter-)Terrorist Discourse as (Anti-)Dialectical Phenomenon

In his seminal study *Writing the War on Terrorism: Language, Politics and Counter-Terrorism* (2005), Richard Jackson argues with reference to Michel Foucault that terrorism must be understood as 'simultaneously a set of actual practices – wars, covert operations, agencies and institutions – and an accompanying series of assumptions, beliefs, justifications and narratives – it is an entire ... discourse' (2005: 8). As a complex system that transcends language as such to include notably the ideological work performed by institutions and organizations, it constitutes a strategic means of exerting power. As Adam Hodges and Chad Nilep observe, discourse 'does not simply reflect events that occur in the world' but also 'infuses events with meaning, establishes widespread social understandings, and constitutes social reality' (2007: 5). Crucially, these mechanisms are exploited by both sides, terrorist and (what is ostensibly) counterterrorist rhetoric – distinctions which, however, ultimately emerge as purely artificial. Thus, as Joseba Zulaika and William A. Douglass demonstrate, counterterrorist discourse can be said to paradoxically 'further [recreate] and [reify] the terrorism paradigm instead of undermining its fictions' (1996: 16), thereby deliberately blurring the boundaries between terrorism and the fight against it. This mechanism has had a particularly pervasive effect in the twenty-first century, as political institutions have successfully appropriated and shaped the discourse in response to 9/11, gaining control over the narrative as a means of legitimizing political action and achieving specific goals, notably 'to empower the authorities and shield them from criticism' and 'to discipline domestic society by marginalizing dissent or protest' (Jackson 2005: 2). Significantly, the discursive patterns which have emerged are organized in rigid dialectical terms, opposing 'us' and 'them', 'victims' and 'perpetrators', 'enemy' and 'friend'. Persistently repeated by the media and adopted by the wider public, an 'official' narrative of the 'War on Terror' has established itself and has become 'naturalized' as well as 'widely accepted, "common sense,"' obscuring the fact that, in truth, it constitutes only 'one among several possible interpretations' (Hodges 2011: 7).

As *Shoot* uncovers, this considerable political and discursive power results above all from a strategic instrumentalization of dialectical categories in (counter-)terrorist discourse. To expose these manipulative practices, the play adopts a conventional dialectical framework, which is reflected in its use of rigorous oppositions on the level of content and form. While the individual playlets are designed as independent entities, they are intricately connected through these recurrent dialectical themes, motifs, structural arrangements and formal devices, creating a haunting cumulative effect despite the overall lack of coherence and linearity. Thus, throughout the cycle, the characters relentlessly evoke the 'Manichean binaries and stark dichotomies that circulate in public discourse' (de Waal 2017a: 74) to the extent that they determine their speech patterns, motivate their actions and thereby become a crucial part of their identity. This is most evident in the characters' attempts to demarcate themselves from what they perceive as the threatening, foreign 'Others' (who are, significantly, never specified and who remain an indeterminate source of danger throughout) by declaring themselves the 'good', 'civilized' and 'normal' citizens and 'innocent' victims as opposed to the 'evil' terrorists, against whom they obsessively try to protect themselves. For example, a member of the chorus in the playlet 'Women of Troy' emphasizes that '[o]ur way of life is the right, the good, it's the right life. It's the only way of life' and disrespectfully treats the alien 'Other' as 'not a person. I don't see you as a person. I've never seen you as a person. You're a bomb' (Ravenhill 2013: 13). Mechanically and unquestioningly reproducing these pseudo-dialectical patterns typical of the discourse of (counter-)terrorism and applying them to their understanding of themselves and to the way they approach their surroundings, the characters thus end up reinforcing these lines of thought through their own behaviour, suggesting not only the characters' ultimate complicity in the politics of (counter-)terrorism but also their fundamental paralysis.

While these rigid dichotomies are at all costs maintained on the surface, the play cycle lays bare that the characters' efforts to uphold these distinctions turn out to be futile: personal and political, war and peace, here and there have become blurred, creating a deeply ambiguous terrain in which 'the means, ends, and limits of (countering) terrorism' (de Waal 2017b: 1) are undefined. This effect is especially underscored by *Shoot*'s domestic scenes, which are set in the private (recognizably Western) sphere and thus reflect how public discourse has become implanted into the most intimate part of the characters' lives. Significantly, a majority of these playlets is rendered as duologues, which does not only reinforce the central role of dichotomous discursive patterns on the level of form but also makes it possible to explore the dynamics underpinning the often tense, conflict-laden relationships from a dialectical perspective. Dan Rebellato has identified two-handers as 'one of the most distinctive forms of the last twenty years' in British playwriting, explaining their dominance with reference to the ethical turn in philosophy as well as theatre and performance studies by drawing attention to their function of 'provid[ing] an opportunity for intense scrutiny of relations between self and other' (2014: 85). While the use of two-handers in *Shoot* is certainly to some extent an economic decision to reduce the costs of staging the epic cycle, the duologues also make it possible to foreground the parabolic quality of the character constellations, as intimate relationships between two individuals are designed to mirror wider political and social concerns.

The playlet 'Fear and Misery', whose title draws a direct parallel with Brecht's cycle, illustrates these mechanisms and serves as a prime example of *Shoot*'s aesthetic strategies and dialectical preoccupations. Strictly speaking, 'Fear and Misery' is not a duologue since, besides Harry and Olivia, two other characters, the couple's child Alex and a Soldier, are also involved in this scene. Yet, Alex is an off-stage character who can only be heard over the baby alarm; similarly, while the Soldier briefly enters the scene, he remains silent throughout and the protagonists ignore his *physical* presence in the room. From a dialectical perspective, therefore, it can be productive to treat the playlet as a two-hander because the *felt* presence of Alex and the Soldier serves to focus attention on the destructive dynamics underpinning Harry and Olivia's relationship. Their marriage is portrayed as a loveless affair, as Harry's obsession with security has overshadowed any genuine feelings that may have existed beforehand. He is preoccupied with protecting his family against external threats, which he perceives to be imminent, and therefore explains to his wife Olivia (in uncannily prescient fashion): 'I want us – you, me, Alex – to build a wall against ... Somehow the world out there got full of ... Somehow there's nothing but hate out there. Aggression' (Ravenhill 2013: 49). Harry's choice of words, in particular his use of simplistic dichotomies between 'us' and 'them', 'inside' and 'outside', shows to what extent the characters have absorbed the patterns of (counter-)terrorist discourse. Their anxieties are displaced onto the most intimate level when Olivia compares sexual intercourse with her husband to an act of violence: 'We really are ... making love. But it feels like, it seems like – there's a sort of ... rape. Sorry. Rape. Sorry. Rape. Sorry' (Ravenhill 2013: 41). Harry reacts harshly to her confession and the increasingly aggressive and violent nature of their conversation is made visible in the script through the use of uppercase letters, which disrupt the text to underscore the brutality of their relationship:

Harry YOU CALLED ME A FUCKING RAPIST FOR FUCK'S SAKE. YOU TOLD ME MY SON WAS BORN BECAUSE OF AN ACT OF RAPE.
Olivia I DIDN'T. I DIDN'T. I NEVER DID THAT. I NEVER DID. WON'T YOU – LEAVE IT. JUST LEAVE IT ...
Ravenhill (2013: 45)

In this sense, 'Fear and Misery' is exemplary of the cycle's use of duologues insofar as it projects the overarching political concerns onto the characters' private lives, thereby revealing how the perceived terror of the public sphere has invaded Harry and Olivia's marriage not only in terms of discourse but also on the level of their thoughts, actions and feelings.

Indeed, what seems to motivate and control Harry and Olivia's behaviour most strongly is an overwhelming sense of anxiety, which attests to the idea that fear constitutes a crucial motor in the discourses of terrorism and counterterrorism alike. This integral role of fear is notably addressed by Michael C. Frank, who defines terrorism as 'the collective apprehension of (more) political violence to come' (2017: 55). As *Shoot* exemplifies, the aim of this 'politics of fear' is to exert control not only over public policy but, more importantly and more insidiously, also over everyday life. The effects of this discursive manipulation of feelings are illustrated by Harry and Olivia's obsessive, anxious and distressed attempts to protect themselves against hypothetical external threats: 'The security. The extra locks. The child locks. Making sure no plug is free. Keeping the mice at bay' (Ravenhill 2013: 42). Despite these measures, they remain hypersensitive: 'THE WORLD IS ATTACKING US, THE TERROR IS EATING US UP AND YOU ... WE NEED GATES. WE NEED TO, TO, TO ... DRAW UP THE DRAWBRIDGE AND CLOSE THE GATES AND SECURITY, SECURITY, SECURITY, SECURITY' (Ravenhill 2013: 50). Thus, creating a self-reinforcing vicious cycle, their efforts to increase security paradoxically increase their anxiety, leading them to adopt ever more absurd strategies and patterns of behaviour without realizing that terror has already become an integral part of their private life at home.

These self-perpetuating dynamics underpinning Harry and Olivia's interaction reflect that both terrorism and the fight against it in fact employ similar strategies, thereby reproducing the very effects counterterrorism ostensibly seeks to combat. This has a profoundly paralyzing impact on the characters. Withdrawing into the isolation of their private home, they display a deliberate denial. Olivia, for example, tries to ignore the omnipresent reality of the war both outside and inside her own house, calming her son by saying '[y]es, darling, there is a war but it's not our war, we don't ... we don't want that war to happen and it's a long way away, that war is such a long, long, long way away' (Ravenhill 2013: 50). The fact that she is off-stage and thus invisible at this moment – just like the war itself, in her understanding – puts her refusal to acknowledge the existence of global conflict even more forcefully on display. In this sense, the characters' behaviour shows that their actions – excessive protection, retreat into the private sphere and denial – cannot be considered active responses; rather, they are motivated by their deep-seated anxieties, which eventually leads them to unquestioningly conform to and participate in the practices of (counter-)terrorism.

In this sense, blurring the boundaries between supposedly distinct categories and concepts while deliberately reinstating these oppositions, the discourse of (counter-)terrorism engages in a strategic manipulation of dialectical thought. As Angelica Nuzzo argues in her insightful essay on 'the challenges that war and terrorism pose today to the project of dialectical reason', dialectical contradiction 'is suffocated and rendered ineffectual' (2007: 294), as war and peace, terrorism and (counter-)terrorism, victim and perpetrator can no longer be clearly distinguished. What results from this deliberate erasure of difference is a form of 'un-dialectical thinking' (Nuzzo 2007: 294), as the characters' lack of critical capacity and their participation in the perpetuation of the status quo reflect. It is this absence of contradiction and opposition which facilitates the emergence of a 'permanent state of war to which, in turn, a perpetual war ought to be waged' (Nuzzo 2007: 304) – a fundamental strategy at the heart of (counter-)terrorist policy. This 'essential formlessness' (de Waal 2017b: 1) of the war on terror is made explicit by the Soldier in the playlet 'War and Peace', where this idea is carried to the extreme: 'But live without war? No human being's ever done that. Never will. It's what makes us human' (Ravenhill 2013: 55–6). Reflecting the self-perpetuating logic of the discourse of (counter-)terrorism, he perspicaciously suggests:

> You know what was wrong with wars before? They ended. There was peace. But this one goes on and on and on. It's a war on terror and it goes on and on and on and on. There's no God, see? There's no end day. There just this war on terror on and on.
>
> Ravenhill (2013: 62)

Thus, the play cycle illustrates how the fight against terrorism is turned into an ostensibly never-ending, indefinite mission without any clear agenda, depriving the participants of any sense of orientation or power. Paradoxically, while the discursive practices seemingly attribute an active, influential role to the characters through the relentless application of polarizing language and dichotomous, structuring concepts, the actual, decidedly anti-dialectical impact of these mechanisms is successfully concealed.

This paradox underlying Ravenhill's play cycle can be brought into fruitful dialogue with Hannah Arendt's understanding of 'banality'. Arendt developed the concept of the 'banality of evil' in her groundbreaking work *Eichmann in Jerusalem*, which documents her report of the trial against Adolf Eichmann, one of the major Nazi officials involved in the organization of the Holocaust. While this specific historical background must of course be distinguished in method, scope and atrociousness from contemporary forms of terrorism, the essential characteristics of the concept of 'banality' are useful to further explain the impact of the discursive practices of (counter-)terrorism, in particular from a dialectical perspective. In Arendt's use of the term, banality describes the normalization of evil under Nazi rule, as a result of which violence and crime were routinized. As Arendt writes, the crimes were thus turned into '[c]lichés, stock phrases, adherence to conventional standardized codes of expression and conduct [which] have the socially recognized function of protecting us against reality' (Arendt quoted in Myers 2004: 96), paving the way for them to become, in Judith Butler's words, 'accepted, routinized, and implemented without moral revulsion and political indignation and resistance' (2011). As a result, it is 'non-thinking itself' which 'had become "banal" … This fact was not banal at all, but unprecedented, shocking, and wrong' (Butler 2011). Hence, this mechanism both hinges on and facilitates a fundamental thoughtlessness on the part of the agent, as the strategic banalization of Nazi ideology had an all-pervading, insidious effect which prevented any form of conscious critical engagement, and thereby made mass murder possible.

Applying Arendt's argumentative framework to the context of (counter-)terrorism, the discursive strategies identified above can be attributed a similar banalizing impact. As *Shoot* demonstrates, the characters are no longer capable of thinking, acting or behaving according to conscious, autonomous decisions, clear intentions or motives. In fact, what is most striking is the extent to which they are portrayed as unaware of their involvement or, indeed, as deliberately denying their participation; either way, they are incapable of critique and distance. Hence, the appropriation of dialectical principles evident in (counter-)terrorist discourse effectively undermines central mechanisms of critique, turning it into a politically dysfunctional, undemocratic and non-emancipatory tool. It is this paralyzing force which Cindi Katz refers to in her definition of 'banal terrorism' as 'everyday, routinized, barely noticed reminders of terror' (2007: 350) – albeit without establishing an explicit connection with Arendt's concept. Similarly, without referring to Arendt, Rustom Bharucha describes terror as '[f]ar from being exceptional', and thus 'as the new banality of evil in our times' (2014: 3). Thus, what the banality of (counter-)terrorism achieves most insidiously and pervasively is to establish a routine which serves to make the manipulative discursive strategies not only ordinary but, above all, also invisible, thereby preventing them from becoming an object of critical inquiry. In short, the anti-dialectical and anti-democratic impact of the discursive practices of (counter-)terrorism evidenced by Ravenhill's *Shoot* results in the characters' complicity, reflecting how these banal dialectical mechanisms are turned into powerful, self-reinforcing discursive tools.

Interrupting Banality

Given the all-encompassing, deeply manipulative force of (counter-)terrorist discourse, the question of how these mechanisms can be resisted and of which role the theatre can play in this endeavour arises. As de Waal insightfully argues with reference to Foucault, it is crucial to acknowledge that 'theatrical events have to be situated within – not outside of, or opposed to – the discursive formation of the "war on terror"' (2017b: 20–1). Hence, the theatre emerges 'as a site of cultural production that participates in a discursive field of force where progressive, conservative, and resistant elements converge and coexist' (de Waal 2017b: 3). This recognition is, however, far from denying the theatre any radical thrust; instead, it poses the challenge of reconceptualizing the particular mode of resistance the theatre can perform under these conditions. In this vein, de Waal suggests that, '[r]ather than countering "war on terror" discourse, what drama might do is inflect its order, elements, correlations, rules and positions; that is, performance might employ the enunciative modalities within this discursive field in a modulated form, with a subtle shift in gesture, pitch, volume, tone, mood, or voice' (de Waal 2017b: 21). Therefore, while the official discourse may impose itself as hegemonic and exclusive, it simultaneously undergoes a constant 'process of recontextualization' with each evocation through which it 'is not only reproduced but also reshaped and resisted across multiple discursive settings' (Hodges 2011: 4). These forms of interpretation of the 'grand' narrative of (counter-)terrorism may thus not only reinforce dominant discursive patterns but may, quite in contrast, also give rise to alternative viewpoints and open up a considerable potential for resistance at the theatre; any interpretive act is, after all, highly subjective and to a certain extent beyond control and manipulation. In this sense, Jackson observes that discourses are 'not monolithic, nor are they ever totally hegemonic; there are always contestations and sites of resistance' (2005: 19–20). As I argue, it is in these interstices that Ravenhill's *Shoot* intervenes through a dialectical aesthetic to explore the possibility of critique and intervention. Crucially, in the light of the banalizing, anti-dialectical effects of (counter-)terrorist discourse, this requires a fundamental reconceptualization of the forms and functions of dialectical philosophy. As Nuzzo explains, 'dialectical reason has now the additional task of producing contradiction for consciousness within a reality whose appearance seems to erase all conflict' (2007: 305–6), foregrounding, in post-Brechtian spirit, the value of negativity and dissensus for twenty-first-century dialectical theatre. In *Shoot*, this is achieved on a discursive, experiential and metatheatrical level, as I will illustrate below.

Neither presenting any positive examples of resistance nor proposing a way out of the vicious cycle of (counter-)terrorism, the playlets nevertheless attempt to challenge these powerful mechanisms through the use of post-Brechtian strategies, first of all on the level of discourse itself. As Jenny Spencer argues, 'Ravenhill experiments with a number of linguistic devices … with the goal of producing social gests – in other words, to make visible an analysis of the relationship between characters' actions, their historical situation, and the current market economy' (2012: 68–9). As a means of establishing a productive connection between theatre, audience and society which facilitates critical analysis, Brecht's concept of gestus represents a privileged device in *Shoot*'s dramaturgy. Crucially, rather than inspiring critique by creating Brechtian distance, gestus is applied as a tool for provocation in *Shoot* to confront and thereby appeal to the audience on the basis of emotional experience. Bringing the spectators closer to the action, the plays' provocative quality serves to spur 'strategic, spectatorial resistance' (Defraeye 2004: 89). The significance of shock as a potentially emancipating force has in fact been foregrounded by Brecht himself, who distinguishes the 'primitive shock effects' employed by 'the theatre of our parasitic bourgeoisie' (2015a: 147) as an end in themselves from a politically inflected 'element of shock necessary for recognition' (2015a: 46). As *Shoot*'s use of gestus illustrates, it is in this political vein that the play's experiential framework is employed to spur conflict and contradiction.

The most prominent gestic strategy employed by the cycle is excessive repetition. Relentlessly reproducing the polarizing language of (counter-)terrorism, the playlets persistently repeat key concepts and categories to show how their original meaning is corrupted through a strategic discursive manipulation in the context of (counter-)terrorist rhetoric. This mechanism is reminiscent of Brecht's 1947 poem 'Freedom and Democracy', which satirizes the establishment of Western democracy in post-World War II Germany as a capitalist undertaking of 'importing' democratic values. In the German original, entitled 'Freiheit und Democracy', this critique is even more poignant, as it uses the English term to satirically underscore the process of importing these allegedly 'Americanized' concepts. Repeated regularly, like a refrain, at the end of nine stanzas, the catchphrase 'Freedom and Democracy' – capitalized in the English translation to underscore its status as a 'brand' – reveals the increasing hollowness of these snappy slogans, which have acquired a considerable rhetorical power while losing their value as fundamental principles of democratic society. *Shoot* adopts a similarly satirical approach to expose that the rhetoric and pursuit of 'freedom and democracy' represent a fallacy for the characters. This is made explicit in 'Crime and Punishment', which stages an allegorical confrontation between a Woman and a Soldier, and thus between occupied and occupier. The Woman accuses the Soldier of thwarting and betraying her genuine hopes for freedom and democracy: 'This is your freedom? This is your democracy? How stupid we were. ... You are just another hell' (Ravenhill 2013: 96). The corruption of these values and the disorientation resulting from their meaninglessness become manifest in a gut-wrenching scene towards the end. After torturing the Woman, the Soldier considers committing suicide, exasperated and weary of his mission: 'I wish I had an order from a superior. ... But there is no order from above. The choice is mine. This is democracy. This is what we call democracy. Democracy – I hate you' (Ravenhill 2013: 97). By displacing these concepts into different contexts, the repetitions acquire a profoundly gestic quality, underscoring the increasing distortion, making visible their corruptive impact on the characters and provoking the audience – as opposed to the inert characters – to adopt a critical perspective on the events.

A similar gestic effect is created through the use of discursive juxtapositions, which uncover the pervasive impact the appropriation of (counter-)terrorist discourse has on the characters. 'War and Peace', which stages the encounter between the child Alex and a headless, wounded Soldier in the boy's bedroom, blends realist and surrealist elements on the level of character constellation, style and discourse. In an ironic reversal, the seemingly innocent Alex has adopted speech patterns typical of adult rather than child language. In a condescending statement, he appeals to the Soldier to

> keep away from me, wanker. You – you – this is my room, this is my property, my family's ... I am so powerful and you're, you're ... you're scum ... you eat bad food, you have numeracy and literacy issues, you will never be on the property ladder ... you don't belong in a gated community. Out, get out, away. You are a monster.
>
> Ravenhill (2013: 61)

Voiced by a little boy, the overlapping of the rhetoric of consumerism and the discourse of (counter-)terrorism offers a disturbing picture of how these discursive practices become implanted and normalized early on. This blending – also evident in 'Fear and Misery', where the semantic fields of love and warfare are juxtaposed – represents a key device for creating *Verfremdung* in *Shoot*, as it exposes these manipulative processes and their pervasive impact on the characters. Through their sheer banality, these juxtapositions deliberately play with audiences' expectations and provoke a shock effect which is instrumental to the plays' dialectical impetus, encouraging the spectators to adopt a critical perspective by confronting them with these disturbing mechanisms.

This intricate combination of shock and recognition is also achieved through the cycle's use of interruptions, which represent a key strategy in Brechtian dialectical theatre. Significantly, Walter Benjamin foregrounds interruptions as a means of creating gestus: 'the more often we interrupt someone in process of action, the more gestures we obtain' (1998: 20). An interruption thus 'has an organizing function. It brings the action to a standstill in mid-course and thereby compels the spectator to take up a position towards the action' (Benjamin 1998: 100). What is decisive for achieving this effect is an experience of 'astonishment' (Benjamin 1998: 18) caused by the disruption. As Stanley Mitchell comments, the aim is 'to "shock" people into new recognitions and understandings' (1998: xiii). This moment of shock is key to the interruptions employed in *Shoot*, where the play's disruptive aesthetic serves to stage a confrontation with the manipulative processes of (counter-)terrorist discourse. Specifically, these interruptions frequently exacerbate the characters' increasing loss of control, as they satirically counteract their obsessive efforts for security and thereby expose the self-defeating mechanisms of the politics of (counter-)terrorism. Employed throughout the cycle, interruptions are mostly realized in the form of sudden entrances or exits, usually involving highly visceral images of explicit violence. In 'Fear and Misery', for example, Harry and Olivia's alertness is caricatured by the appearance of '*[a] Soldier covered in blood and mud*' (Ravenhill 2013: 49) of whom they are entirely unaware. In 'War and Peace', the absurdity of the discursive blending described above reaches its visceral climax when Alex shoots the Soldier in the arm, finishing the playlet with the words '[a]nd then the soldier went but Alex kept his gun. And the war went on' (Ravenhill 2013: 63). Reinforcing *Shoot*'s depiction of the vicious cycle of violence, these atrocious and confrontational interruptions are, in post-Brechtian spirit, decisive for the cycle's political thrust. By making visible what the characters are manipulated to ignore, the violent disruptions function as an antidote to the detachment and denial of responsibility manifest in the characters' behaviour. In this sense, Clare Finburgh argues that 'rather than providing spectacles of war', the playlets 'stage the violence of war in ways that challenge and interrogate audiences' (2017: 104–6). Underscoring the characters' lack of critical reflection, these provocative post-Brechtian devices force the audience to confront and negotiate these images and actions and to acknowledge, in gestic spirit, their wider sociopolitical implications. It is, as Benjamin writes, only 'against this rock of astonishment' and shock that 'the stream of things breaks' (1998: 13).

Experiencing Spectatorial Manipulation

This provocative quality does not only unfold on a discursive level but also in the relationship between stage and auditorium, which may be experienced as profoundly unsettling by the audience members. Crucially, the spectators also perform a central role in the context of (counter-)terrorism, as Frank explains: 'Terror is never in the hands of the violent actors alone. It is at least partly also a phenomenon of reception, in which the entire public participates' (2017: 47–8). As the playlets show, the implementation of (counter-)terrorist measures depends to a great extent on the characters' responsiveness and willingness. Significantly, this mechanism of complicity also represents the pillar of *Shoot*'s strategic positioning of the audience. Mirroring the characters' lack of control and agency, it enlists and manipulates the spectators by turning their participation into an experience of paralysis. Based on this deliberate provocation, the audience is therefore involved in the performance 'on visceral, emotional, and cognitive levels', as Spencer explains: 'the goal of the cycle is not simply to promote detachment in the service of analysis, but also to amplify audience affect in ways more likely to produce political change' by 'put[ting] affect in the service of political dissent' (2012: 67). Hence, the experiential quality of the performance is employed as a means of fostering awareness and critique and is therefore decisive for turning the audience's complex participation into a dialectical experience, as I will demonstrate in the following.

At first sight, the majority of the playlets seems unremarkable and straightforward with regard to the role of the audience. These are dialogic plays with a conventional set-up, as the spectators can supposedly watch from a safe distance behind the fourth wall without being directly involved. This specific constellation reflects what has been identified as the theatre's intrinsic voyeuristic quality. In this sense, George Rodosthenous describes the theatrical event as 'a voyeuristic exchange between the performer and the audience, where the performer (the object of the audience's gaze) and the audience (the voyeur of this exchange) are placed in a legalized and safe environment for that interaction' (2015: 3). Given its visceral dramaturgy and its explicit representations of violence, *Shoot* can be said to exploit this inherent voyeuristic dimension as a means of radicalizing the spectators' experience of the performance. As described above, the scenes are all characterized by intense moments of physical, sexual and psychological violence, realized through both direct enactment and verbal descriptions which invite audience members to imagine the incidents and thus to be even more closely involved in the production of these images. Crucially, behind the fourth wall, the spectators are involuntarily exposed to these scenes and positioned as silent and (ostensibly) passive witnesses of the events. Being forced to observe without being able to intervene, they are incapable of voicing resistance and the very fact that they are present in the auditorium, that the unfolding of the performance depends on their attendance in the first place, renders them complicit with the plays' strategies.

In this sense, the spectators are forced to undergo an experience which is not dissimilar from the characters' conspicuous lack of agency. Cast as passive participants incapable of interfering, the audience is, however, made all the more acutely aware of the potentially paralyzing and banalizing impact of these mechanisms. Thus, the highly provocative effect of this voyeuristic constellation may trigger a wide range of emotional reactions such as '[s]ympathy, anger, and guilt', which may, crucially, 'force a radical reassessment of values' (1992: 119), as Mary Karen Dahl argues in her analysis of dramatic responses to terrorism. In this sense, voyeurism 'can go beyond an exploitative thirst for watching' (Rodosthenous 2015: 17) to acquire a fundamental political and ethical relevance, blurring the lines between passive voyeurs, on the one hand, and active participants, on the other. *Shoot*'s provocative positioning of the audience may thus give rise to a form of emancipated spectatorship in Rancière's sense of the term. Facilitating a heightened experience of voyeurism, the plays pursue a post-Brechtian strategy which aims to incite the spectators to adopt a different perspective on what they have been exposed to on stage, as a prerequisite for reinitiating critique and intervention.

While the dialogic playlets provide a more implicit form of participation, the five choric plays involve the spectators immediately, as the members of the chorus appeal to the audience by directly addressing them with a collective 'you'. Pervasively, the spectators are cast according to the dichotomies of (counter-)terrorist discourse as the 'Other', functioning, for example, as the occupied population of an invaded nation in 'War of the Worlds', 'The Odyssey' and 'Birth of a Nation', as perpetrators in 'Women of Troy' or, indeed, as a theatre audience suspected of having attacked an actor in 'Yesterday an Incident Occurred'. The first play of the cycle, 'Women of Troy', sets the tone for this provocative arrangement:

– We want to ask you this. I want to ask you: why do you bomb us?
– We all ... All of us: why do you bomb us?
– Yes. Why ...?
– Just ... tell us – why?
– You see. We are the good people. Just look at us. Take a look at us. Take a good look at all of us. Gathered here today. And what do you see? You see the good people.

Ravenhill (2013: 7)

Addressing the spectators as potential terrorists, the play 'explicitly attributes an oppositional stance to the audience' (Grochala 2017: 216), accusing them of having bombed the women's city and threatening them with revenge. In a daring move, the scene ends with a Soldier's menace to kill the audience members. The confrontational quality of this set-up was accentuated by the London production, as the spectators 'were harangued from three edges by the choric women, and jostled into confusion by the suicide bomber who walked through their midst' (McGinn 2008). Crucially, while thus implicated in the performance, the spectators are never given any opportunity of responding to these accusations; they function as silent participants in the spectacle. In this sense, Sarah Grochala argues that, in dialectical terms, '[c]onflict is absent from the stage' because '[t]here is only thesis. Antithesis is banished ... and with it the hope of any synthesis' (2017: 216–17). Forced to perform the role of the dichotomously opposed 'Other', the spectators undergo a visceral, confrontational experience of paralysis and manipulation.

Therefore, rather than on the stage itself, it is the highly provocative and tense quality of the relationship between chorus and audience and the extent to which spectators are both implicated in and excluded from the action which may reinvigorate conflict and pave the way for developing a more critical standpoint towards the chorus. In her subtle analysis of *Shoot*'s choral aesthetics, de Waal shows how Ravenhill's playlets strategically undermine any 'affirmative' bond which conventionally underpins the relation between audience and chorus by deliberately destabilizing the chorus's identity in the respective plays, as the members fail 'to articulate a collective/choral voice' (2017b: 99–100). As a result, the values which the chorus embodies and which the audience is implicitly called to share are rendered highly problematic. This impression of insincerity is reinforced in the playlet 'War of the Worlds', which offers a particularly critical perspective on the chorus's emotional investments. Commemorating the victims of a terrorist attack, the citizens reunite for a public, mediatized performance of grief:

> YOU HAVE BEEN BOMBED. WE ARE SICKENED. WE ARE GRIEVING. WE FEEL PAIN. YOU ARE FAR AWAY FROM US. BUT OUR HEART IS YOUR HEART. YOUR PAIN IS OUR PAIN. YOUR WORLD HAS CHANGED FOREVER. WE LOVE YOU. WE WILL ALWAYS LOVE YOU BECAUSE WE ARE AS ONE WITH YOU FOR EVER.
> Ravenhill (2013: 129)

That the chorus's emotions are far from authentic is underscored by the play's excessive repetitions, its explicit use of theatrical vocabulary and the members' constant need for acknowledgement: 'Please see my grief. See it. Watch. Watch. See. *(Acts out this grief)*' (Ravenhill 2013: 127). Their performance is, however, disrupted by their sudden '*[h]ysterical laughter*' (Ravenhill 2013: 132), which reveals their hypocrisy and pretence. This is followed by an implicit but genuine acknowledgement of their fundamental indifference and disrespect, resulting first in condescending, even abusive behaviour towards the victims, whom they now refer to as 'fucking stupid … Phantoms. I piss on you. Piss on you' (Ravenhill 2013: 132), admitting that in fact they 'feel – well – nothing' (Ravenhill 2013: 133), and then, eventually, in their disengagement from the events by 'turn[ing] off the images' (Ravenhill 2013: 133). Confronted with this 'judgmental, and hypocritical underside' of these 'rituals of solidarity with, and mourning of, the victims of terror' (Spencer 2012: 74), the spectators are not only invited to question the chorus's politics but, given the playlet's strategic self-reflexivity, also their own emotional reactions, as they are self-consciously made aware of their status as audience members and, hence, as the plays suggest, as participants in the atrocities. This provocatively metatheatrical set-up, which forces the audience to confront their potential complicity, may produce, in Brechtian terms, a 'shock of recognition' (Spencer 2012: 67) – one which may challenge the emotional artificiality of the chorus's performance and which invites the audience to dis-identify from the stance the chorus attributes to them as well as to emancipate themselves from the plays' politics of positioning. Therefore, given the play cycle's manipulation of spectatorial participation, 'the audience must actively build their own argument in opposition to the argument presented on stage' (Grochala 2017: 217) – and, in addition, to the argument they themselves are enlisted to embody in relation to the chorus. It is thus in the relationship between stage and audience that conflict is reinitiated, that awareness can be raised, and resistance encouraged.

Performing Dissensus

Significantly, stage productions have capitalized on the playlets' experiential dimension by creating a potentially emancipating space which facilitates a performance of Rancièrean dissensus on the part of the spectators. Given *Shoot*'s epic dimensions, stage productions require creative solutions and selective approaches, specifically regarding the cycle's fragmentary and improvisational nature. While the Berliner Ensemble's 2010 adaptation was comparatively conventional with its spatial separation between stage and auditorium, other performances adopted a decidedly more innovative approach. Both the premiere in Edinburgh in 2007 and the subsequent London run in 2008 foregrounded the texts' experiential quality and, in the spirit of the Brechtian *Lehrstück*, turned the stagings into a more imaginative, individual and interactive event for the spectators. In this sense, they also offered an antidote to the provocative experience of banalization the audience undergoes in the dialogic and choric scenes described above.

Thus, when the playlets were first staged as part of the 2007 Edinburgh Fringe festival under the title *Ravenhill for Breakfast*, with a new play chosen for each day of the event, the scenes were performed as rehearsed readings, which, along with the fact that the process of creating the plays was still ongoing during the festival, reflects the improvisational and imaginative quality of the project. That the playlets were read rather than acted out had a considerable impact on the role of the spectators, who, in the spirit of Elisabeth Angel-Perez's notion of 'in-yer-ear' theatre, had to imagine the events themselves (2013). Hence, the audience was enabled to experience the performances in a decidedly more vivid and direct fashion precisely by being denied any explicit representation on stage. The shift from visualization to imagination implies that each spectator can, indeed has to, establish individual connections and thereby creates their own unique versions of the stories recounted verbally – an approach which offers, on a metatheatrical level and in Rancièrean spirit, 'alternative ways of seeing and participating in ... theatre events' (Svich 2011: 418) and may thus encourage to develop a different perspective on the action.

This individualized form of participation was a particularly central element of the London stagings, where the playlets were 'scatter[ed]' across the city, as Katalin Trencsényi describes:

> The pieces were presented in various spaces, from the traditional stage of a theatre to less conventional locations: in a bus stop, a hotel room, the bar of a theatre, or promenade. BBC Radio 3 chose two plays that were amalgamated into one radio drama that was not only aired but also simultaneously made available for the public to listen to on headphones. (2015: 92)

Thus, the production's unusual format underscored the significance of the plays' experiential dimension. Significantly, leaving it up to the spectators to decide which playlets they wanted to see, the London performances most notably succeeded in presenting the audience with a potentially empowering experience of choice, which effectively countered the deliberate manipulation of this central dialectical concept by the plays both on stage and in the relationship with the audience. Indeed, the cycle foregrounds a considerably distorted notion of choice which is exclusively framed in terms of neoliberal ideology and therefore severely limited. This is made evident in 'The Odyssey', in which the members of the chorus celebrate 'the power and the thrill and the beauty of the ... choice. We have so much choice. Who will provide my electricity? Who will deliver my groceries? Which cinema shall I go to? There is a choice at home' (Ravenhill 2013: 190). These examples satirically reflect how ideas of choice and agency have become conflated with purely economic interests, thereby fundamentally restricting rather than expanding the individual's freedom. The discourse of (counter-)terrorism similarly exploits these notions for neoliberal purposes. This manipulation is implicitly acknowledged and problematized by the play cycle's title, *Shoot/Get Treasure/Repeat*, which is borrowed from video game terminology and has a 'brutal banality' (Ravenhill 2008b) at its heart which gestures to the profoundly anti-dialectical impact of (counter-)terrorist discourse. At the same time, however, the title also hints at a certain potential for spectatorial agency which is central to the cycle's political agenda – even though, admittedly, the choices available in video games are strictly predetermined, too. This was put into practice in the London stagings, which granted the audience a considerable degree of choice to determine their own trajectory through the performance.

Thus, depending on each spectator's decisions, participating in the cycle was turned into a strongly individual and unique experience, in which each audience member could establish their own associations, connections and interpretations. In this respect, the spatial 'scattering' of the playlets across London also represented an attempt to give expression to the radically fragmented nature of the cycle. Rejecting 'a grand narrative with linking plot and characters' (Ravenhill 2008b), this emphasis on fragmentation can be understood as a direct response to contemporary lived experience. Therefore, both in the absence of 'grand', orientating narratives and, as I suggest, in a simultaneous effort to counter the pervasive meta-narrative of (counter-)terrorism, *Shoot*'s fragmentary style provides a disruptive experience that materialized in the London run in each spectator's individual journey. It is on the basis of these individual, small narratives that connections between past, present and future, as well as between individual and collective, private and political, can, in a post-Brechtian vein, be re-established. Oscillating between a manipulation of spectatorial participation in the dialogic and choric scenes, on the one hand, and a stimulus to reclaim and actively practise choice and agency in the specific performances, on the other, it is this paradoxical experience which represents a strong impetus to emancipate ourselves from the 'grand' narrative of (counter-)terrorism.

Self-Reflexivity as Resistance

What the play cycle's intricate implication of the audience exposes is, as mentioned above, that not only the spectators but also the institution of the theatre as a whole are to some extent entangled in the very structures it sets out to critique. It is worth dwelling on this potential complicity a little longer to understand how *Shoot* negotiates this problematic constellation. Thus, as de Waal argues, the theatre's resistant potential cannot be taken for granted, as theatre events may 'not only combat hegemonic representations ... but also often work to replicate them' (2017b: 3). Indeed, theatrical concepts and mechanisms are frequently exploited in the discourse and practice of terrorist warfare, to the extent that (counter-)terrorism can be described as a highly efficient type of performance: it depends on previous rehearsal, a carefully choreographed staging and a large audience in order to achieve its effects (Taylor 2009: 1888; Juergensmeyer 2017: 155). *Shoot* addresses the issue of the performative nature of war most explicitly in the playlet 'Crime and Punishment', in which a Woman is interviewed by a Soldier about her experience of living under dictatorship and about the specific day when '[t]he statue [came] down' (Ravenhill 2013: 87) – a reference to the invasion of Iraq and the toppling of the statue of Saddam Hussein in Baghdad in 2003. In her report, the Woman describes how the events were effectively 'stage managed' (Finburgh 2017: 97) by the occupying forces. Nothing was left to chance: witnesses were specifically cast for the live broadcast, the process was meticulously planned, indeed plotted by the media, and designed to achieve a highly symbolic, far-reaching impact on a global scale. Exposing this manipulation, the scene provides an example of 'the theatre of war' (Finburgh 2017: 39) through which the local population is turned into participants in the performance. The artificially created enthusiasm clashes, however, with the reality of life under occupation. The Woman's profound disappointment with the developments after the invasion, which, rather than introducing 'freedom' and 'democracy', has in fact perpetuated violence and brought 'just another hell' (Ravenhill 2013: 96), self-consciously reflects on *Shoot*'s own potential contribution to the cycle of violence and underscores the playlet's 'mistrust of [its] own [voice] by reflexively commenting on the deceptions of a decorative act of performance during times of crisis' (Hughes 2011: 121).

This self-reflexive acknowledgement of the theatre's fundamental complicity is also echoed by the chorus play 'Birth of a Nation', which sheds a sinister light on the theatre as a medium of resistance. Exposing the hypocrisy behind artistic endeavours in destroyed areas, the playlet hints at the potential shortcomings and limitations of using art for therapeutic purposes. In the play, a chorus of artist facilitators arrives in a '[s]hattered city' with 'shattered people' (Ravenhill 2013: 199) with the intention of helping the population heal:

> Hi. We're artists. ... And what we do is, what we do, we come to a place like this, a place like this where there's been the most terrible pain and horror and there's ... We come to a place where everyone's been hurting and we start the healing process by working through, by working with art.
>
> Ravenhill (2013: 202)

The artists' investment is, however, directly tied to wider economic purposes and their mission is thus revealed not as a genuine support for the local population to rediscover their own culture, but rather as an attempt to reshape it according to Western values and ideals (de Waal 2017b: 219): 'You want inward investment? You want tourism? You want civilization? You want freedom and democracy? ... [Y]ou want all that then let some culture in, sign up for some culture, embrace some culture, let some culture into the ruins of this shattered city' (Ravenhill 2013: 207). While the artists identify themselves as former Marxists, the politics of their intervention is nevertheless exposed as corrupted. The fact that they explain their commitment with the demise of Marxism, their resulting lack of orientation and their eventual discovery of 'the whole performance art installation bonkers sort of thing', which 'really seemed to, seemed to, seemed to give meaning to the lack of meaning' (Ravenhill 2013: 206), raises strong suspicions regarding their sincerity, as their frank admission gives away the essentially selfish and self-indulgent nature of their so-called engagement.

The playlet's cynical and bleak ending, during which a Blind Woman who 'has lost her tongue and ... her eyes' is brought on stage in order to prove '[t]he healing power of art' (Ravenhill 2013: 208), mercilessly reveals the artists' profound ignorance, their lack of understanding as well as the inappropriateness of their endeavours, as they misinterpret the woman's suffering 'as artistic expressions of the therapeutic self' (de Waal 2017b: 223). The chorus's self-congratulatory applause at the end accompanies the woman's screams and spasms, underscoring the artists' condescension and hypocrisy. As de Waal compellingly argues, by ending the playlet with this metatheatrical gesture, 'Birth' also raises urgent questions regarding the spectators and their involvement. Notably, de Waal points to the same issues explored with regard to the audience's positioning in the dialogic and choric scenes above, as 'their own applause during the curtain call [could] be seen as mimicking the chorus, and thus as an endorsement of the violent imposition of the therapeutic habitus' (2017b: 223). Yet, while *Shoot* does shed a particularly critical light on the theatre as a means of resistance, I do not share de Waal's conclusion that, according to the plays, 'the only response available to those neoliberal subjects who would occupy an anti-war position' is to 'disengage from a war launched by "their" elected representatives' (2017b: 223). On the contrary, I would suggest that the cycle's metatheatricality, its awareness of its own shortcomings as well as its self-reflexive acknowledgement of its potential entanglement in the processes it sets out to challenge represent the very prerequisite for re-establishing critical analysis in an environment hostile to opposition and resistance. Most importantly, the provocative quality of the metatheatrical scenes does not only draw attention to the theatre's but also the audience's problematic position with regard to these processes, and thereby reinforces the cycle's post-Brechtian strategy of inspiring critique through an experience of provocation, which serves to draw the audience in precisely as a means of fostering analytical distance. *Shoot*'s self-reflexivity and its acute awareness of these issues thereby emerge as key to a contemporary form of post-Brechtian political theatre which aims to reinitiate dissensus in the relationship between stage and audience on the basis of experience and ambivalence.

Conclusion

This chapter has offered a fresh examination of the politics of 'in-yer-face' drama by foregrounding the productive intersections between this visceral theatrical style and Brechtian dramaturgy. As Ravenhill's work demonstrates, provocation is employed as a dialectical tool to express a crisis of dialectics both as a means of social analysis and as an aesthetic strategy. As a self-reflexive parable, *Some Explicit Polaroids* illustrates the challenges of making political theatre at the turn of the millennium. Exposing the strategic manipulation of dialectical categories in the Cool Britannia ideology, *Polaroids*'s conventional dialectical framework diagnoses the dysfunctionality of traditional political dramaturgies and the value of emotions as a means of reconnection, mirroring the fundamental role of the audience in post-Brechtian theatre in the light of epistemological uncertainty and ambivalence.

The play cycle *Shoot/Get Treasure/Repeat* illustrates that these concerns are not limited to the Cool Britannia era, but indeed represent a wider trend in Ravenhill's oeuvre. Critically examining the discourse of (counter-)terrorism from a dialectical vantage point, *Shoot* uncovers a pervasive rhetorical instrumentalization of dialectical concepts and its profoundly banalizing impact on public and private life. Searching for a way of resisting these manipulative processes, the playlets offer a revised dialectical dramaturgy based on a strategic provocation which displaces the mechanism of contradiction from the stage into the auditorium. Forcing the spectators to undergo a deeply provocative and paradoxical experience of the performance, *Shoot* employs self-reflexivity as a post-Brechtian tool to reinitiate dissensus in the relationship between stage and audience. Heralding a new approach to Brecht's dialectical drama, it is Ravenhill's emphasis on experience, ambivalence and self-reflexivity that is indicative of a wider trend in contemporary forms of dialectical theatre which critically examine, recycle and innovate Brechtian dialectics as a progressive theatrical model for the new millennium.

2

Reimagining Brecht: David Greig's Theatre of Dissensus

In the history play *The Speculator* (1999), Scottish playwright David Greig critically investigates the opportunities offered by globalization through the lens of eighteenth-century Paris by exploring the values and risks of speculation – understood as both an economic and creative practice. In a key scene, (the fictional characters of the) French playwrights Marivaux and Dufresny discuss the question of speculation from the perspective of the theatre-maker:

> **Dufresny** ... We are not – playwrights – really we're gamblers.
> **Marivaux** Not gamblers.
> Speculators.
> **Dufresny** What's the difference?
> **Marivaux** Gamblers stake blind.
> Speculators imagine a possibility
> And have the courage to force it into existence.
>
> Greig (1999: 85)

What characterizes the work of a dramatist, according to Marivaux, who serves as a mouthpiece for Greig's ideas in this instance, is the ability – or, indeed, responsibility – to 'imagine a possibility', to dare to envision fresh perspectives and to open up new horizons through the medium of the theatre. While Marivaux implies that this task is not without its risks, in particular because it requires 'for the people to, temporarily, suspend their disbelief' (Greig 1999: 69), as Scottish banker John Law explains to Dufresny earlier in the play, theatrical speculation is nevertheless different from gambling because, as Marivaux seems to suggest, rather than 'staking blind', it follows a specific plan and purpose. Yet, even though enthusiastically arguing for the power of the imagination as a means of renewal and progress, the play ultimately stages the failure of the characters' various speculative projects, thereby compromising its initial optimism by offering a considerably more ambivalent and sceptical outlook.

Self-reflexively documenting Greig's self-understanding as a playwright, *The Speculator* attests to the fundamental role of the imagination in Greig's oeuvre, where it performs vital functions as a central element of the political fabric of his plays. Crucially, while it represents first and foremost a highly subjective activity, political thought has recently foregrounded the fundamental social and collective significance of the imagination. With reference to Hannah Arendt, Chiara Bottici defines the imagination as 'the very basis of the possibility of action' (2011: 24) and thus as an active, potentially transformative mode of engagement. Problematically, however, while the increasing global interconnectedness has expanded the horizon of individual and collective consciousness, late-capitalist globalization has also facilitated a strategic instrumentalization of the imagination which has undermined its potentially emancipating and liberating qualities, resulting in a 'contemporary crisis of imagination' (Kearney 1998: 9). In this context, Henry A. Giroux has described the emergence of a 'politics of disimagination' (2013: 26), reflecting the extent to which the imagination has been co-opted by neoliberalism to stifle our capacity to reimagine reality and envision alternatives. Significantly, searching for ways of reactivating its critical functions, Greig's plays target this 'management of the imagination by power' which has fostered 'the narrative superstructure around which our imagination grows' (2007: 214), as he explains in his manifesto for a 'Rough Theatre'. For this purpose, Greig probes the potential of theatrical acts of imagining as a means of inspiring change under the conditions of neoliberal ideology, conceptualizing the imagination as a key device both for the playwright's process of creation and, crucially, for the spectators' work of interpretation. More precisely, as a source of possibilities, the imagination serves as a central dialectical mechanism within the essentially post-Brechtian framework of Greig's plays, where it is employed to stage the contradictions shaping life in times of globalization as well as to inspire ways of resolving the paradoxes presented by the plays.

While a Brechtian influence on Greig's playwriting has frequently been acknowledged in scholarship, analyses have mainly focused on a practical level, identifying formal manifestations of Brechtian devices in the texts (Holdsworth 2013: 171; Wallace 2013: 31–68; Rodríguez 2019b). Yet, as I argue in this chapter, what Greig's works reflect above all is a distinct engagement with Brecht's philosophical and theoretical ideas, which can be connected to Greig's oft-cited interest in Adornian theory. Although critics have demonstrated the significance of Adorno's concept of negative dialectics for Greig's plays (Wallace 2013: 36; Rodríguez 2019a: 13–16; Rebellato 2003; Botham 2014), what has so far been omitted from the discussions is the crucial intersections between Adorno's dialectical theory and the imagination, which Greig employs as a fundamental dialectical tool. More precisely, Greig's use of the imagination can be understood with the help of Adorno's notions of the rational and the irrational – highly resonant terms, which, well beyond their literal meanings in everyday usage, unfold a significant critical potential in Adorno's dialectical analysis of capitalist society. Thus, in Adorno's view, capitalism has, as Karoline Gritzner summarizes, resulted in a 'rationalisation of all aspects of human existence', which has, in turn, led to a 'de-mystification of the world' (2015: 8). This is above all manifest in 'a rejection of reality's irrational, mythical, spiritual and heterogeneous elements' (Gritzner 2015: 8). For Adorno, it is precisely in what is suppressed from the surface of reality, in what he conceptualizes as the irrational, that a potential for spurring resistance to the status quo may reside. However, 'far from implying an endorsement of irrationalism' (Tiedemann 2008: xv) *per se*, the irrational is understood in Adornian theory as encapsulating a subjective, creative force that seeks to disrupt the logic of capitalism and thus denotes a guided and purposeful rather than purely unreasonable and instinctive form of behaviour. In fact, as Adorno writes, rationality and irrationality are mutually dependent, as the paradoxical notion of 'speculative *ratio*' illustrates: 'We might also say that speculative *ratio*, the kind of *ratio* that goes beyond the conceptual of an already owned, positive given, necessarily possesses an *irrational* element in that it offends against the secure knowledge it already has. There is no rationality without this intrinsic element of irrationality' (2008: 78). Situating art in 'profound opposition to the empirical reality that has been colonized by identity-thinking and exchange' (Rebellato 2003: 68), and thus as supposedly autonomous from capitalist rationality, Adorno implies that fiction represents a particularly important realm where the power of the irrational in the form of a speculative *ratio* can be cultivated.

This interdependence between rationality and irrationality which Adorno posits is useful for analysing the imagination as a central thematic and aesthetic device in Greig's plays. More precisely, I suggest that the dialectical potential of the imagination as it is employed by Greig can be described in terms of the disruptive and progressive power Adorno attributes to the irrational. Bringing conflicting perspectives between the familiar and the unfamiliar, the conventional and the radical, the imaginable and the unimaginable into a productive, seemingly unresolvable tension, Greig uses the imagination in the spirit of Adorno's negative dialectics to create an experience of Rancièrean dissensus. Emphasizing 'dissonance' (Wallace 2016: 32) rather than straightforward utopian hope, this strategy may give rise to a moment of 'transcendence' (Greig 2007: 220) – a term which Greig employs not in its metaphysical, idealist meaning, but rather as a metaphor 'to explain and explore the potentialities of political theatre' (Wallace 2013: 65) and, more precisely, to challenge the simple binary between rational and irrational as a means of providing new perspectives on reality which disrupt the status quo. It is therefore in Adornian terms that the irrational dimension Greig explicitly ascribes to his concept of Rough Theatre must be understood (2007: 220). Whereas the playwright himself identifies a shift from dialectical theatre to 'the multiple possibilities of the imagination' (Greig 2007: 212) in his projects, these tendencies are far from mutually exclusive. In an attempt to bring these supposedly contradictory strands between the irrational or imaginative and the rational or political into dialogue, the following sections will explore what I consider the fundamental dialectical potential of the imagination in Greig's work. As this chapter argues, rather than leaving dialectics behind, the plays' emphasis on the playwright's, characters' and spectators' imaginative capacities can be understood as a means of reinvigorating dialectical critique on the basis of an experience of paradox, ambivalence and indeterminacy.

Appropriating the Imagination: *Dunsinane*

Appropriation as Post-Brechtian *Verfremdung*

Dunsinane emerged in a moment of radical transition. The play's premiere in 2010 coincided with profound shifts not only globally – especially with regard to Britain's increasing military involvement in conflict zones around the world – but also within the UK itself, as Anglo-Scottish relations had become heavily contested since devolution in 1997 and in the run-up to the referendum on Scottish independence in 2014. In this respect, *Dunsinane* has remained prescient and acutely relevant, particularly in the wake of Britain's decision in 2016 to leave the European Union. Reimagining the reign of Macbeth and his wife Gruoch in Scotland in the eleventh century, Greig envisions the violent struggle for the Scottish throne in the aftermath of the murder of the king and stages the English army's attempts to re-establish order by restoring Malcolm, the supposedly legitimate heir, to the throne. Practising a post-Brechtian form of *Verfremdung* and historicization, the play refracts contemporary developments through a historical lens by bringing the deep transformations of the past into conversation with the present. Crucially, however, it is not to the historical events *per se*, but to William Shakespeare's dramatization of the story in *Macbeth* that Greig's version responds most immediately. Through this technique of appropriation, *Dunsinane* establishes a complex dialogue between different texts and contexts, bridging the gap from the Middle Ages to the Renaissance to the new millennium. What these disparate historical moments share is that they all mark instances of substantial political and social change in the formation of the English, Scottish and British nations. *Dunsinane* explores the challenges arising out of these unstable and fluid periods. Preoccupied with how fundamental notions of identity, knowledge and commitment are being revised, the play offers critical reflections on pressing national and global concerns, as well as on the crucial functions literature can perform in the processes of constructing and renegotiating conceptualizations of history and nationhood in times of transformation.

Foregrounding issues of national identity, both *Macbeth* and *Dunsinane* attest to the fundamental role of the literary imagination as an active participant in the construction of national self-consciousness. Defining the nation as 'an imagined political community' (1991: 6), Benedict Anderson has drawn attention to the imagination as a constitutive factor in the process of creating a cohesive sense of nationhood shared by individual subjects. As Jen Harvie explains, Anderson's emphasis on imaginative creativity notably entails that national identities must be understood as 'dynamic' (2005: 3), and therefore as adaptable. In this sense, Homi K. Bhabha underscores the particular significance of narrative for shaping ideas of the nation, stressing that it is always a preliminary, subjective and partial product 'in the process of being made' (1990: 3) and therefore an 'ambivalent' (1990: 2) rather than absolute concept. Thus, literature is attributed vital functions in processes of (re)writing the nation, for which the theatre seems particularly well suited by virtue of its ephemeral and performative character (Holdsworth 2010: 7).

Preoccupied with the shifting nature of the nation both then and now, *Dunsinane* examines these ideas through the lens of the complex and tense relations between England and Scotland as they are reflected in Shakespeare's *Macbeth*. For this purpose, it creates a 'contact zone' which, according to Mary Louise Pratt, represents a '[space] where cultures meet, clash, and grapple with each other' (1991: 34; Müller and Wallace 2011: 2). Bringing decisive moments of transition in English and Scottish history into dialogue with each other, *Dunsinane* presents a deeply unsettling confrontation between different periods, geographies and value systems with the aim of destabilizing any fixed ideas of nation, identity and community. Hence, as Ariel Watson contends, *Dunsinane* stages 'the *Verfremdungseffekt* of performing nation outside its boundaries' (2014: 244) by offering 'a portrayal of *nation as conflict* that is profoundly dialogical, humane, and ambivalent' (2014: 230). Crucially, *Dunsinane* also turns this into an aesthetic strategy: through its appropriation of Shakespeare's play, it becomes a textual contact zone itself (Müller and Wallace 2011: 10). It is on this metalevel that the play draws attention to the role of the literary imaginary in the construction of nationhood.

In this sense, *Dunsinane* takes Shakespeare's *Macbeth* as its cornerstone and point of departure. The play begins with the English conquest of Scotland after the murder of Macbeth and, adopting, but also substantially revising, central features of Shakespeare's plot and *dramatis personae*, imagines a different outcome of the events. In *Dunsinane*, the English forces struggle with the unexpectedly intricate political situation in Scotland, where Macbeth's wife Gruach, for whom Greig uses a version of her actual name, and her son Lulach claim the throne against Malcolm, and where, in addition, different clans compete for power and influence. Challenging the supposedly straightforward ending of Shakespeare's play and replacing it with a profoundly complex political situation that defies expectations, *Dunsinane* represents a sequel which engages in a 'speculative continuation' (Saunders 2017: 119) of *Macbeth* and thereby also implicitly re-evaluates the preceding story and characters familiar from Shakespeare's text.

It is for these reasons that Greig's play has been widely understood as historically more 'accurate', indeed as an effective counter-narrative which aims to set the historical record – supposedly misrepresented in Shakespeare's piece – 'straight' as well as to offer an arguably more 'authentic' version of the past closer to the 'facts' (Price 2018: 22–5; Brown 2016: 196; Reid 2013: 66). In line with the Scottish dramatist's own statements about wanting 'to reclaim a bit of our [Scotland's; AH] history' (qtd. in McGlone n.d.), Clare Wallace, for example, describes *Dunsinane* as a project of 'writing back to and beyond Shakespeare' (2011: 202) and as a subversive 'act of repossession' (2013: 92). In this context, critics have particularly tended to foreground *Dunsinane*'s critique of what is often perceived as Shakespeare's deliberate distortion of historical events, as Macbeth is – in contrast with the historical sources – depicted in the tragedy as a ruthless tyrant whose rule was infamously short-lived. Yet, while *Dunsinane* may indeed to some extent 'question the "truth" of Shakespeare's *Macbeth*' (Wallace 2013: 93) by offering a different account, the bifurcating way in which these interpretations tend to present Greig's piece as opposed to *Macbeth* obscures the complexity of the intertextual relations that can be established between both plays.

Offering a more nuanced approach, I argue that *Dunsinane* pursues a profoundly ambivalent strategy in its retelling of the story of Macbeth based on a post-Brechtian form of *Verfremdung*. Significantly, Brecht's concept is derived to a large extent from his engagement with Shakespeare, whose works he, too, appropriated for the purposes of dialectical theatre, and whose theatre practice represented a rich source of inspiration for the development of his theoretical model (Brecht 2015b: 55–8). In the 'Messingkauf' dialogues, for example, the Dramaturg describes early modern theatre as 'earthly, profane and unmagical' (Brecht 2015b: 56) because, by convention, it did not, indeed could not, rely on illusion – a characteristic which strongly appealed to Brecht. Thus, the Dramaturg goes on to explain that Renaissance performance traditions, among which the use of boy actors, the absence of stage props and the resulting need for word scenery to evoke setting and atmosphere, created '[a] theatre full of V-effects' (Brecht 2015b: 58) which required spectators to 'use their imaginations' (Brecht 2015b: 56). What Brecht considers most valuable with regard to Shakespeare is 'the contradictory, unpredictable, dialectical element' (Heinemann 1994: 228) in his plays and the extent to which 'the work is connotative rather than denotative' (Barnett 2013a: 115). Significantly, Brecht connects the ambivalent quality of Shakespeare's texts to the English playwright's preference for depicting periods of transition and moments of rupture, which he describes as 'those valuable fault-lines in his works where what was new in his age collided with what was old' (Brecht 2015b: 92), highlighting the value of (political as well as aesthetic) instability as a productive source for interrogating relations between past and present, from Shakespeare's time to the present day.

It is this emphasis on the critical value of such 'fault-lines' and their potential for *Verfremdung* and change which connects Shakespeare's oeuvre not only to Brecht but, crucially, also to *Dunsinane*. As I will argue in this chapter, Greig's play stages a post-Brechtian form of *Verfremdung* by juxtaposing different texts, contexts and perspectives to create a complex and rich dialectic in which binaries – between England and Scotland, past and present, war and peace, and not least between *Macbeth* and *Dunsinane* themselves – are destabilized. Hence, *Dunsinane* deliberately evokes motifs and elements familiar from Shakespeare only to undermine the well-known narrative by contrasting it with alternative scenarios, thereby playfully exposing it as a cliché which is taken for granted and perpetuated rather than interrogated. While *Dunsinane* certainly targets central aspects of Shakespeare's text, it is important to emphasize that its aim is not exclusively to offer an explicit counter-narrative, but to create a fundamental indeterminacy with regard to the authenticity and accuracy of the respective versions presented on stage. In this respect, *Dunsinane* draws attention to the seminal status of Shakespeare's dramatization, which has shaped the predominant image of the Scottish king as a savage warrior and tyrant (Aitchison 1999: v). Crucially, by doing so, it also raises awareness of its own participation in the ongoing mythologization of the historical figure. Rather than responding to *Macbeth tout court*, therefore, I argue that Greig opens the material up to address broader issues with regard to the intersection between literature, nationhood and the cultural imaginary.

Employing ambivalence and self-reflexivity, *Dunsinane* challenges rigid dramaturgical and conceptual structures, engrained notions of history and identity as well as straightforward intertextual relations, and it is in this sense that its appropriation of Shakespeare's text emerges as a distinctly post-Brechtian strategy. Associated with 'questions of ethics and politics' (Saunders 2017: 6) and with a subversive agenda, the practice of appropriation has been defined as distinct from the more general practice of adaptation in Julie Sanders's influential *Adaptation and Appropriation* (2006). As Graham Saunders succinctly summarizes Sanders's argument, 'appropriation challenges and subverts, whereas adaptation mostly confirms and confers an already assumed authority held by the source text' (2017: 7). Notably emphasizing 'agency' as well as 'political, cultural, and ... ethical advocacy' (Huang and Rivlin 2014: 2), appropriation can be described as a useful tool for the kind of political theatre Greig envisages. Moreover, bringing several texts into dialogue with each other, appropriation directly appeals to the (playwright's and spectators') imaginations. Yet, rather than hierarchical and one-sidedly exploitative, as the etymological origins of the word may suggest, appropriation must be understood as a 'dialogical' (Desmet 2014: 42) process in which both source and adapted product inform each other. In this sense, *Dunsinane*'s intertextual relation to *Macbeth* can be considered collaborative to the extent that it 'does not trace its texture back to a single matrix. Rather, it is a palimpsestic artefact in flux and in transit' (Capitani 2016: 29). It is from this perspective that the dialectical dimension of *Dunsinane*'s technique of appropriation can be identified. Rather than offering a binary logic, the play pursues a more open, heterogeneous and ambiguous approach as a means of inspiring a critical, interrogative attitude toward the material, which attests to the play's fundamental post-Brechtian qualities. This complex strategy is employed on three levels, as the remainder of this chapter will show: on the level of content itself, where common ideas of nationhood are estranged in the relationship between English and Scottish characters; on an intertextual level, where conventional understandings of historical knowledge and of writing the past are questioned; and in the interaction between stage and auditorium, where spectators' expectations are deliberately undermined to foster an experience of dissensus. Hence, at the core of its appropriative strategy, *Dunsinane* employs a post-Brechtian form of *Verfremdung* to create a flexible and pluralistic contact zone which brings into focus not only the significant role of Shakespeare's *Macbeth* but also the wider network of stories about the historical figure circulating in the cultural imaginary, thereby offering a nuanced comment on the politics of literary appropriation and on its potential for constructing, reinforcing and revising concepts of nationhood, history and culture in times of transition – both then and now.

Reimagining the Nation: England and/or Scotland

The significance of *Verfremdung* as a central aesthetic strategy is first and foremost evident in the confrontation between England and Scotland in a profoundly indeterminate cultural and political contact zone. *Dunsinane* focuses on the perspective of the English rather than the Scottish soldiers, who thereby come to represent the most decisive point of reference for the play and, indeed, a mirror for the spectators. The English characters' experience is marked by a deep sense of alienation and displacement, as the conditions they encounter in Scotland radically defy their expectations. Harking back to Ancient Greek theatre traditions, the voice of the English regiment is realized in the form of a chorus which intervenes both at the beginning of each of the play's four sections and in-between individual scenes, in which their everyday life during their occupation of Scotland is illustrated. It is especially the prologues, rendered in direct address to the audience, which help establish a specific intimacy between the English characters and the spectators and offer insight into the soldiers' thoughts and feelings. Spoken in verse, their rhythmic and poetic quality clashes with the hardships and feelings of insecurity expressed in these lines, thereby reinforcing the soldiers' estrangement also on the level of form. Describing their journey to Scotland as an expedition into the unknown, they state that what reunited them initially was their uncertainty: 'Some of us new and eager for a fight and others / Not so sure but all of us both knowing and not knowing / What lay ahead of us' (Greig 2010: 9). From the very beginning of the play, therefore, the oscillation between the familiar and the unfamiliar is established as a central trope.

Despite the English soldiers' acknowledgement of their feelings of otherness, however, they refuse to genuinely engage with Scottish culture, which spurs a growing sense of alienation and culminates in a deeply felt disillusionment and frustration. Most problematically, they insist on their superiority and the rightfulness of their mission against all the odds. Thus, the English general Siward stubbornly continues to pursue his plan, which he defines in an unequivocal way: 'We'll set a new king in Dunsinane and then summer will come and then a harvest and by next spring it'll be as if there never was a fight here' (Greig 2010: 24). To settle the conflict, Siward relies on what he considers objective facts and numbers, rationality and common sense, which is reflected in his rigid application of dichotomous structures and fixed categories; indeed, he 'incarnate[s]' these 'binary opposition[s]' (Pattie 2016a: 25). Aiming to establish clarity based on distinctions between, for example, war and peace, winning and losing or good and bad, Siward is obsessed with 'draw[ing] a line' (Greig 2010: 108) and creating 'consensus' (Greig 2010: 38). Yet, the play goes on to expose the sheer banality of Siward's way of thinking. As a result of his and the soldiers' repeated failures, Siward is not only more and more isolated – in the end, he is even deserted by his sole remaining companion, the Boy Soldier (Greig 2010: 138) – but crucially also develops increasingly violent methods to enforce his vision of Scotland's future, notably by burning members of the Scottish population alive, a strategy which scandalizes even the disloyal and ruthless English lieutenant Egham (Greig 2010: 93–4).

Thus, the supposedly rigid distinctions on which the English soldiers' rationality is built begin to blur. Siward's mission to bring peace in fact ends up causing even more violence, and the idea of leading war in pursuit of peace creates a fundamental paradox at the heart of the play (Greig 2010: 94). Gruach makes this critique explicit when she ridicules Siward's 'good intentions' (Greig 2010: 138). Appearing more and more brutal and savage, therefore, the English soldiers seem to acquire precisely those qualities which are stereotypically associated with and attributed to the Scots, both in Shakespeare's play and the cultural imaginary (Alker and Nelson 2007: 382–3). This confusion of values exposes Siward's insistence on clear-cut distinctions between English and Scottish causes as entirely futile; indeed, the English army 'fight[s] in the service of a Scottish contender for the throne. Siward is, therefore, unable to disentangle himself from the power struggles that follow on from the invasion' (Pattie 2016a: 25). This fundamental dissolution between what the play seems to establish as characteristic of 'Englishness' and 'Scottishness' is also epitomized by Siward's affair with Gruach, through which the countries and identities they embody literally merge: 'Which of us is really the conqueror here and which of us the conquered?' (Greig 2010: 77). Obstinately pursuing his mission and sticking to his ideals, however, Siward fails to realize the extent to which the categories he insists on have already become meaningless and inefficient.

While reproducing the stark contrast between English and Scottish characters which Shakespeare's *Macbeth* has often been understood to stage (Alker and Nelson 2007: 383), *Dunsinane* to some extent reverses the conventional image of these intercultural relations by prioritizing a Scottish perspective on the events. As representatives of their respective nations, the characters are contrasted in their understanding of politics, culture and history. Whereas the English army is presented as too rigid in their preconceptions and intentions, the Scots pursue a more ambiguous and flexible approach. The complications arising from these intricate conditions are particularly evident at the level of language. While Siward bases his mission on the conviction that communication establishes clarity and comprehension, his 'insistent literalness' (Greig 2010: 29) clashes with the Scottish characters' approach. Gruach and Malcolm embrace ambivalence as a key principle of interaction, strategically exploiting the insight that meaning is never solid, fixed or objectively given, and creating a complex cultural and political territory in which alliances and allegiances are radically unstable. In this uncertain territory, even the difference between life and death has become insignificant. Siward assumes that by killing Gruach's son Lulach, the legitimate heir to the throne, he can resolve the conflict and finally install Malcolm as king. Paradoxically, however, killing Lulach only ends up reinforcing Gruach's claim for the throne. Thus, Malcolm concludes: 'I think it's more likely that by killing this boy you have given him eternal life' (Greig 2010: 125). As 'Scotland will find a new child' (Greig 2010: 135) no matter what Siward does, Lulach – alive or dead – emerges less as a character than as a powerful symbol of the paradoxes and ambivalences reigning in the country, against which the English army is, despite all their efforts, entirely powerless.

As the *modus operandi* in Scotland, ambivalence and contradiction thus serve to make strange, in the Brechtian sense of the term, any conventional understandings of nationhood and identity. The English soldiers' expectations are radically undermined by their confrontation with an entirely different political and cultural reality in Scotland, notably because the dichotomous contrasts structuring both the English characters' way of thinking and the play as such dissolve in this unstable and complex contact zone. Conventional markers of national identity, in particular a shared language, a collective culture and a common political system, are estranged and problematized in *Dunsinane*, which serves to complicate habitual understandings of 'Englishness', 'Scottishness' and, by extension, the very concept of nationhood as such. Instead, situated liminally in-between England and Scotland, the play creates a highly complex picture which emphasizes contradiction and paradox over clarity and resolution. Associating Scotland with an infinite range of possibilities, *Dunsinane* thus draws attention to the necessity of careful and ongoing interpretation, an openness to adopt different perspectives and a willingness to engage with otherness – none of which the English soldiers display.

In this respect, the play's specific understanding of Scotland as a nation can therefore be read as a metaphor for the principles underpinning *Dunsinane*'s own dialectical strategy. Rejecting clear-cut categories as they are incorporated by the English characters in the play, *Dunsinane* exposes the tensions and contradictions inherent in the period of transition it envisions, underscores their potential for transformation and emphasizes the significance of continuous negotiation. This appeal to engage with the paradoxes of the play crystallizes at the end, when Siward, acknowledging his 'mistake' (Greig 2010: 132) but unwilling to give in and surrender, remains in uncertain territory. Still convinced of his mission, he disappears into the infinity of the snow-white countryside, deprived of any remaining sense of purpose or orientation, ultimately incorporating the very ambivalence and indeterminacy he set out to fight in the first place. The play's complex dialectical conflict between England and Scotland, between different concepts of national identity and, by extension, between different stories, assumptions and interpretations thereby remains radically unresolved. It is this emphasis on indeterminacy which underscores the possibility of revising, redefining and reimagining the nation as a powerful source for change.

Appropriation as (Meta-)Historicization

As the last section has shown, *Dunsinane* undermines conventional understandings of nation and identity through the specifically post-Brechtian way it stages the encounter between English and Scottish characters. The play does not envision the Anglo-Scottish conflict as clearly structured and oppositional, but locates it in a profoundly liminal contact zone in which commonly accepted categories and distinctions dissolve. This impression of ambivalence is reinforced on an intertextual level through the complex interplay between *Macbeth* and *Dunsinane*. While any adapted text can be described as 'haunted' by its source text (Hutcheon 2013: 6), I would suggest that *Dunsinane* exacerbates this oscillatory movement to rethink the relation between past and present texts and contexts as well as to interrogate the functions of history for developing a sense of national consciousness. Thus, embracing a variety of perspectives on the historical events around the figure of Macbeth, Greig's appropriative strategy does not only explore the complex intersections between history and nationhood, as any sense of national identity fundamentally depends on the shared understanding of an imagined past; more importantly, it also draws attention to its own role in shaping these narratives. Estranging, in post-Brechtian fashion, the predominant image of the Scottish king as shaped by Shakespeare's version of the story, *Dunsinane* complicates any straightforward approach to history, and raises awareness of the essential instability of any form of historical imagination. Crucially, while offering a self-critical perspective on these processes, it also underscores the potential of reimagining history as a source for redefining national identity in times of transformation.

Foregrounding the nexus between history, nationhood and the literary and cultural imaginary, *Dunsinane* critically engages with Shakespeare's text as a form of historical knowledge which has shaped widespread understandings of Anglo-Scottish relations. For this purpose, it establishes a complex dialectic that brings into focus contradictory versions of the story of Macbeth. Thus, as Nick Aitchison argues, 'Shakespeare's Macbeth is so well known that the historical Macbeth has been almost completely eclipsed by his dramatic counterpart' so that 'the Macbeth of modern consciousness is almost invariably Shakespeare's Macbeth' (1999: 125). In response to this problematic constellation, *Dunsinane* is written from a Scottish rather than English perspective and stages a series of reversals which challenge central elements of Shakespeare's play. For example, complicating Shakespeare's depiction of Lady Macbeth, Greig presents the character as a powerful leader and emancipated woman. Most importantly, Gruach explicitly rejects the widespread myth of Macbeth as a tyrant which the English soldiers had firmly believed in and draws a considerably more positive and sympathetic picture of the figure, who, significantly, is never referred to by his name:

> He was a good king.
> He ruled for fifteen years.
> Before him there were kings and kings and kings but not one of them
>   could rule more than a year or so at most before he would be killed
>   by some chief or other.
> But my king lasted fifteen years.
> My king was strong.
>
> Greig (2010: 32)

It is with a focus on these explicit reversals of central elements in Shakespeare's text that Greig's play has been widely understood not only as a form of 'writing back' to the English playwright but also as an ostensibly more 'authentic' story which seems closer to historical records (Wallace 2013: 92; Price 2018: 22–5; Brown 2016: 196; Reid 2013: 66). While it is true that *Dunsinane* is invested in reversing certain aspects of Shakespeare's version, problematizing the negative portrayal of the Scottish king and queen and, by implication, of the country, its history and national identity more broadly, such interpretations overlook the fact that Greig's strategy is decidedly more subtle, as it stages its critique by introducing a fundamental ambivalence at the heart of the play. Thus, rather than merely fashioning a new image of Macbeth, *Dunsinane* juxtaposes multiple perspectives without, however, resolving the resulting contradictions in the end. In this respect, the fact that Macbeth himself never appears on stage makes it possible for Greig to draw attention not to the protagonist himself, but to the wider context in which Macbeth ruled, and to foreground more explicitly the relations between the characters and the nations they represent, emphasizing the intricacy of Anglo-Scottish relations and suggesting that the conflicts between both nations cannot be as easily resolved as the English army may believe.

The complexity of this specific strategy of appropriation comes to the fore in *Dunsinane*'s reflections on the forms, functions and implications of (re)telling the past. More precisely, Greig's text is characterized by a distinct self-reflexivity, as it acknowledges its own participation in the construction and perpetuation of stories about Macbeth. This is particularly evident in the strategic distribution of information through the Scottish characters. Thus, most of the English soldiers' expectations with regard to the situation in Scotland turn out to be false, as Siward is forced to realize. In response to Siward's accusations that he deliberately lied, Malcolm explains that Scottish culture is characterized by a radically different approach to historical knowledge and the uses it is put to, rejecting notions of objectivity and facticity in favour of a more context-sensitive and adaptable understanding of the past:

> In Scotland to call me a liar is really unacceptable ... the way we manage this sort of thing in Scotland is by being careful not only not to tell lies – but also to be very very careful about the way we hear and understand words. ... people have to pussyfoot around when obviously one simply wants to ... describe the facts of the world as they are.
>
> Greig (2010: 28)

Malcolm's emphasis on nuance, subtlety and subjectivity creates profound misunderstandings on the part of the English soldiers. His negotiations with the English army are deliberately paradoxical, as he self-consciously shapes his accounts to meet his own ends. Foregrounding processes of constructing historical narratives and underscoring the significance of context and interpretation, the Scottish characters' understanding of history is thus fundamentally shaped by storytelling and mythology. Depending on the repetitive and circular nature of the practice of retelling, these Scottish principles radically clash with Siward's belief in a linear, chronological and teleological approach to historical development.

By self-reflexively exposing these processes of constructing the past, *Dunsinane* refrains from any claim to accuracy and authenticity and instead raises awareness of the multiplicity of versions which circulate in the cultural imaginary. It acknowledges that it constitutes itself one participant among many in the wider (inter)textual web built around Macbeth's reign in Scotland. While certain elements of *Dunsinane*'s rewriting of Shakespeare's play may indeed be 'historically grounded' (Brown 2016: 196) and hence potentially more truthful – if such parameters can be meaningfully applied in this context at all – it would be misleading to interpret Greig's version as a counter-narrative *tout court*. In his reimagination of the story of Macbeth, Greig in fact deliberately 'creates his own improbabilities' (Brown 2016: 196) and complicates any stable understanding of the past. Thus, '[t]he foundation of *Dunsinane* as a history play is not verifiable fact, not even orthodox "facts of history"' (Brown 2016: 195); rather, the play participates in the creation of 'new mini-myths' (Brown 2016: 189) through its strategic ambivalence. In this sense, *Dunsinane* can be understood with Douglas Lanier as a rhizomatic form of adaptation, which conceives of the process as horizontal and non-binary, and foregrounds the 'multiple, non-hierarchical nodes of meaning and interpretation (rather than one centralized, hierarchical system of base and branches)' (Desmet, Loper and Casey 2017: 4; Lanier 2014: 25; Capitani 2016: 29). It is in this spirit that *Dunsinane* contrasts different narratives of the past to bring them into a dynamic and paradoxical dialogue, neither asserting authority for its own account nor explicitly rejecting Shakespeare's version – or any other variant, for that matter. Through its rhizomatic appropriation of *Macbeth*, *Dunsinane* shows that history is never a given, but always created, indeed performed, in the present moment, where it may also be exploited for furthering specific political aims.

This complex interplay between competing versions of the past can be understood as a specifically post-Brechtian form of *meta*-historicization which *Dunsinane* employs to explore the intricate intersections between history and nationhood as well as the role of the (literary) imagination in creating a sense of national self-consciousness. Brecht's concept of historicization, which emphasizes change and rupture rather than continuity and consensus, has a considerable self-reflexive potential to the extent that it also serves to interrogate the nature, forms and functions of history. In this sense, Linda Hutcheon argues that Brechtian theatre to some extent anticipated postmodernism's interest in challenging 'concepts of linearity, development, and causality': 'Brecht's theater and postmodernist art ... parodically rewrite the historical events and works of art of the past, thereby questioning the stability of the meaning of both. By incorporating known historical events and personages within their texts, both manage to problematize historical knowledge' (1988: 220). It is in this vein that *Dunsinane*'s appropriation of *Macbeth* must be understood, as Greig draws on Shakespeare's text to lay bare how narratives of past and present are developed, how they get anchored in the cultural imaginary and how they may thereby shape and perpetuate popular understandings of history, nation and identity. In this sense, *Dunsinane*'s ambivalent appropriation of *Macbeth* 'illuminates' and, more crucially, as I would add, interrogates 'Shakespeare's role as a writer of history' and 'suggests that we need to rethink our reading of *Macbeth* and reconsider where authority lies' (Linneman 2010). More generally, the case of Shakespeare's *Macbeth* highlights 'questions about the playwright's' – and this includes Greig's – 'own role in using, recreating, reinterpreting and adapting history' (Price 2018: 27). Contrasting different perspectives without ultimately resolving the conflict, *Dunsinane* embraces a more nuanced and pluralistic understanding of history. At the same time, however, the play also attests to the power of these mechanisms and acknowledges their vital functions for imagining a cohesive, shared sense of national identity. By drawing attention to the necessity of subtlety and nuance for an interpretation of the relationship between past and present, *Dunsinane* reintroduces history as a dialectical medium of critique and intervention. Promoting an unstable, flexible and open understanding of the historical and national imaginary, the play powerfully reasserts the potential of the (literary) imagination as an ambivalent tool for rethinking, reinventing and reimagining past and present as the basis for creating a different future. It is this emphasis on indeterminacy and radical openness which creates an implicit appeal to the audience not only to critically approach the play's depiction of the past but, more to the point, also to imagine their own version by engaging with the paradoxes presented on stage.

Dissensus and Speculation

Employing a post-Brechtian form of *Verfremdung* in its appropriation of Shakespeare's *Macbeth*, *Dunsinane* creates a complex and rich dialectic through which different texts, contexts, perspectives and values are juxtaposed in an indeterminate contact zone. Notably, this emphasis on ambivalence particularly foregrounds the role of the audience. As adaptation is as much 'a product and process of creation' as of 'reception' (Hutcheon 2013: xvi), it vitally depends on the readers' and spectators' cooperation and can be attributed a significant mobilizing potential with regard to the audience. Focusing specifically on the theatre, Nico Dicecco goes so far as to conceptualize adaptation as an exclusively performative and receptive practice altogether, arguing that a text's adaptive dimension only materializes in the very moment of performance and thus depends on the presence and participation of the spectators (2017: 614). To the extent, however, that 'not every audience knows precisely the same things, and what they happen to know about a precursor text changes the way they attend (to) the adaptation'

(Dicecco 2017: 614), this entails a highly subjective form of interpretation. In the case of appropriation, the pivotal role of the spectators is emphasized even more strongly. Through its less overt and more intricate relation to the source text and its explicitly subversive intent, appropriation attributes a considerable degree of interpretive freedom, but also of responsibility to the audience members. In this sense, the spectators' interpretive and imaginative capacities constitute a crucial factor for the politics of appropriation.

It is in this critical and political vein that *Dunsinane*'s appropriative strategy casts the audience as vital participants in its post-Brechtian dialectical strategy. In fact, the various techniques of *Verfremdung* described in the previous sections are first and foremost directed at the spectators themselves. Yet, this effect depends on the audience's awareness of the text's adapted nature, as Hutcheon explains: 'To experience it *as an adaptation*, however, ... we need to recognize it as such and to know its adapted text, thus allowing the latter to oscillate in our memories with what we are experiencing' (2013: 120–1). The resulting interplay between the texts serves above all to 'set up audience expectations' (Hutcheon 2013: 121). In the case of canonical works such as Shakespeare's, these may not only be nurtured by 'direct experience' (Hutcheon 2013: 122) but also by 'a generally circulated cultural memory' (Ellis 1982: 3), which reflects the seminal role of these texts within the national and cultural imaginary and draws attention to the wider intertextual networks in which they operate. Thus, *Dunsinane*'s political impetus is, if not entirely dependent on, decidedly fuelled by the audience's awareness of its appropriative strategy, and thus by the extent to which the play raises and undermines the spectators' expectations with regard to the sequel. As Emily Linneman explains, *Dunsinane* does '[acquire] independence as it develops, shifts, and moves away from *Macbeth*' so that 'a knowledge of that play is not a prerequisite to understanding' (2010) Greig's version. Crucially, however, 'to lose the connection between *Macbeth* and *Dunsinane* would be to lose a great part of both the past and the present' (Linneman 2010). Therefore, it is in the play's engagement with 'preconceived ideas of how a response or sequel to *Macbeth* should look' (Linneman 2010) that its politics becomes most tangible.

The title serves to establish this intricate interplay, as it directly refers back to Shakespeare's text by foregrounding its infamous setting, while also already indicating a decisive alteration with regard to the source by foregrounding the importance of place and, indeed, displacement. This is reflected at the beginning of the play, which stages the battle of Birnam Wood – familiar from Shakespeare – but ironically undermines the English soldiers' mission to defeat Macbeth by depicting their disguise as a clumsy and inadequate endeavour, thereby implicitly questioning the ending of Shakespeare's play.

Hence, it soon turns out that '*Dunsinane* is not the play we thought we knew. ... At the end of *Macbeth*, we are certain of several things. ... In *Dunsinane*, most of our suppositions turn out to be false' (Linneman 2010). Constructed first and foremost as 'a challenge to its audience' (Linneman 2010) – and not to Shakespeare – *Dunsinane* interrogates the 'facts' supposedly established by Shakespeare's version, which has become firmly anchored in the cultural imaginary, and directly implicates the audience in its appropriative strategy.

These estranging effects on the audience's interpretation are particularly pertinent to *Dunsinane*'s *dramatis personae*, as Greig's play complicates any straightforward process of identification with the characters. Even though most dramatic figures are appropriated from Shakespeare, they are depicted in a radically different and, crucially, decidedly more ambivalent light, thereby undermining the spectators' expectations with regard to the characters. This is evident in *Dunsinane*'s treatment of Siward as the protagonist of the sequel, as the play destabilizes his central position as tragic hero. While the play adopts Siward's perspective and closely maps his development, he is unlikely to be perceived as a heroic figure the audience would empathize with. As argued above, *Dunsinane* satirically critiques Siward's rigid attitude, presents his behaviour as misleading and questions his status as leader of the English army. This is underscored by the play's ostensible moment of anagnorisis. Even though Siward recognizes his mistake at the end, he does not draw any significant conclusions from this acknowledgement (Greig 2010: 132). Vice versa, while the Scottish characters are presented as much more adept at negotiating intercultural differences and political conflicts, their strategies emerge as equally ambivalent. Relying on manipulation and fostered by selfish interests, their approach cannot be considered a genuine alternative to Siward's obstinacy, as it prevents any successful communication and negotiation between the enemies. Thus, Siward perspicaciously remarks that Malcolm's so-called 'subtlety is dangerously close to corruption' (Greig 2010: 108). As a result, the relations between stage and auditorium emerge as complex and tense, encouraging the audience to engage with paradoxical character constellations which contrast with their preconceptions. Instead of facilitating identification, *Dunsinane* juxtaposes a variety of possible perspectives on the figures to encourage critical reflection.

Crucially, this paradox between the audience's expectations and the conflicting alternative perspectives made available on stage remains unresolved at the play's conclusion, as Siward is resolved to continue his futile search for a way of defeating Gruach and Lulach, and of safely installing Malcolm on the throne. This is underscored by the play's structure, which is based on the cycle of the seasons rather than on a progressive division into acts and thereby defies any straightforward reading of the final scene. Suggesting a cyclical rather than linear development as well as infinity and openness rather than closure, the play remains indeterminate about the future of the characters. This evocative and associative approach can be seen to inspire the spectators' imagination to speculate about and negotiate the differences which prevail in the complex contact zone at the end. Hence, even though the play may offer an experience of ambivalence and disorientation for the audience – which to some extent mirrors the English army's confusion – the spectators are assigned an active role in resolving the conflicts. While the English soldiers are depicted as incapable of revising their prejudices, *Dunsinane* makes a tentative, but nevertheless effective appeal to the audience to negotiate the contradictions presented on stage through its emphasis on ambivalence and paradox. This was also made explicit in the Royal Shakespeare Company's production, as the specific seating arrangement of the auditorium forced spectators to interrogate their viewing habits. Thus, as Linneman explains, the feeling of alienation dominating the play

> is made apparent to the audience in the jagged stage that juts awkwardly into the theater. Set into the right hand corner of the auditorium, the stage is surrounded by an oval of seats. The audience, used to looking at a stage straight ahead of them, are required to crane their necks, swivel in their seats, and adopt an uncomfortable position. ... Like the soldiers, we are uncomfortable and in unfamiliar territory. (2010)

This specific set-up thus challenged habitual patterns of spectating and thereby underscored the fundamental role of the spectators for the play's appropriative strategy, physically reinforcing the text's appeal to the spectators to critically engage with the conflicting positions and to adopt a fresh perspective on the events.

Appropriating the spectators' imagination by directly implicating them in its complex dialectic, *Dunsinane* creates an experience of dissensus in the Rancièrean sense of the term. Emphasizing ambivalence and paradox, the play seeks to establish a dialogue with the audience to explore concepts of nationhood, history and culture within an open, heterogeneous and non-binary (inter)textual and political contact zone, foregrounding the imagination as a critical tool in the dynamic processes of shaping (national) identities. The significance of the nexus between theatre and nation at which *Dunsinane*'s politics of appropriation must be situated is particularly significant from a contemporary perspective. *Dunsinane*'s foregrounding of the (Scottish) nation as 'an identity fundamentally in relation, fundamentally linked to and in dialogue with all the other identities that surround and inform it' (Pattie 2011: 57) and thus as 'a radical space in the simplifications of a politics based on national identity' (Rebellato 2009: xxii) remains timely and acutely relevant. This focus on the possibility of change in moments of political and social, local and global transition is what continues to spur Greig's explorations of the nation in times of globalization more generally, and his commitment to the Scottish independence movement more specifically:

> The Scotland whose independence I seek is more a state of mind: cautious, communitarian, disliking of bullying or boasting, broadly egalitarian, valuing of education, internationalist in outlook, working class in character, conservative with a small c. ... It's a multicultural, shared, open polity. (Greig 2013b)

Thus, envisioned as a paradoxical and open 'field of debate, enquiry and at times resistance' (Wallace 2013: 70), the specific idea of Scotland that Greig conceptualizes in his plays can be understood as a metaphor for the politics of his dramaturgy more broadly, reflecting the open and contradictory agenda of his dramatic works as well as the critical 'state of mind' they aim to foster. In this sense, it also encapsulates the significance of a dialectical way of thinking and theatre-making in Greig's works, which are profoundly indebted to the Brechtian tradition in their emphasis on contradiction and their commitment to change. As *Dunsinane*'s complex appropriation exemplifies, it is on an insistence on conflict, tension and paradox that Greig's post-Brechtian dialectics are based, and it is out of the resulting ambivalence that critique and renewal may emerge in the relationship between stage and audience. Appealing to the spectators' imagination, *Dunsinane* initiates a post-Brechtian act of speculation which both interrogates and reinvigorates the potential for transformation at the critical intersection between nation, history and the literary and cultural imaginary.

Interrupting Empathy: *The Events*

Community in Crisis and the Post-Brechtian *Lehrstück*

As the discussion of *Dunsinane* has shown, communities are at the heart of Greig's oeuvre – be they national, local, social, political, cultural or, indeed, theatrical in nature. As the place of 'a transaction between two communities: the performers onstage and the improvised community that constitute what we call an audience' (Gray 2013: xi), the theatre represents by definition an ideal locus for exploring the challenges and potential of fictional and real communities. In *The Events*, which premiered at the

Edinburgh Fringe festival in 2013 before touring extensively both nationally and internationally, Greig examines these questions on a more abstract level by focusing on the relationship between the individual and the collective. Inspired by Anders Breivik's mass shootings in Norway in 2011, the play is set in the aftermath of a terrorist attack on a multicultural choir and therefore portrays an extreme situation of a community in crisis. As Martin Middeke argues, the play stages a 'deconstruction of community' (2017: 221), probing its limits and values on the threshold between the urge to take revenge and the struggle for forgiveness.

For this purpose, the play foregrounds the tensions within a community through a politically and culturally confrontational arrangement. It envisions Claire's – the only survivor and leader of the choir – urge to make sense of the events, and to understand the motives for the mass murder by focussing on her interactions with the antagonistic character of The Boy. Performed by a single actor, The Boy assumes the multiple identities of the people Claire encounters or, rather, imagines encountering in her desperate search for answers – from the perpetrator himself to Claire's partner to a psychologist – slipping in and out of character almost imperceptibly. This conflict is heightened by the inclusion of a choir in the stage action. As a constant and acute reminder of the community – and thus of what has been lost and of what is at stake in the play – *The Events* features a collective of amateur singers, who play an integral role both for the characters and as mediators in the relationship between stage and auditorium. While in this way reflecting Claire's healing process after the traumatic 'events' to the extent that audience members might feel 'caught in Claire's mind' (Brantley 2015), *The Events* goes beyond this psychological dimension to explore urgent political and ethical questions by foregrounding the challenges of living together in the face of risk and violence.

To initiate a reconsideration of the notion of community and the individual's role in it, *The Events* employs, as I argue, the imagination as a central thematic and aesthetic strategy. Thus, on the level of content, the play offers 'an engagement with "the unimaginable,"' which Marilena Zaroulia defines as 'events that violate one's sense of normality' (2016: 71). As Greig writes in his manifesto 'Rough Theatre', '[t]error and violence are certainly one way in which the imaginable is disrupted by the unimaginable' – a disruption which forcefully demonstrates 'that things are not "as they are" but can be suddenly and horribly different' (2007: 217–18). Yet, as the playwright goes on to explain, this violent action does not qualify 'as a method of resistance' because 'violence is, in itself, unimaginative. To commit violence, one must suppress empathy. ... [V]iolence in the service of resistance relies upon the same inhuman suppression of the imagination as violence in the service of power and is, therefore, not a fruitful way to seek to resist it' (Greig 2007: 218). Crucially, while dealing with such an intervention of the 'unimaginable' in the form of a terrorist attack, *The Events* attempts to avoid this trap by refusing to visualize the crime itself. Instead, it stages, in an imaginative and profoundly empathetic way, its aftermath, revolving around Claire's repeated and obsessive, but eventually futile attempts to put herself in the terrorist's shoes in order to gain understanding: 'I don't want to understand what happened to me, / I know what happened to me. / I want to understand what happened to him' (Greig 2013a: 27). By contrast, the perpetrator himself is described as 'empathy impaired' (Greig 2013a: 25), as failing to imagine the potential consequences of his behaviour. Through this constellation, the play forces both characters and spectators to engage with the unspeakably violent events and the challenges they pose for both on- and off-stage communities: how can we make sense of these atrocities? What is the value of the collective in the face of such destruction? Can there be forgiveness in the relationship between self and Other? And ultimately, how can and how should violence be resisted? Implicating the audience in the exploration of these questions, *The Events* stages processes of trying to understand and forgive through the conflict-laden interaction between Claire and The Boy, exploring the possibility of a new and different form of living together.

In this context, *The Events* notably investigates the potential of empathy as a decisive means of (re)connecting individuals and communities. Defined as 'an imaginative reconstruction of the experience of another person's experience' (Nussbaum 2001: 302), empathy represents above all a fundamental 'capacity of the imagination' (Clohesy 2013: 1). As a central element shaping literary and theatrical communication between text/performance and recipients, empathy has, however, occupied a notoriously problematic place within Brechtian theory. Notably, as Lindsay B. Cummings writes, Brecht rejected empathy as a form of 'emotional identification *without thought*' (2016: 29; Brecht 2015a: 194). While it is certainly undeniable that Brecht opposes spectatorial identification as the basic premise of 'bourgeois' theatre practice, his fierce critique must be situated in the historical context of his time, as it represents an explicit reaction against the rise of German Nazism and its seductive emotional manipulation of the masses (Brecht 1978: 178; 1993: 561–6; 2015a: 86, 238). The provocative quality of his theoretical writings has often led to reductive understandings of the role of emotions, particularly of empathy, in his theatre practice. Thus, a fresh and more nuanced approach to Brecht's texts is rewarding as it reveals that his stance towards emotions is far from straightforward. In fact, Brecht 'tried to find productive uses for it' (Barnett 2015: 66) and, indeed, never entirely rejected empathy *per se* for the purposes of dialectical theatre. What he dismissed was, more precisely, a lack of critical reflection on the part of both actors and audiences which he felt was facilitated by empathetic identification. Therefore, while Brecht was suspicious of 'simple, undisturbed processes of empathy' (Barnett 2015: 69), he was also invested in a search for dialectical uses of empathy at the theatre.

Thus, in his theatre practice, Brecht productively experimented with the critical potential of empathy, most explicitly in the *Lehrstücke*, which provide a vital point of reference for *The Events*, both thematically and aesthetically speaking (Hartl 2018b). In Brecht scholarship, the *Lehrstücke* have represented a bone of contention, especially because theoretical material is scarce and definitions have therefore remained fragmentary; as Jonathan Kalb writes, the '*Lehrstück* is probably the most widely misunderstood concept in Brecht's theory' – a diagnosis which is particularly acute 'among Anglophones' (1998: 24) because of conflicting translations and a limited reception of Brecht's fractured writings. In recent years, however, the *Lehrstücke* have been rediscovered as a productive source for contemporary theatre and performance practice. Crucially, Hans-Thies Lehmann emphasizes the importance of this often-marginalized genre for the twenty-first century, specifically with regard to its political potential, as it provocatively undermines conventional forms of institutionalized theatre-making; what Lehmann particularly foregrounds in his assessment is the participatory nature of the *Lehrstücke*, as they blur the distinction between actors and spectators, stage and auditorium (2012: 260–1). Brecht's definition notably underscores the key role of the audience for staging and productively engaging with the plays: 'The *Lehrstück* teaches through being played, not through being watched' (Brecht 1978: 177; my translation). Thus, the *Lehrstücke* aim to initiate an important dialogue between all participants through their specific implication of the audience. Significantly, this form of spectatorial involvement depends on empathetic identification. Indeed, Brecht – albeit reluctantly – acknowledges the dialectical potential of empathy in these plays, arguing that he specifically developed the *Lehrstück* for the purpose of empathy (Brecht 1978: 179). Crucially, the significance of identification and participation is intimately tied to the central thematic concerns addressed by these plays, which foreground the relationship between community and individual, and emphasize 'the capacity for decision-making, the availability of political and ethical options' (Ridout 2009: 48) – issues which are explored in collaboration with the spectators. In the *Lehrstücke*, empathy is thus a necessary technique of interpretation for the audience and an indispensable source of the genre's political potential, as spectators are encouraged to embody, engage with and compare different perspectives, combining both emotional identification and critique at the heart of dialectical theatre.

It is therefore from a thematic as well as aesthetic viewpoint that Brecht's *Lehrstücke* offer a useful framework for an analysis of *The Events*, as I will show in the remainder of this chapter. Exploring ethical questions arising in the relation between self and Other on an individual and collective level, *The Events* probes the potential of empathy as a politicizing and mobilizing tool both within the play itself and, most crucially, in the interaction with the audience. For this purpose, it leaves the more straightforward approach pursued by Brecht's *Lehrstücke* behind to foreground the complexities and ambivalences of communities in liminal and precarious moments of crisis, in which the foundations of social, political and ethical premises of living together are radically unsettled. The resulting indeterminacy complicates both the characters' and the audience's processes of identification and interpretation, destabilizing the relationship between stage and auditorium, and implicating the spectators as performers in the spirit of the Brechtian *Lehrstücke* as a productive means of inciting critique and of reimagining forms of living together in the twenty-first century through the medium of the theatre.

Unstable Identities

The play's critical examination of different concepts of community crystallizes in its innovative treatment and constellation of the characters. The conflict between Claire and The Boy can, to some extent, be read as a confrontation between their supposedly diametrically opposed notions of living together. This is emphasized by the fact that the play opens with the terrorist's vision of a racially and ethnically pure and exclusive community, which is framed in terms of an aboriginal tribe. Thus, The Boy imagines an aborigine who only knows 'his land, his tribe, and the tribes beside' (Greig 2013a: 11), which he is willing to defend against any outside influence. The contrasting notion of a heterogeneous, cosmopolitan community is embodied by Claire's choir, which is rejected by the extremist party The Boy joined as an example of 'state-funded propaganda for multiculturalism' (Greig 2013a: 36). Clashing with the perpetrator's emphasis on cultural essentialism and purity, Claire, a liberal-minded, lesbian priest, describes her choir as 'one big crazy tribe' (Greig 2013a: 68) which 'brought together vulnerable people, old people, asylum-seekers, immigrant men, young mums and so on' (Greig 2013a: 14), underscoring the significance of the choir as a symbol of the play's interrogations of the politics and ethics of communities. Situated in a cultural and political moment in which the limits of multiculturalism as a form of living together are acutely felt, *The Events* refracts this conundrum through its two main characters and the dialectical conflict their relationship initiates, thereby participating in the debates about the forms and functions of communities and the value of notions of difference and heterogeneity in the contemporary context.

By representing these issues through a minimalist, ostensibly clear-cut confrontation between protagonist and antagonist, *The Events* notably seems to adopt the straightforwardness, formal sparsity and tendency towards condensation characteristic of Brecht's *Lehrstücke* (Willett 1997: xii; Hartl 2018b: 158). In a post-Brechtian turn, however, the play simultaneously employs specific 'strategies of contingency' which complicate this apparent simplicity on the surface, thereby introducing 'an air of uncertainty and perhaps improvisation' (Riedelsheimer 2017: 208) which exposes a fundamental tension at the heart of the play, and which reveals the issues under discussion as considerably more complex and ambivalent. Any straightforward dialectical oppositions are dissolved and replaced with an intricate set of unresolvable paradoxes, which serves to reinforce the intricacy of the play's central conflict.

This effect is notably created by Greig's specific treatment of the characters, who lack a coherent sense of identity, thereby undermining any clear attribution of traits and stances. The notion of character is conventionally associated with the idea of '*one fictional person*' who is 'impersonated by *one actor*' (Delgado-García 2015: 2) and connotes 'understandings of the subject as a self-identical, unique, coherent and rational individual' (Delgado-García 2015: 14). This concept is radically challenged by Brecht, for whom 'a unified character did not actually exist' (Barnett 2015: 58). Rather, Brecht conceptualizes dramatic figures in dialectical terms as 'unfixed and flexible' (Barnett 2015: 59) and as defined by social context. Significantly, Greig's ambivalent approach transcends this model to self-reflexively raise urgent questions about notions of identity, belonging and difference. Thus, traumatized and haunted by the terrorist attack, Claire appears 'fractured' to the extent that she 'embodies multiple, contradictory responses to trauma ranging from spiritual crisis, depression, anger, rationalization, self-destructiveness and violence' (Wallace 2016: 37). This fragmentary strategy is radicalized in the figure of The Boy and the multiple subject positions he adopts throughout the play. These shifts in identity – ranging from the perpetrator's at one end of the continuum to Claire's partner's at the other – occur unexpectedly between, but also within the scenes and undermine any fixed, antagonistic understanding of the relationship between Claire and The Boy. Rather than functioning as one single character, the different personae embodied by The Boy overlap to the extent that they become indistinguishable from each other.

In this sense, The Boy functions as a 'blank canvas' (Zaroulia 2016: 77), as the figure is exclusively defined by the various conflicting perspectives offered by the people Claire encounters in the course of the play, such as the terrorist's father, the leader of a right-wing party or a friend – and therefore through the eyes of others and, in Brechtian spirit, in terms of his relationship with the community. Hence, '[t]he Boy does not exist unless he is spoken about' (Zaroulia 2016: 77); he can only be approached socially and in context. This is particularly evident in a scene during which individual members of the choir are asked to adopt the voice of the perpetrator by reading out answers in response to Claire's question '[w]hat *are* you?,' which she addresses to The Boy:

> I am a Europe-wide malaise
> I am a point on the continuum of contemporary masculinity
> I am an expression of failure in eroded working class-communities
> I am unique
> I am typical
> I am the way things are going
> I am the past
> I am the product of the welfare state
> I am the end point of capitalism
> I am an orphan
> A narcissist
> A psychopath
> I am a void into which you are drawn.
> I am sick.
> Dead.
> Lost.
> And alone.
>
> Greig (2013a: 53)

These replies are exemplary of the play's strategy to expose any potential explanation Claire might embrace in her attempt to understand the perpetrator's motives – through her reading of The Boy's manifesto, for example, or in her conversations with those who supposedly knew him – as misleading: all answers represent well-rehearsed, familiar clichés frequently evoked in the aftermath of terrorist attacks and must ultimately fail to provide any insight for Claire. The Boy – and, one might add, the events – cannot be 'understood through psychology' (Zaroulia 2016: 74). Through this technique, *The Events* conceptualizes the 'unimaginable' (encounter with the) terrorist figure as a paradoxical form of absent presence/present absence and as a blend of multiple identities, which complicates the interaction between the characters on stage, and radically disrupts Claire's attempts to empathize with the perpetrator. To the extent that The Boy's identity cannot be grasped because it is never settled, understanding is out of reach for Claire. Ultimately, the terrorist has to remain 'a blankness out of which emerges only darkness' (Greig 2013a: 53). It is in this acknowledgement of 'darkness', rather than in rational understanding, that a reinitiation of community is conceivable, as the play seems to suggest.

Crucially, Greig's unconventional treatment of character does not only destabilize identities but also 'ideological positions that reproduce specific, often racially or ethnically driven understandings of self and Other' (Zaroulia 2016: 77). In this respect, the play complicates the distinctions it evokes between Claire and The Boy as victim and perpetrator of the attack, as well as between the respective ideals of community they embody. Thus, Claire's obsession with the perpetrator increasingly threatens her relationship with Catriona, who compares Claire's behaviour to 'a form of masochism' (Greig 2013a: 39) in its own right. Indeed, through her inability to acknowledge the futility of her endeavour, Claire appears more and more self-centred and egoistic. Preparing for revenge as a last resort to find inner peace by killing the terrorist with a poisoned cup of tea (Greig 2013a: 65-7), Claire is finally on the brink of committing a crime herself. Through this questioning of boundaries, the conflict at the heart of the play between the characters' dichotomously opposed notions of community is rendered decidedly more complex. What the play undermines through its specific conceptualization of dramatic characters is the possibility of a fixed identity and thus of categorizations based on notions of difference, inclusion and exclusion – which paradoxically represent integral mechanisms of both The Boy's pure, 'tribal' understanding of community and Claire's multicultural approach which, while aiming to reunite, still upholds cultural distinctions. In a critical vein, then, *The Events* 'works against a community where its members classify as either red, German, Muslims, or activists' and interrogates notions of 'meaning, identity, belonging, or the essence of a unified collectivity' (Middeke 2017: 224). Destabilizing these markers of identity and offering a decidedly more ambivalent picture, the play addresses the potential and challenges of communities in an age of terrorism and globalization in an attempt to imagine a new form of living together.

Significantly, Greig's decision to break away from conventional understandings of dramatic character also has crucial implications for the audience's interpretation of the play. Thus, *The Events* is structured and organized in a way which puts the spectators in a similar position to

Claire's. Instead of providing a clear exposition and a coherent, teleological and chronological development of the plot, *The Events* proposes an episodic, fragmentary structure by presenting a scattered array of perspectives on Claire's – and, by extension, the community's – attempts to come to terms with the traumatic events. The unconnected scenes blur into each other almost indistinguishably, creating a structural indeterminacy which forces audience members 'to piece together information' in order to understand and follow the play: 'Audiences … are only able to synthesize and imaginatively reconstruct the version of the events that lie at the heart of the play by the end of the live performance' (Thomaidis 2018: 219). Like Claire, the spectators are involved in a search for explanations and experience a lack of orientation that mirrors Claire's own confusion and desperation, which makes it impossible to approach the characters through conventional forms of identification. While *The Events* 'calls for empathy for and understanding of a character that is unlike us' (Zaroulia 2016: 77), these attempts to determine The Boy's identity are repeatedly frustrated.

Hence, *The Events* paradoxically both invites and denies the spectators' empathetic identification with the characters. Processes of empathizing with the protagonists are, on the one hand, presented as necessary in order to try and understand the play, but are, on the other hand, immediately interrupted through various 'strategies of contingency' on the level of structure and character constellation. This form of interruption represents, according to Walter Benjamin, a key principle of Brechtian theatre practice for fostering critical reflection (Benjamin 1998: 19). In a post-Brechtian turn, it is through its emphasis on ambivalence and uncertainty that *The Events* creates an interruptive, estranging aesthetic which deprives the spectators of any interpretive clarity. Thus, it does not only compel us to take a distance from the play but also from ourselves. In a self-reflexive vein, therefore, '[i]t is precisely our empathy that is estranged' (Cummings 2016: 76), inciting us to enquire into both our relationship with the characters on stage and our own involvement in the action. In this respect, 'interruptions to empathy may enhance rather than curtail dialogue' (2016: 40), as Cummings argues with regard to contemporary theatre practice more generally, thereby reconceptualizing empathy as an ongoing dialogic process in which meanings and relations are constantly renegotiated. Crucially, through this heightened self-awareness, the paradox of interrupted empathy may also 'challenge us to engage others *even when we cannot understand*, to make room in our dialogue for gaps and fissures' (Cummings 2016: 76). In this vein, interrupted empathy represents a crucial tool for dialectical analysis in *The Events*, as it is in this acknowledgement of indeterminacy that an engagement with the unresolvable contradictions surrounding the question of community and the individual's relation to the collective can emerge.

The Paradox of the Choir

The importance of the community for the play's interrogations is not only reflected in the confrontation between the two protagonists, but above all in the collective of the choir as the third participant in the action. As an emblem of the play's central thematic and aesthetic concerns, it is visible and active on stage throughout the performance and fulfils a variety of tasks, ranging from singing or interacting with the characters to silently witnessing the action. The choristers' participation through word, music and movement is integral to an interpretation of the play. Through its very presence, the choir represents a 'fixed point of reference' (Pattie 2016b: 56) for both Claire and the audience; rather than encouraging identification, however, it is employed to enhance the intricacy of the conflict. Performing contradictory functions, the choir invites a wide range of different interpretations and responses and thereby further problematizes the characters' interactions as well as the spectators' relation to the action on stage. Heightening the paradoxical quality of *The Events*, it is thus designed as an ambivalent metaphorical and dramaturgical device which connects all participants in the performance while refusing to provide any clear answers to the questions raised by the play. Thematically speaking, as the central metaphor of *The Events*, the choir evokes contradictory associations which underscore the play's critical approach to the idea of community. As an on-stage community, it embodies the essence of the play, but, crucially, stands in for different, seemingly mutually exclusive notions of community. While symbolizing the ideal of a harmonious community, it also draws attention to the potential dangers inherent in any community and its constitutive processes of inclusion and exclusion. More than that, the choir may also be perceived as 'oppressive' (Greig 2016: 249) to the extent that it forces its members into a certain degree of consensus and oneness and may therefore foster anxieties. Through this paradoxical constellation, the play's specific use of the choir thus also implicitly raises the question of the forms, functions and values of communities in times of crisis. Given Claire's attempts to come to terms with the traumatic experience by setting up and rehearsing with a new choir, it also serves as a powerful prospective – if ambivalent and conflict-laden – symbol of the play's search for a potential community of the future.

Crucially, the choir does not only serve as a metaphorical point of reference in the play but also represents the core of its dramaturgy. As a central device in both Ancient Greek theatre practice and Brecht's model, the choir has been attributed a complex range of functions. In Brechtian theatre, it is notably the *Lehrstücke* which make ample use of the chorus as an embodiment of the collective which critically intervenes in the action of the play (Hartl 2018b: 161). In this context, Brecht emphasizes the chorus's musical function, which is why Klaus-Dieter Krabiel has situated the *Lehrstücke* in the context of avant-garde music rather than in a theatrical environment (2001: 28). While Brecht's use of the chorus and of music in the *Lehrstücke* is primarily designed to create *Verfremdung*, it may also enhance the participants' collective experience and '[facilitate] communal participation' (Calico 2008: 23). As Joy H. Calico explains, this might also produce 'a quasireligious effect that [is] highly emotional and difficult to manage' (2008: 34). Encouraging identification and cohesion, on the one hand, while critically interrupting these processes, on the other, the Brechtian chorus thus represents a complex device. Indeed, Brecht reinforces the 'essentially ambiguous nature' the chorus has acquired over the course of its long history, as it reunites, according to Patrice Pavis, both 'cathartic and ritual power' and 'distancing force' (1998: 55) in its dramaturgical range.

The Events exploits this inherent complexity in order to foster an intricate engagement with the play's interrogations into different conceptualizations of the community. This is above all reflected by the contradictory dramaturgical functions the choir fulfils. Thus, it can first and foremost be attributed a strong emotional and 'cathartic' force, which is reflected in the soothing hymns which accompany Claire's healing process and evoke feelings of togetherness (Hartl 2018b: 162). At the same time, however, this naive affirmation of community is radically undermined by a more subversive, 'distancing' quality of the choir's musical interventions. In this respect, the songs acquire a gestic dimension to the extent that they bring the sociopolitical context into view. In Brechtian theatre, music is attributed a particularly important function for realizing the gestic principle in performance. Contrasting dramatic with epic uses of music, Brecht emphasizes that the latter aim to '[communicate]', to '[take] up a position' and to '[present] behaviour' (2015a: 66). While thus interrupting the action and the audience's identification with the characters, songs may also encourage emotional forms of engagement. Indeed, Brecht stresses the importance of 'fun' and 'enjoyment' that dramatic and epic forms of opera provide and ascribes a 'culinary' (2015a: 63) quality to both. The crucial difference is that gestic music invites critical analysis with regard to the music's emotional effects: 'It was necessary to fashion something instructive and direct from the fun, so that it would not simply be irrational' (Brecht 2015a: 66). In this respect, gestic songs are characterized by a tension between fostering emotional attachment, on the one hand, and disrupting these processes to create distance, on the other.

The Events capitalizes on this gestic function of music in Brechtian theatre practice by countering the 'cathartic and ritual' effects of the choir's interventions described above. Challenging Claire's quest for understanding, the choir critically comments on the events through a variety of gestic songs. Their disruptive quality derives not only from their 'rough' (Greig 2007: 213) style and content, which sharply contrasts with the more soothing tunes of the play, but also from the fact that they critically point to the wider political and social context, as I have argued elsewhere (Hartl 2018b: 162-4). Hence, the choir critically comments on and consciously undermines Claire's attempts to recreate a sense of community. This is made explicit by the gradual dissolution of the choir, in a scene later added in the revised edition of the play. Critical of Claire's practices, the singers have left and the last remaining participant, Mr(s) Sinclair – performed by a member of the local choir – explains their motives: '*We don't want to do choir any more. ... The things you've asked us to do lately. ... They're not fun. ... We don't want to dwell on what happened. We want to forget. Perhaps forgetting is best*' (Greig 2014: 41). Thus, both supporting and resisting Claire, the choir performs a decidedly paradoxical role in the play, underscoring the complexity of the conflict between Claire and The Boy, and resisting any straightforward solution or ultimate conclusion.

Dissensus and the Community of Emancipated Spectators

While the choir's paradoxical dramaturgical functions seem to defy any attempt to resolve the conflict between the protagonists, it nevertheless represents a crucial device for the play's investigations into the notion of community in the contemporary context. Indeed, in *The Events*, the very ambivalence of the choir functions as a vital source of critique and emancipation. This potentiality results above all from its indeterminate status in relation to the spectators. As I will argue in the following, it is precisely within the unstable and ambiguous relationship negotiated with the audience during the performance that a possibility of reimagining the idea of the community may arise, which underscores the centrality of the spectators for an interpretation of the play.

Crucially, the intricate connection between the choir and the audience in *The Events* particularly hinges on the playwright's decision to integrate a local ensemble of amateurs instead of professional actors or singers for taking over the part of the choir. In an unusual experiment, a new group of singers from the region where the play is performed is specifically cast for every single show, which reinforces the uniqueness of each performance. To reflect the liberal, open nature of Claire's fictional choir, the producers aim for diversity 'in size, in gender split, in repertoire, in age range etc.' (Actors Touring Company n.d.: 4). Apart from music rehearsals, the choristers are only provided with very little additional information about their role within the play prior to the show. Witnessing the events on stage for the first time, they are thus relatively unprepared for the performance during which they have to interact spontaneously with Claire and The Boy, for example by reading out parts of the dialogue or by improvising and contributing text spontaneously (Greig 2013a: 41, 52). Consequently, the choir's improvised interventions sharply contrast with the professionalism of the other actors, thereby enhancing the play's emphasis on contingency. As a result, the spectators are not only incited to follow the plot as such, but they are also made aware of the amateurs' (lack of) performative skills and their inexperience as participants in the production, which is consciously put on display and turned into a significant source of meaning. It is this double awareness which emerges as decisive for the audience's productive engagement with the contradictions presented by the play.

By virtue of its amateur status, the choir can be said to occupy a problematic, ambiguous position in-between theatre and reality. On the one hand, it is firmly integrated into the fictional world of the play and performs a crucial role in the action. On the other hand, however, it is also intimately connected to the 'real' world of the audience beyond the theatre. Asked to dress casually 'as you would normally ... for your choir rehearsal' (Actors Touring Company n.d.: 7), the singers appear as ordinary people on stage, which helps foster a certain intimacy with the audience. As members of the local community, they are also likely to share the spectators' background and, significantly, they are as uninformed about the events which are about to unfold as the members of the audience. The choir is therefore located in a liminal space, on the 'threshold': it represents the 'precarious hinge' of the play 'between the fictional world on stage and reality, between the fixed lines in the playscript and the differences and contingencies brought about by the changing choirs every night' (Middeke 2017: 221). Hence, the singers' amateurism is what both connects them to and disconnects them from the spectators, creating a complex and uncertain relationship between stage and auditorium.

This in-betweenness has a significant impact on the audience's interpretation of the play, as the intricate tension between fiction and reality is turned into a productive source of enquiry for the spectators. Notably, the use of amateurs represents an 'interruption of the real' which spurs what Lehmann describes as an '*aesthetics of undecidability*' (2006: 100), and thereby performs vital functions as part of the play's political fabric. In this context,

Brecht's theatre projects mark an important development in the history of the 'Theatre of Real People', a term coined by Ulrike Garde and Meg Mumford to describe current trends to include amateurs in performance (2016: 5). Aiming to establish an intimate connection between theatre and everyday life, Brecht attributed considerable importance to the 'proletarian actor' (Brecht 2015a: 206) not only as a means of disrupting illusion and estranging the action but first and foremost also as a way of 'authenticat[ing] and democratiz[ing] art' (Revermann 2013: 167). This is above all reflected in the *Lehrstücke*, which require by definition the participation of the audience as amateur performers on stage; in this sense, they have also been understood as early forerunners to contemporary performance practices. Brecht privileges the amateur over the professional actor and the value of the 'professional naiveté (rather than ineptitude)' (Gruber 2010: 102) they introduce to the performance as vital for the politics of the plays.

Greig's *The Events* illustrates this potential and radicalizes Brecht's intentions by staging an improvised and highly self-reflexive encounter between professional and non-professional participants. More precisely, the choir's amateurism and the indeterminacy it creates serve as efficient tools for the play's interrogations into the forms and functions of communities through the shifting relations between choir and audience. As I have argued elsewhere, this specific approach prompts urgent questions regarding the political and ethical implications of the use of amateurs in performance, in particular regarding their intimate exposure and heightened vulnerability on stage (Hartl 2018b: 164). A successful cooperation between professional and amateur performers thus depends on an ongoing process of negotiation – a relationship that has to be built anew with each local choir as part of the show itself. Notably, the 'undecidability' of the singers' status, as part of both the fictional world on stage and the reality beyond the theatre, enhances the 'ethical confusion or cross-purposes' between 'truth and untruth' (Ridout 2009: 15) inherent in any theatrical transaction, thereby directly implicating the spectators in the play's ethical enquiries. This critical interrelation between stage and auditorium is self-reflexively heightened in *The Events* through its confrontational stage design, as the singers are positioned on a platform from which they face the audience (Actors Touring Company n.d.: 7). While the choristers may intervene verbally, musically or physically in some phases of the performance, in others, they witness the action as an onstage audience, sitting down on the rostrum during those scenes which do not require their active intervention. Through this arrangement, *The Events* self-consciously raises awareness of the 'situation of mutual spectatorship', which Nicholas Ridout describes as intrinsic to the theatre; thus, as spectators, we 'watch ourselves watching people engaging with an ethical problem while knowing that we are being watched in our watching (by other spectators and also by those we watch)'

(2009: 15). *The Events* capitalizes on this self-reflexive dimension precisely by disrupting these reciprocal dynamics. As David Pattie explains, 'we look to them [the singers; AH] to mirror our response to the performance, but they only mirror us sometimes – at other moments they are performers, as distanced from us as the actors themselves' (2016b: 55). Therefore, 'by emphasising the act of spectatorship' through this interruptive strategy, *The Events* 'strengthens the audience's involvement in the stage action' (Riedelsheimer 2017: 212). Complicating the relation between amateurs and spectators, the play's self-reflexivity creates an acute awareness of the instability of the connection between on- and offstage communities, which forces audience members to constantly renegotiate their relationship with the choir.

As a result of this complex arrangement between the ensemble on stage and the spectators in the auditorium, the boundaries separating not only professionals from amateurs but also actors from audience members blur, as the supposedly 'safe distance' between on- and offstage spaces is dissolved. In this sense, the mirror constellation between singers and audiences can be said to inspire the spectators' own integration into the action. These intricate forms of spectatorship and participation can be usefully connected to the *Lehrstücke*. While the genre has frequently been 'taken to mean that it is only for actors and that an audience has no place in a *Lehrstück*' (Wood 2018: 173), Brecht's theoretical approach is more nuanced, as it does precisely not posit the abolition of the spectator as such, but rather emphasizes the uses spectators can be put to (Brecht 1978: 177). Thus, spectators still perform vital functions in the *Lehrstücke* and, indeed, in Brecht's own productions 'the Lehrstücke were staged for nonperforming audiences more often than performing ones', as Calico (2008: 17) notes. Hence, Michael Wood revises widespread misunderstandings by emphasizing that 'those not physically engaged in the process of performing the *Lehrstück* are actors in a dialectical thought experiment', participating actively 'in the form of studying' (2018: 182). Consequently, the *Lehrstücke* fundamentally interrogate the distinction between acting and spectating, doing and watching and, as it were, feeling and thinking. Through their specific focus on the audience as a vital element of the plays' production and interpretation, they rewrite theatrical conventions by 'unify[ing] the production and consumption of art in a single reciprocal process that challenged the concept of audiences as mere consumers of cultural products' (Calico 2008: 17). As such, their reconceptualization of spectatorship anticipates Rancière's notion of the 'emancipated spectator', which acknowledges the inherently active nature of any form of interpretation and oscillates 'between a Brechtian-style critical specular relation to the stage and a more Artaudian immersive, experiential connection to the performance' (Stevens 2016: 13).

It is this emancipated concept of spectatorship which emerges out of the complex constellation between actors and spectators which is integral to an interpretation of the play. This effect particularly crystallizes in the play's last lines, which represent a final appeal to audience participation. At the end, her former attempts having failed, Claire tries once again to start a new choir. Welcoming new members, she turns to face the audience to invite all present, on- and offstage, to join:

> Come in.
> Don't be shy.
> Everyone's welcome here.
> Why don't you sit with us and if you feel like singing –
> sing. And if you don't feel like singing
> Well that's OK too.
> Nobody feels like singing all the time
> …
> Are we all here? Good. Sing.
>
> Greig (2013a: 68)

Crucially, what is underscored in this direct address to the audience is the availability of choice. Rather than forcing the spectators to sing along, Claire's words raise awareness of the fact that it is up to each individual to make a decision, thereby highlighting the fundamental role of the audience – who, even though seated in the auditorium, supposedly at a distance from the stage, is far from merely passively consuming the action in this moment.

Yet, while the idea of singing together may initially 'feel like a blessing' and a 'moment of comfort' (Pattie 2016b: 49), this impression is undermined by a heightened sense of paradox which prevails at the end of the play. In the revised edition, rather than finishing with a repetition of the choir's own song, as in the first version, *The Events* finishes with the song 'We're All Here' (Greig 2013a: 68), which describes the new community of singers as a supposedly safe, protected space open to everyone (Greig 2014: 65). However, the Choir Pack indicates that some singers are meant to disturb this apparent harmony by singing 'I'm not [here]' (Actors Touring Company n.d.: 10). In addition, in the Actors Touring Company's production, The Boy moved away from the choir to the back of the stage during this closing scene and was thereby also visually excluded from the community Claire has attempted to re-establish with the amateurs and, by implication, the spectators. In this respect, the profoundly affective quality of the choir's song is heavily compromised: it 'does not allow the audience a simple moment of emotional catharsis' (Pattie

2016b: 59). While the music to some extent illustrates 'the power of empathy' (Wallace 2016: 38) explored in the play, it is yet again disrupted, depriving the participants of any cleansing effect. Thus, the paradoxical rendering of the hymn serves to emphasize the tensions between conflicting understandings, forms and functions of the community at the heart of the play, reinforcing the contradictions shaping the conflict between Claire and The Boy, on the one hand, and between stage and auditorium, on the other. Ultimately, the question of whether this song represents 'a sign of healing, a promise for the future' or, instead, 'a perpetuation of the conditions that produce the violence' (Zaroulia 2016: 80–1) remains unanswered.

Therefore, rather than proposing a sense of 'unity, coherence, origins, ends, and closure' (Middeke 2017: 225) which would to some extent reinscribe conventional understandings of the community, the openness and uncertainty at the heart of *The Events* can be said to serve as a means of exploring the limits of the community by probing the limits of empathy. Encouraged by Claire to make an ethical choice – to join or not to join – the members of the offstage audience find themselves in a strongly ambivalent situation at the end: they are enticed to identify with the choir, get involved and sing along, on the one hand, while, on the other, they are acutely aware of the potential implications and risks this decision might entail. By providing an experience of unresolvable paradox for the spectators, the play underscores the significance of ambivalence and undecidability as sources for its attempts to rethink community for the contemporary context. Rather than on the stage, it is in the fundamentally unstable and ambiguous relationships established between performers and audiences that this reimagined community can be found: it is effectively formed in the very moment of the performance as an ephemeral, provisional, processual and therefore always unfinished form of collectivity (Zaroulia 2016: 80). Most importantly, it can be said to be based on an experience of Rancièrean dissensus, which is manifest in the play's emphasis on fragmentation, contingency and liminality. Rejecting any fixed concepts and categories and constantly renegotiating the terms of its own arrangement, the community which develops between the individuals on- and offstage is thus characterized, in post-Brechtian spirit, by an awareness of difference as well as a radical openness towards revision, renewal and change.

Conclusion

In Greig's theatre, the imagination is employed as a dialectical technique for staging the contradictions shaping life under the impact of globalization, as well as for speculating about alternative realities. While diagnosing a crisis of the imagination that seems to paralyse our capacity to challenge the status quo, the plays experiment with the possibility of reactivating the imagination as a creative means of inspiring change. For this purpose, it creates a rich and paradoxical dialectic in which the irrational and imaginative are, in an Adornian vein, juxtaposed with the rational and political.

Dunsinane emphasizes the fundamental role of the (literary) imagination for constructing and re-envisioning a sense of nationhood and history. Turning its appropriation of Shakespeare's *Macbeth* into a post-Brechtian strategy of *Verfremdung*, the play estranges common narratives within a complex contact zone in which different texts, historical and political contexts as well as interpretive perspectives are brought together without resolving these contradictions, suggesting that any attempt to (re)imagine the nation must be understood as provisional and open to change. By emphasizing the pluralistic and rhizomatic nature of its appropriative strategy, *Dunsinane* does not only expose the seminal status of Shakespeare's version within the cultural imaginary but also opens the material up to address broader issues, offering a nuanced comment on the politics of literary adaptation and its potential for reinforcing as well as revising concepts of nationhood, history and culture.

The Events pursues a more explicitly experiential approach in its exploration of the imagination by adopting the participatory model of Brecht's *Lehrstücke*. Proposing a reconsideration of the concept of community in the context of terrorism, the play probes the potential of empathy as an imaginative capacity and as a means of critique in the relationship between individual and collective as well as stage and auditorium. Through an interruptive and estranging approach which seeks to destabilize conventional aesthetic and epistemological parameters – between performers and spectators, victims and perpetrators, real and imagined as well as professionals and amateurs – *The Events* creates a deeply ambivalent framework in which the ethical challenges of reimagining the community in the face of violence are, in post-Brechtian spirit, effectively handed over to the audience.

3

Strategic Naivety: The Dialectic of Sincerity in Andy Smith and Tim Crouch's Work

Theatre practitioners Andy Smith and Tim Crouch have frequently collaborated throughout their careers, co-writing plays as well as acting in and directing each other's works. Their individual and joint projects offer an innovative approach to theatre-making which radically disrupts the aesthetic status quo and clearly distinguishes their pieces from other, arguably more conventional forms of contemporary British theatre. Pushing the boundaries of the theatre as such, Smith and Crouch also stand out from other examples of post-Brechtian theatre discussed in this study. While the Brechtian dimension of their plays may, in comparison, emerge in more oblique ways, significant intersections can be established which open up fresh perspectives, both on the role of Brecht's legacy in twenty-first-century British theatre and on Smith and Crouch's idiosyncratic dramaturgy. Crucially, it is their uncompromising use of metatheatricality – a key concept for Brecht, too – which determines the decidedly experimental quality of their plays, as Smith and Crouch's performances are above all self-conscious examinations of the formal premises of the theatre, its functions and its relationship with the audience. For this purpose, they privilege minimalism as a guiding aesthetic principle. Focusing attention on the theatre as such, they reduce spectacle by rejecting mimetic representation and by leaving traditional categories of character, setting and action behind, thereby returning to the very basics of the theatre – while deftly breaking new ground.

The characteristic 'dematerialised' (Smith 2015c: 55) quality of their texts and productions has, however, been heavily contested and has even at times been perceived as profoundly irritating. Elizabeth Sakellaridou, for example, describes Smith and Crouch's *what happens to the hope at the end of the evening* (2013) as 'blunt' and 'random', displaying 'a lack of skill or inspiration or a thinly prepared script' (2014: 26). Similarly, Ann Treneman considers Crouch's most recent piece, *Total Immediate Collective Imminent Terrestrial Salvation* (2019; co-directed by Andy Smith and Karl James) 'a stilted and rather baffling event' which left her 'more bored and impatient than anything else' (2019). Other plays – notably Crouch's *ENGLAND* (2007) or *The Author*

(2009) – have pushed conventional thematic and aesthetic boundaries in such a profoundly provocative way that audiences have experienced the performances as shocking and overwhelming. It is this paradox between (the playwrights' claim to) simplicity, indeed aesthetic innocence, on the one hand, and the fierce reactions triggered by this approach, on the other, that is the focus of this chapter. As I will argue, it is precisely in this strategic provocation of conventions, and in the resulting implications for the relationship between stage and auditorium, that not only a significant political potential but also a distinctly Brechtian dimension arises.

This complex political fabric has so far not been explored in any detail, which reflects perceptions of the plays as being, in Cristina Delgado-García's words, 'relatively apolitical' (2014: 71). Despite their emphasis on metatheatricality and their aesthetic proximity to conceptual art forms (Morin 2011), however, all of Smith and Crouch's works are in fact explicitly preoccupied with questions of politics, specifically exploring the impact of neoliberalism on political engagement and committed art. Whereas Crouch concentrates on more abstract questions by addressing the increasing commodification of art as well as issues of ownership, value and justice, as for example in *ENGLAND* or *Adler & Gibb* (2013), Smith's plays, such as *The Preston Bill* (2015) or *Summit* (2017), more concretely examine the effects of consumerism and economic precarity on individual lives and communities. Significantly, these issues are self-consciously explored through the lens of the theatre itself, which functions as a blueprint for the broader social context, critically examining the possibility of politically progressive playwriting against the background of the institution's own entanglement with the neoliberal processes it seeks to critique.

Hence, the use of self-reflexivity, a central postmodernist technique, is, as I suggest, far from self-sufficient in these plays; instead, it is refunctioned in Brechtian terms as a means of dialectical interrogation. Building on Delgado-García's observation on the significance of the legacy of 'avant-garde, popular and political theatre' (2014: 74) for Smith and Crouch's works, I contend that it is in particular this post-Brechtian dimension, only briefly mentioned by Delgado-García, which is important for identifying the political thrust at the heart of their plays. Thus, Smith and Crouch's metatheatrical investigations can be understood on a theoretical level as participating in a wider search for a new form of Brechtian-inspired political theatre after postmodernism. By realizing a fundamental *Verfremdung* of dramaturgical conventions, their plays offer an explicit meta-commentary on the challenges of re-establishing a productive connection between theatre and reality – perceived as disrupted by postmodernist notions of relativism and epistemological uncertainty – and of reasserting, in a Brechtian vein, ideas of change and engagement. For this purpose, Smith and Crouch foreground the role of the spectators, who are conceptualized as co-creators and co-producers of the performances. Referring to forms 'collaboration', 'conversation' and 'dialogue', the playwrights suggest that they understand their theatre-practice as a gentle, trusting and careful encounter between equal participants. Thus, their approach reflects the growing interest in sincerity which has manifested itself in literary and theatrical works, as well as in scholarly criticism in the new millennium. While postmodernist conceptualizations of selfhood have radically questioned notions of genuineness, truthfulness and intimacy associated with the concept, the contemporary cultural moment has above all been shaped by a renewed desire for experiences of the sincere and authentic (Kelly 2010; Schulze 2017). Drawing on Lionel Trilling's influential study *Sincerity and Authenticity* (1972), Wolfgang Funk explains that sincerity, in contrast to authenticity, 'is always aimed at an external point of reference' and is therefore 'comparable, relative, relational, heteronomous and describable in terms of social and intersubjective norms' (2015: 24). Given this essentially performative and processual nature, the theatre represents a privileged place for negotiating and establishing sincerity in the interaction between stage and audience, as Smith and Crouch's projects exemplify. Crucially, however, as critics' and spectators' contentious reactions to the performances mirror, the quest for sincerity at the heart of their plays seems to be less straightforward than the playwrights' own assertions may suggest; in fact, their naive claims seem to be perceived as radically alienating and unsettling by audiences.

Hence, while, on the surface, pretending to aim for an earnest dialogue with the spectators, the shift towards a new form of engagement envisioned by Smith and Crouch emerges as a decidedly ambivalent endeavour. The negotiation of sincerity as the basis for their cooperation with the audience is based on a strategic juxtaposition. What the plays reflect is the challenge of initiating a new form of political theatre and spectatorial involvement in the (post-)postmodernist moment through an oscillation between sincere collaboration, on the one hand, and an ironical undermining of these attempts, on the other. This paradox reflects what Siân Adiseshiah has usefully defined as a 'new' (2016: 186), decidedly more ambiguous form of sincerity, in which 'residues of an ironic affect continue to trouble the encounter, ironic moments exist within the space of sincerity, and the authentic is always in question' (2016: 189). Analysing the work of Forced Entertainment, Adiseshiah proposes the term 'critical sincerity' to describe this shift in emphasis, which can also be identified in Smith and Crouch's plays – reflecting not only the precarious nature of this new ideal but also the space it creates for critique and analysis. Essentially, the turn to sincerity can thus be understood as a dialectical process which determines the complex encounter between performers and spectators, as Adiseshiah insightfully argues.

Proposing a post-Brechtian perspective on these intricate mechanisms, this chapter is dedicated to critically exploring Smith and Crouch's dialectical negotiations of sincerity on the basis of a close analysis of Smith's *all that is solid melts into air*, which represents a prime example of the metatheatrical mechanisms typical of both playwrights' aesthetic style. Focusing in particular on the potential implications for the audience's experience of the performance, I will investigate the possibilities and difficulties of fostering spectatorial engagement afforded by the precarious oscillation between irony and genuineness that underpins the plays. While this ambivalence may create space for the spectators, the strategic provocation at the heart of this self-reflexive theatre practice may in fact also stifle productive forms of participation and commitment. This is particularly evident in Crouch's *The Author*, which I will consider by way of conclusion as an illustration precisely of the limits of the dialectic of sincerity as an example of post-Brechtian theatre on the contemporary British stage.

Post-Brechtian Meta-Theatre: *all that is solid melts into air*

Performing Theory

It is in Brechtian spirit that Smith's dramatic works are preoccupied with the possibility of social and political change in the contemporary moment and that they explore these questions through the theatre as a potential medium for encouraging action. For this purpose, Smith conceives of the theatre – paradoxically the very cradle of the spectacular – as a place for thinking, providing a mental space for critical analysis, as well as an opportunity for thereby reconnecting with social reality as a first step towards intervention. In this light, the solo play *all that is solid melts into air* (2011) represents a particularly significant example because of its heightened self-reflexive framework. Offering a complex *mise-en-abyme* structure, *all that is solid* is a play about (the creation of) a play and, in fact, gives the impression of being a play about itself. Thus, the unnamed performer, usually played by Smith himself, introduces himself as the author and meditates on how 'this' play has come into being, considering his motivations, thoughts and decisions in the working process. With the disarming straightforwardness typical of Smith's texts, he announces his agenda at the beginning of the performance:

So this ... this is about how we change the world. ... I've been thinking a lot about how we might do it. How we might do that. I've spent a lot of time just imagining the situation. Just imagining it. This situation. What we could do here. What I could tell you here. Here in the theatre.

Smith (2015b: 68)

At its heart, therefore, the play specifically addresses the problem of how to create a politically mobilizing piece of theatre. The epigraphs preceding the playtext anticipate this investigation into the potentially transformative and emancipatory quality of the theatre. Playwright John McGrath's famous claim that '[t]he theatre can never cause a social change' (Smith 2015b: 65) is provocatively juxtaposed with theatre practitioner Chris Goode's assessment that '[w]e've barely begun to make the theatre that dares to believe that change is possible' (Smith 2015b: 65), reflecting a certain ambiguity and awareness of the limitations of the theatre's politicizing potential. While acknowledging that it may be illusory to directly influence social and political reality, these quotations seem to suggest that theatre-making can nevertheless fulfil vital functions in working towards change, thereby setting the tone for *all that is solid*'s self-conscious interrogations.

Hence, the play explicitly inscribes itself into a left-wing tradition – both politically and aesthetically speaking. This is above all reflected by the title, which is taken from Karl Marx and Friedrich Engels's *The Communist Manifesto* (1848). Self-reflexively justifying this choice in the play, the performer explains that the phrase is used by Marx and Engels to describe 'what happens to us when capitalism takes hold. When our values change. When our relationships to things and each other start to alter. When our infrastructures break down' (Smith 2015b: 79). These speculations establish the communist legacy as a central point of reference for the play. At the same time, however, communism is also treated with some suspicion, gesturing to the question of its ongoing relevance and acknowledging the difficulty of thinking with and through communist ideology today (Smith 2015b: 79). In this respect, the title can also be connected to Marxist-inspired philosopher Zygmunt Bauman's concept of 'liquid modernity', which Smith cites to foreground the implications of postmodernism and neoliberal globalization on communities, raising the question of the possibility of resisting these processes at the theatre by foregrounding the value of social bonds as a means of 're-solidifying' life and, ultimately, of changing the system (Smith 2017). Hence, the performer wonders 'how we can break these systems, change these systems. Make some cracks in these systems. ... How we might get out of this situation' (Smith 2015b: 77). Convinced that 'there must be something we can do' (Smith 2015b: 70), he locates this resistant potential at the theatre, where individuals can 'just get together' (Smith 2015b: 81) and 'try and have conversations with each other' (Smith 2015b: 80). It is thus through an emphasis on the value of social connections that the play envisages the transformation of reality as a possibility.

Exploring these questions in a post-Marxist moment, *all that is solid* raises issues which are central to current debates about political theatre in general, and about Brecht's legacy more specifically. In its endeavour to reconnect theatre and social reality, and to reinvigorate drama's political potential, the play critically engages with conventional forms of theatre practice. Thus, sharing his considerations in preparation for the show, the performer explains that he did not only have to decide which 'things to write about. Subjects to cover. Questions to ask' (Smith 2015b: 68) but also which formal means to choose. Significantly, in this context, he also offers an implicit critique of Brechtian stagecraft. Sceptical of its ongoing radical power, he argues for the need for innovation:

> I thought about using lights. … I thought about using some technology. … I wrote a list of slogans that I thought about projecting on the wall. … Slogans that might provoke us or entertain us. Make us think. … And of course I had plans for great music to play as we came in at the start. And sound effects. … I thought all of these things would serve as great illustrations or support, but none of them seemed to capture the essence of the work for me. They ended up feeling clichéd or not quite right. It just didn't feel that these things alone could do justice to the subject or to us. … All the stuff that I think we need to change, that I want us to change, with this piece.
>
> Smith (2015b: 71–2)

Assigning the function to provoke change by means of social analysis to these dramaturgical devices, the performer establishes a significant connection with Brecht. Hence, while Brecht's fundamental belief in the transformative capacity of the theatre represents a crucial point of departure for *all that is solid*, the play offers a critical perspective in its search for a new form of political drama which is capable of responding to the radically different contemporary context. It is thus through an interrogation of Brecht's legacy that *all that is solid* self-reflexively seeks to reinvigorate the progressive potential of dialectical theatre for the present moment.

In this respect, *all that is solid* can be brought into fruitful dialogue with Brecht's 'Messingkauf, or Buying Brass'. Written between 1939 and 1955, the unfinished 'Messingkauf' project stands out from Brecht's oeuvre not only because it represents the 'single most extensive and … most significant exposition of his views on theatre' (Giles 2014: 1) but also because it is located on the threshold between theory and practice. The overarching thematic focus of the eclectic 'Messingkauf' fragments is on the forms and functions of the theatre. Thus, five characters – the Philosopher (usually interpreted as Brecht's *alter ego*), the Dramaturg, the Actor, the Actress and the Lighting Technician – discuss their respective expectations with regard to the theatre. Guided by the Philosopher's questions, they notably engage in a critique of conventional forms of theatre-making. For this purpose, 'Messingkauf' employs a strategic naivety, as the Philosopher's lack of practical theatrical experience makes it possible for him to interrogate the very foundations of the theatre from an amateur perspective. This form of naivety reflects the wider significance of this concept in Brechtian theatre. As a central aesthetic strategy, it encapsulates the intuitive, natural and fresh approach to dramatic works that Brecht demanded of both theatre-makers and audiences. As David Barnett summarizes, Brechtian naivety denotes 'the ability to perform or respond to material without reducing it with prejudices or preconceptions' (2015: 76). Thus, rather than implying, as in everyday usage, a lack of knowledge, naivety is employed as a meaning-making device, as it estranges the familiar to inspire new perspectives and encourage critical thinking.

Crucially, in their naive rejection of fundamental principles of theatre-making, the dialogues reflect a profound 'mistrust of the theater' (Puchner 2002: 148). Eschewing representational illusion, the play consists entirely of philosophical discussions. However, while fiercely critical of the theatre, 'Messingkauf' is far from abandoning it: it does not constitute 'the theater's negation' (Puchner 2010: 111), but is rather discursively concerned with the search for a new theatrical form based on a rigorous critique of previous traditions. Reflecting this tension, Martin Puchner describes 'Messingkauf' as an example of 'philosophical theater' because it 'view[s] epic theater through a philosophical lens' and adopts 'the form of a philosophical dialogue' (2010: 108) in the Platonic and Socratic tradition. At the same time, however, the discussions also create a lively, open 'forum' (Barnett 2015: 39) for debate, and can therefore be attributed an important performative dimension. Hence, the dialogues are themselves a 'kind of drama' (Puchner 2010: 110); indeed, the text 'performs theory' (Barnett 2015: 53). Thus, located on the threshold between philosophy and theatre, the dialogues 'do work that discursive essays cannot', as Barnett elucidates: their conflict-laden, open character creates 'space for a spectator to stand back and process the arguments on stage and reach conclusions' (2015: 45). In this respect, it is particularly noteworthy that Steve Giles qualifies 'Messingkauf' 'as a sophisticated variant of the *Lehrstück*' (2014: 7) because of its engagement with a diversity of opinions and attitudes, and, as I would add, because of its specific conceptualization of spectatorship. Just as the *Lehrstücke* rely on the audience's active participation, the paradoxical quality of 'Messingkauf's' fragmentary discussions and its naive aesthetic approach serve to foreground the role of the spectators and to encourage them to engage with the issues presented on stage – both on a theoretical and, crucially, also on an eminently practical level.

Similarly situated at a crossroads between philosophy and theatre as well as theory and practice, *all that is solid* can thus be described as a Brechtian-inspired form of philosophical anti- as well as meta-theatre which paradoxically articulates its call for a renewal of the theatre by self-reflexively performing it on stage. For this purpose, *all that is solid* pursues a Brechtian-inspired strategy of naivety which not only questions but indeed also does away with the very foundations of the dramatic genre. While the piece represents, in contrast with 'Messingkauf', a monologue, it can in fact be understood as a dialogue – not between different characters on stage, but rather between the performer and the spectators, thereby underscoring the pivotal role of the audience for the play's interrogations. Directly addressing the audience members, Smith interpellates them in a decidedly more explicit and experiential way than Brecht to create a collaborative collective of co-creators, as the following sections will demonstrate.

Strategically Naive Storytelling

At the heart of *all that is solid*'s naive aesthetic is a metatheatrical story about the function of the theatre and its relation to social reality in the contemporary moment. Emphasizing diegesis over mimesis, and telling rather than showing the dramatic events (if this term is applicable at all in this case) by enacting them on stage, this form of self-conscious storytelling paradoxically fulfils vital functions for reinvigorating the progressive and radical potential of the theatre. Choosing an extract from Walter Benjamin's 'The Storyteller' as an epigraph for his collection of plays, Smith attributes a crucial significance to stories in a rapidly transforming world, while also critically pointing to their decreasing role. Thus, taking this diagnosis as its point of departure, *all that is solid* foregrounds storytelling as a means of reconnection both with our own lives and with each other. Explicitly telling the story of the creation of a piece of theatre (indeed, one is led to assume, of its own creation), the play is constructed around an intricate framework which offers a self-reflexive perspective to critically reflect on its own status as a theatrical story, and to reassert the fundamental value of storytelling for contemporary culture.

Significantly, Smith's specific understanding of the story as the political core of his plays to some extent chimes with Brecht's concept of the *Fabel*, which Brecht defines as 'not just ... an episode from people's lives together as it might have taken place in reality', but as a rearrangement of 'incidents in which the plot inventor articulates ideas about people's lives together' (2015a: 258). Hence, as Barnett explains, the *Fabel* 'is not simply a summary of [the events of a play]'; rather, it can be described as 'an account of a play's action from a dialectical point of view because it teases out contradictions in order to emphasize them in performance' (2015: 86). As such, it is 'at the heart of the theatrical event' (Barnett 2015: 89) and plays a decisive role not only for the actors' but also for the spectators' interpretation of the performance. While Smith shares Brecht's interest in the political, indeed dialectical potential of the *Fabel*, *all that is solid*'s story is fragmentary, consisting of multiple, highly self-referential micro-narratives. Hence, in Smith's adaptation of Brecht's model, the dialectical conflict encapsulated by the *Fabel* resides in the very question of the forms and functions of the theatre in the contemporary context as it is articulated through the relations established between the participants in the play. 'Retain[ing] only the barest framework of a narrative', Smith's work is, as Liz Tomlin argues, designed to '[invite] each spectator to fill in the details from their own imagination' (2019: 127). Thus, as a means of facilitating the spectators' connection to both the work and each other, storytelling is attributed a decidedly political and emancipatory purpose in Smith's play; it aims to reinvigorate this radical potential not only by looking for new kinds of stories but also by seeking creative and innovative ways of telling them at the theatre.

The importance of storytelling for Smith's dramaturgy is also made explicit by the minimalist stage design, which is characteristic of Smith's style. On an almost empty stage, the actor sits down on a chair at the beginning of the show and (seemingly) reads out the text from the script in front of him. Conspicuously present throughout the performance, the script thus functions 'as a prop' (Love 2017: 2), which underscores the importance of the story as the core of the play. As Smith explains, this approach provides a highly unusual experience for audiences and actors alike, as it challenges conventional techniques of acting and spectating (2015a: 90–1). Thus, in an unspectacular but all the more intriguing beginning, the performer in *all that is solid* enters, welcomes the audience with a brief '[h]ello' and then announces that the story he is going to tell 'is about how we change the world'. Crucially, this ambitious mission is immediately connected to the idea of the theatre as a medium 'full of possibility' (Smith 2015b: 69) for thinking about '[w]hat we are doing' (Smith 2015b: 68). Through this intersection, then, thinking about the theatre is turned into a powerful means of inspiring change.

Rather than developing an elaborate and complex narrative, the story can thus be said to pursue a seemingly simple agenda, which is also reflected in its supposedly artless, formal linguistic style. The text mostly consists of paratactic, short sentences in which key words, expressions or entire sentences are frequently repeated. As a result, the story acquires a rhythmic dimension, almost like a mantra, as if reinforcing the performer's ambition to change the world. However, the programmatic nature of this statement somewhat contrasts with the associative structural organization of the story, as the performer's thoughts and memories are loosely combined in what appears to be an improvised account. Crucially, the story is told in a decidedly conversational tone, which does not only enhance the seemingly spontaneous impression given by the storyteller but also strengthens his efforts to establish a close relationship with the spectators. For this purpose, a conspicuously private and personal atmosphere is established, most notably through direct appeals to the spectators, which structure (and, significantly, also disrupt) the fictional narrative to acknowledge their importance and to integrate them into the story. For example, he repeatedly admits that the audience might feel alienated by his approach, perhaps 'thinking Andy, shut up! You sound like some sort of self-help book or quasi-Buddhist monk. Or Andy, we know all this. We know that the world is in bad way, what is your point exactly?' (Smith 2015b: 81). Nevertheless, he explicitly calls on the spectators to 'stay with me' (Smith 2015b: 67) and to engage with the narrative. As a result, the monologue acquires a dialogic quality which foregrounds the audience members as both narratees and participants in the creation of the story.

While the play's political core seems to reside in its revaluation of storytelling as a means of genuine connection, this ostensible 'affirmation of storytelling' in *all that is solid* must be considered strongly 'ambivalent', as Catherine Love (2014) astutely observes. Indeed, on closer inspection, the seemingly artless, simplistic arrangement of the story – on the level of both subject matter and form – emerges as profoundly naive, thereby to some extent self-reflexively problematizing and undermining the play's assertion of the radical potential of storytelling. This strategic naivety is particularly explicit with regard to *all that is solid*'s use of exaggerations and stark contrasts, which serve to both reinforce and ironize the performer's speech. For example, his exclamation '[t]his is amazing!' ironically clashes with his 'total despair' (Smith 2015b: 69) about life only a few lines later. Similarly, listing his wishes and aims, the performer betrays a certain pettiness and self-righteousness. Thus, on the one hand, he explains: 'I want to want something. I'd like a new computer maybe, or a bed that doesn't squeak so much. I want a quality cup of coffee, another room or a bit more space in the house,' while on the other hand demanding 'more peace than there currently is in the world', 'an end to poverty' as well as 'a new form of government' (Smith 2015b: 76). In fact, the storyteller calls for change and intervention – but neither during the story itself nor during the performance does anything remarkable happen. No action – in the conventional sense of the term – develops as the story keeps turning on itself, raising the question of whether *this* is in fact really everything, and whether the play will lead anywhere at all. Crucially, this naivety is never concealed, but self-consciously acknowledged throughout. As illustrated above, the performer repeatedly acknowledges that his approach may seem unconvincing, even alienating, but nevertheless appeals to the spectators to give him a chance. Through these insertions, the speaker apparently substantiates his claim to the sincerity of his intentions, which he asserts at the beginning of the show: 'I'm being honest with you. I want to be honest with you' (Smith 2015b: 67). Yet, the very optimism with which the performer relentlessly repeats his mantra that the theatre can contribute to change, the self-consciously bare, minimalist aesthetics, as well as the deliberately and excessively straightforward, simplistic style may raise suspicions with regard to his genuineness, thereby potentially unsettling the dialogic connection the monologue aims to generate between storyteller and spectators. As a result, the performer's naivety emerges as strategic to the extent that it serves to ironically interrogate the play's own mechanism, creating a problematic oscillation between sincere and insincere intentions that foregrounds the contradictory, paradoxical and ambivalent dimension at the heart of the play.

Hence, *all that is solid*'s seemingly artless and unsophisticated approach to storytelling as a means of reinvigorating the progressive potential of the theatre emerges as decidedly more complex than it may initially appear. Its strategically naive form spurs a process of *Verfremdung* through which the performance as a whole is made strange, thereby introducing a profound degree of uncertainty into the play's dramaturgy. The resulting ambivalence is particularly conspicuous with regard to the distinction between reality and fiction, which is radically undermined through an emphasis on presence over representation. Through an obsessive repetition of 'this', 'here' and 'now' as well as through regular comparisons of 'likeness' and 'unlikeness', the fictional and the real begin to blur and the boundaries between different spatial and temporal layers are erased. This confusion is particularly problematic with regard to the persistent use of personal pronouns such as 'I', 'you' and 'we', whose respective referents are deliberately unclear. For example, it is tempting to assume that Andy Smith – the scriptwriter and, usually, the performer – refers to himself and the creation of his play *all that is solid* in these instances. This strongly autobiographical quality creates 'realesque' (Rebellato 2013c) effects, inviting us to mistake fiction for reality and vice versa. In a similar vein, the storyteller makes use of the collective 'we' to integrate the spectators into the story, attributing an ambivalent position to the audience. Cast as the performer's addressees, the spectators perform a dual role as both fictionalized and real audience. These doublings enhance the overall impression of ambiguity which emerges under the surface of the play's supposedly simplistic, but strategically naive storytelling style. At the same time, however, these distinctions are never entirely abolished. Ultimately, as Hans-Thies Lehmann argues with regard to similar trends in postdramatic performance, what is decisive for a play's political impetus is precisely 'not the assertion of the real as such ... but the unsettling that occurs through the *indecidability* whether one is dealing with reality or fiction' (2006: 101). In this sense, *all that is solid*'s tension between the fictional and the real represents the nexus of its critical interrogations, as the resulting 'indecidability' may encourage interrogation and spur the play's radical thrust.

Hence, storytelling represents a decidedly paradoxical device in *all that is solid*. On the one hand, the story serves as a metatheatrical tool for interrogating the forms and functions of the theatre, while also representing a means of reactivating its transformative impact. On the other hand, however, these processes are self-reflexively undermined and critically examined, suggesting a profound scepticism with regard to the play's own attempt to innovate theatrical conventions, and raising doubts about the emancipatory potential of the theatre in the contemporary moment. Revealing a profoundly contradictory and ambivalent impression, the play's naive aesthetics thus reflect the performer's own sense of crisis, as he admits that 'I've begun to wonder what places like this – what spaces like this – are really for now. Maybe it's a crisis in confidence but sometimes I feel a bit unsure' (Smith 2015b: 81). Thus, while *all that is solid* may display an unequivocal commitment to optimism on the surface, it is a much more ambivalent and uncertain impression which ultimately prevails. Crucially, however, it is this complex juxtaposition which may pave the way for the critical, dialectical form of sincerity Adiseshiah has described. Whereas Tomlin proposes that it is precisely Smith's 'rejection of ironic interpellation' which 'enables him to embrace the "new sincerity"' (2019: 119), the ironic undertones of Smith's play are undeniable. Indeed, contrary to Tomlin's argument, I would suggest that *all that is solid* illustrates the vital functions irony may fulfil in the context of contemporary renegotiations of sincerity: the performer's interaction with the audience is characterized not by an unequivocal (re)turn to genuineness but rather by a precarious liminality between the sincere and the ironic. Thus, rather than pessimistic about the future of the theatre as a place for sincere encounters, the play seems to assert that it is, in a post-Brechtian vein, the very indeterminacy at its core which may unfold a critical and radical impulse and prompt urgent questions – at and about the theatre as well as beyond. Instead of offering an optimistic perspective which would straightforwardly pave the way for the renewal of the theatre, the play withholds such simplistic gestures as a tentative, but efficient way of raising awareness and spurring critical analysis. As such, *all that is solid*'s progressive impetus vitally depends on the spectators' involvement. It is out of this diagnosis of ambivalence that the fundamental role of the audience for negotiating the play's contradictions and, by extension, for rethinking the theatre as a locus of critique, engagement and transformation emerges, as the following section will elucidate.

Strategic Intimacy and Relational Antagonism

At the heart of *all that is solid*'s metatheatrical story about the theatre as a place for reflection and intervention is the question of the audience. As the story centres on the role of the collective and its capacity to take action and effect change, it is the idea of togetherness which underpins the performer's search for a new theatre. Therefore, the community created between all participants during the performance can be said to represent the core of the play's political fabric. More precisely, it is through the specific connections initiated between the audience members and the performer that *all that is solid*'s attempt to innovate theatre practice is performed and put into practice. Indeed, while the story as such 'never really begins' (Frieze 2012: 8), turning, as it does, continuously around itself, it can in fact be said to take shape in the auditorium, and thus to develop through the spectators' relationship with the performer as a crucial part of their imaginative engagement with the play. This is, however, an intricate process given the paradoxical quality of the play's storytelling style. Through its strategically naive approach, the very sincerity and optimism that *all that is solid* aims to promote is self-consciously undermined, with profound implications for the spectators' experience of the performance. Yet, it is precisely out of this rejection of a romanticized ideal of harmonious togetherness and out of the resulting critique of the theatre's community-building qualities that a fresh perspective on its politicizing potential is articulated, as I will show in the following.

Significantly, the ambiguous and unstable nature of the relationships between stage and auditorium essentially hinges on a profound degree of intimacy which is established between the performer and the audience members, and which is key to an understanding of the play's complex relational dynamics. With the aim of developing a communicative, dialogic bond between performer and spectators, *all that is solid*'s storytelling mode seems committed to introducing a sincere form of intimate closeness at the heart of the performance. As outlined above, the play explicitly implicates the spectators in the story's collective 'we' and thereby effectively foregrounds the idea of community. This collaborative spirit is enhanced by the spatial proximity which results from the self-conscious lack of sophisticated stage design. While the spectators still face the performer in an oppositional arrangement, the fact that no further efforts are made to conceal the artificiality of the theatre situation establishes an intimate relationship between actor and audience. Indeed, the absence of elaborate costumes and props even suggests a certain similarity between the spectators and the performer, foregrounding what they share rather than what separates them. Above all, this emphasis on intimacy serves to redefine the role of the spectators, as the boundaries between stage and auditorium are erased on an experiential (if not spatial) level through the spectators' identification. Radicalizing Brecht's efforts to break down the fourth wall, spectators and performer form one community in Smith's play. This is further enhanced by the fact that the audience members are conceptualized as participants in the performance. The auditorium is thereby to some extent turned into the stage, as the spectators become performers themselves and seem to be attributed not only a certain equality but also authority and responsibility as part of their involvement. Hence, bridging the gap between theory and practice, the performer's wish for collective action is both discursively expressed and directly realized through the intimate relationships built with as well as among audience members. In this way, the specific strategies applied in the play's narrative mode may give rise to an alternative theatrical community based on a supposedly sincere and equal encounter.

While undoubtedly encouraging closeness, trust and collaboration between performer and spectators, however, specific strategies are at work which serve to undermine these very processes, complicating any straightforward understanding of the play's negotiation of intimacy in the relationship with the audience. In particular, the specific form of participation offered to the spectators does in fact seem to question rather than affirm the notions of equality and co-creation ostensibly underpinning the play. Thus, although the audience's involvement is explicitly solicited by the performer, the spectators do not have any noticeable or decisive influence on the performance; in truth, their options are very limited and at all times controlled by the storyteller, who orchestrates the plays' relational dynamics. Even when they are directly addressed, an actual verbal or physical reaction to these (rhetorical) questions is not expected or necessary for the performance to continue. Most conspicuously, the only truly 'active' form of spectatorial participation is to '[sit] in silence for a moment' (Smith

2015b: 67) at the very beginning of the play as well as towards the end. Thus, the performer anti-climactically announces that 'one of the things that we might do here ... is to just get together and sit quietly for a bit. Maybe just listen to the sound of our breathing' (Smith 2015b: 81). The ensuing silence is visualized through two empty pages in the playtext and followed by the performer's '[t]hanks' (Smith 2015b: 83). The blankness on the page as well as the silence in performance seem to offer a deeply ironic comment on the only actual participatory action the spectators contribute to the play, raising the question of whether coming together at the theatre really is, as the performer asserts, enough to achieve the radical effects the play supposedly aims for. Ultimately, therefore, the relational aesthetics proposed by *all that is solid* remain decidedly hierarchically structured and thereby complicate the very notions of spectatorial equality, authority and emancipation the play seems to strive for.

Thus, the relationship evolving between the participants on- and offstage acquires an indeterminate quality, as the spectators' status, role and position with regard to the performance are rendered ambivalent. Through an emphasis on naivety and intimacy, the play deliberately 'untether[s]' the audience members 'from their usual position, from what might feel like an anchored position' (Smith 2011: 413–14), thereby undermining central dramatic categories and blurring fundamental distinctions between theatre and reality, actor and audience as well as presence and representation. In this respect, *all that is solid* privileges dissensus over harmony in the relationship between stage and auditorium by providing a paradoxical experience for the spectators, oscillating between genuine dialogue and sincere encounter, on the one hand, and insincere indeterminacy, on the other. Rather than a gentle form of togetherness, what emerges is a form of 'relational antagonism' (Bishop 2004: 79) – a concept Claire Bishop proposes with reference to Ernesto Laclau and Chantal Mouffe, who revalue conflict over consensus as a powerful source of democratic debate and emancipatory politics. In this sense, rather than naively taking the resistant force of intersubjective encounters in performance for granted, Bishop offers a more nuanced framework for evaluating spectatorial interpellation and argues that 'the relations set up by relational aesthetics are not intrinsically democratic' (Bishop 2014: 67). Above all, instead of a harmonious, gentle and consensual relationship between performers and audience members, it is through an antagonistic form of spectatorship based on tension and conflict in the interaction between stage and auditorium that a potentially progressive impulse may arise.

In Smith's *all that is solid*, this self-reflexive interrogation of the play's relational aesthetics is most explicitly reflected at the end, which marks a moment of insight and critique with regard to the play's own limitations, as the performer suddenly self-consciously relativizes his own ambitions. After relentlessly repeating his optimism about the political potential of the theatre as well as his affirmation of the intrinsically empowering value of the social relations established with the audience, the storyteller acknowledges a profound scepticism. This is most notably reflected in an increasing distance between stage and auditorium, which is articulated through a movement from an enthusiastic and inclusive 'we' to an isolated and more hesitant 'I' in the monologue. Thus, the performer's assertion that '[w]e are changing all the time. The world is changing all the time. And we are changing it' sharply contrasts with '[w]ell actually, I don't know what you are thinking. I don't know that. I can't know that. How can I know that?' (Smith 2015b: 84). This shift is remarkable to the extent that it represents an implicit recognition of the precarious nature of the play's naivety and the impossibility of directly changing the world through the theatre.

Crucially, however, while conceding a certain degree of scepticism, this acknowledgement is juxtaposed with a final reassertion of the performer's refusal to give in to the potential futility of his project as well as a powerful reaffirmation of the political value of theatre-making, which justifies – indeed makes indispensable – the ongoing attempt to create political theatre against all the odds:

> Anyway, thank you for listening to me.
> In a minute I am going stand [*sic*] up and walk out of that door.
> In a minute we all are.
> I'm going to walk towards change and optimism, towards complicated struggles and joyful celebrations, towards our houses and homes and our cities and our streets, towards families and friends and strangers and enemies.
> I will walk towards all these things and more.
> I am walking towards them now.
> *The performer stands.*
> I hope someone is with me.
> *They exit.*
>
> Smith (2015b: 86)

This corporeal appeal to the audience to join the performer and 'walk towards change and optimism' encapsulates the naivety of the piece as a whole. Yet, it is out of this strategic emphasis on naivety as well as out of the play's specific relational dynamics that a powerful critical appeal to the spectators may be seen to emerge. Thus, while leaving the theatrical space inevitably implies that the fictional universe and the ephemeral theatrical community created therein are dissolved, this call to join the performer may literally contribute to bridging the gap between the theatre and the world outside. Hence, in this final moment the tension between potentiality and failure, sincerity and irony tangibly culminates. Rather than representing a moment of inertia, however, this profound ambivalence is construed as potentially empowering, with the play opening up, in post-Brechtian spirit, to the spectators and initiating a productive engagement with the play, its indeterminacy and its profoundly ambiguous and naive conclusion. Through the performer's call for action, a limbo is created which foregrounds the importance of the spectators by implicitly asking them to decide for themselves how to interpret the performer's appeal, to reflect on what it means for each of them to exit the theatre, and the extent to which this may represent a first step towards a different life – or, indeed, if it is, on the contrary, entirely without any meaningful consequences for them.

Therefore, through its ambivalent conceptualization of spectatorship, *all that is solid* ultimately offers a critical perspective on its own strategies and their supposedly progressive impetus. Proposing an antagonistic understanding of theatrical community, spectatorship and interpretation, it is on the basis of these contradictions and ambivalences and the questions they prompt that a new form of collectivity and, thus, of theatre emerges that attempts to respond to the complexities and ambiguities of the contemporary moment. Indebted to fundamental principles of Brechtian theatre, *all that is solid* is committed to a dialectical approach to theatre-making in its emphasis on contradictions and change. At the same time, however, the relationship between theatre and reality at the heart of Brecht's concept can no longer be understood in terms of conventional dialectical structures and binary categories. It is, as *all that is solid*'s relational aesthetics reflect, through an emphasis on the antagonistic, irreconcilable and paradoxical that this connection can be fruitfully re-established as a prerequisite for emancipation and change.

The Limits of Sincerity: *The Author*

As the previous section has argued, Smith's *all that is solid* is characterized by a careful balance between sincerity and insincerity, created through the play's use of post-Brechtian naivety to spur a potentially emancipating relational antagonism between performer and spectators. While employing similar aesthetic strategies, Crouch's *The Author* goes decidedly beyond this playful ambiguity and pushes at the boundaries of this specific dialectical framework. As the result of a fruitful collaboration between Crouch and Smith, who was involved as co-director (alongside Karl James) in the development and production of the play, *The Author* has attracted considerable attention in the media and academia – despite or, rather, precisely because of its unusual and daring approach. Indeed, the play has polarized public opinion and provoked contentious audience responses, ranging from celebration and appraisal to outright rejection, with spectators regularly walking out of the performance, 'physically threaten[ing] actors' or 'throw[ing] copies of the text at the playwright' (Crouch 2011c). Probing the limits of re-establishing sincerity as a prerequisite for critical engagement, the play offers an altogether more sceptical perspective on the questions raised by all of Smith and Crouch's projects: what degree of agency and authority can audiences acquire, if at all? To what extent can ambivalence facilitate an empowering form of spectatorship? Can the theatre offer a model for social commitment through its relational dynamics? And how successfully can the complex contradictions and paradoxes to which the theatre has to respond provide the basis for genuine engagement? For this purpose, *The Author* deliberately capitalizes on the precariousness of the relationship between stage and auditorium by employing a strategic insincerity which foregrounds the manipulative potential inherent in this constellation. Quite in contrast with *all that is solid*, Crouch's play seems to undermine any genuineness in the theatrical encounter right from the start by offering a disorientating experience for the audience. Through a pervasive ambivalence of meaning, any productive form of exchange between actors and spectators seems to be undermined, thereby also self-reflexively interrogating the play's own aesthetic approach.

Diegetic and Structural Insincerity

Reflecting Smith and Crouch's shared emphasis on metatheatricality as a central strategy of post-Brechtian *Verfremdung*, *The Author*, too, is a play about a play with a highly complex structure. Its storyline is concerned with the rehearsal process, performance run and aftermath of a fictional play about abuse and violence in a father-daughter relationship. The characters, whose names are always the same as those of the real actors, participate in the performance of this play as author and director (Tim), actors (Vic and Esther) or spectator (Adrian). In Smith and Crouch's typical monological and diegetic style, they reflect on their involvement in this theatrical project. Even though the audience is provided with only little information about the production, unequivocal references to rape, suicide, murder or pornography accumulate and provide hints to its profoundly disturbing content. Gradually, if reluctantly, the characters also acknowledge the deeply unsettling and desensitizing impact of their involvement in the fictional play, foreshadowing to some extent the spectators' own experience of shock as a result of attending a performance of *The Author*.

Preoccupied with issues of violence and voyeurism, the ethics of its representation and glamorization as well as the question of the legitimacy of its consumption, *The Author* itself seemingly attempts to eschew the very glamorization it thematizes by rejecting mimetic forms of representation in favour of a minimalist, storytelling style in a 'deconstruction of the theatre as spectacle' (Henke 2018: 78). Consisting of the characters' personal accounts, the play may therefore at first sight seem naive and indeed unspectacular in approach. The stories are told in a casual manner and the play-within-the-play's atrocities, which only slowly come to light, are narrated rather than shown through graphically explicit and visceral scenes on stage. However, despite its implicit critique of aesthetic realism and its potential for sensationalist exploitation of violence, *The Author* paradoxically and deliberately reintroduces spectacle at the very heart of its own dramaturgy. This is achieved through its specific approach to storytelling, as it shifts the production of images from the stage to the spectators' imagination: 'the atrocities ... are graphic even in their narratively distanced form' (Henke 2018: 86–7). Actively participating in the production of these disturbing images, the spectators are made complicit with the play's exploitation of violence. Hence, provocation is not only created through the play's disturbing content alone, but first and foremost through *how* the characters tell their stories. While the play may superficially appear simple and straightforward in its naive storytelling style, the underlying strategy emerges as carefully calculated and deeply insincere on a textual and structural level. Underneath its uneventful façade, a radical confrontation with violence gradually builds up, which may have a shocking and profoundly destabilizing impact on the audience's relationship with the performers.

A key device for creating this impression of insincerity is the choice of a complex *mise-en-abyme* structure. The 'real' play *The Author* represents the external frame; in this play, the characters tell, in a loose and associative style, a story about another fictional play written by the fictional author-figure Tim Crouch (referred to as Tim in the following), which, in turn, constitutes the innermost core of the construction. A similar effect is created from the perspective of the audience. The real spectators attend a performance of *The Author*, in which they are addressed as spectators and invited to perform the part of the fictional audience – more precisely the role of the narratees of the story, in which the characters also recapitulate the reactions of the absent spectators of the fictional play. In addition, the *dramatis personae* includes a spectator figure, Adrian, who explicitly sides with the members of the audience and invites their contributions, thereby gaining particular significance for the spectators' identification with the performers. Owing to the play's metatheatricality, the different layers to some extent mirror each other and become almost indistinguishable: to which play are the characters referring, the fictional play or *The Author*? Are *The Author* and the fictional play maybe even the same? And which audience is addressed – the absent spectators of the fictional play or the people who are present in the auditorium for *The Author*? This confusion is also spurred by the intertwinement of different temporalities in the narrative, as characters speak from various points of time and move freely in-between past and present tenses without providing further contextualization. While the layers remain distinct throughout, the play's fragmentary structure renders orientation increasingly difficult for the audience, as boundaries between here and there, now and then, begin to dissolve.

The play's strategic confusion is further exacerbated by the deliberate erasure of the distinction between fiction and reality that is typical of Smith and Crouch's plays. Radicalizing *all that is solid*'s arguably more playful approach, *The Author* produces harrowing effects through its deliberate confusion of real and fictional figures. This culminates in the case of the author-figure Tim Crouch, which is the name of the playwright of both *The Author* and the fictional play. His name is always Tim Crouch, no matter whether or not (the real) Tim Crouch himself performs the character Tim. Explicitly introducing him as 'Tim Crouch, ... the author' (Crouch 2011a: 169), the play consciously draws attention to the overlap between fiction and reality only to make it even more difficult for the spectators to draw a clear line. This is underscored by the wide range of roles Tim performs in the play: he represents at one and the same time a 'writer, performer, audience member and director, ... master of the narrative, head of a company, friend, husband, and transgressor' (Angelaki 2013). The complexity of the character crystallizes in the final moments of the play, when Tim tells us that he decided to watch pornographic material of child abuse after a dinner party with the cast. Not only his detached, neutral storytelling mode but also the unresolved questions of whether Tim is 'merely' consuming paedophile material or, indeed, is abusing the baby lying next to him while sitting in front of the screen are particularly jarring. This moment in the performance has frequently incited fierce reactions from the audience, as Crouch recalls: 'Once, one audience member, sitting directly behind me, threatened to hit me. On one performance, six people left during the speech. At many times people called on me to stop' (Crouch 2011b: 417). Hence, by 'short-circuiting ... reality and fiction' (Henke 2018: 86) the play provocatively draws a parallel between the characters' exposure to violence and the audience's (involuntary) consumption of it as witnesses of the performance. In this respect, it is precisely the extent to which the play capitalizes on the spectators' confusion of fiction and reality as well as of the different structural layers which fuels its provocative impetus.

Intricately intertwining an episodic, palimpsestuous structure, an associative storytelling style as well as a radical confusion between fiction and reality, *The Author* thus creates a profoundly unsettling experience for the spectators, as an understanding of the play's content, its strategic mechanisms and the role of the audience members themselves only gradually – and belatedly – emerge. In fact, the play more and more entangles the audience in its intricate set-up. This effect is particularly daring at the beginning, when the spectators are forced to realize that the actors have been 'unspectacularly seated throughout the audience' (Crouch 2011a: 164) all along and that the performance actually started as soon as they entered the theatre space. At the '*easy, playful*' (Crouch 2011a: 165) beginning of the text, Adrian casually chats away with members of the audience. As Chris Goode, who took over the part of the spectator-figure from Adrian Howells, recalls, spectators frequently 'weren't sure that the play had begun by the time that first intervention by "Chris" had ended' (2015: 241). Hence, while Crouch may claim that he is not 'attempting to deceive' (Crouch 2016: 179) the spectators, the indeterminacy of '*[n]o sense and every sense of a beginning*' (Crouch 2011a: 165) and the deliberate withholding of information raise suspicion with regard to the ostensible sincerity of the performers. While giving the impression of casualness and improvisation, the naive beginning quickly degenerates into a disconcerting experience for the audience. When the spectators finally begin to see through the mechanisms of the play's strategic provocation, they will already have become implicated as witnesses and, indeed, as participants themselves. Thus, rather than establishing, as in *all that is solid*, a careful dialectic between gentleness and genuineness, on the one hand, and irony and insincerity, on the other, *The Author* one-sidedly radicalizes this insincerity, with a profound impact on the audience's experience of the performance. The play's metatheatrical *Verfremdung* is thereby refunctioned as a tool for provocation which not only undermines spectators' expectations but also manipulates their participation in the performance.

Participatory Insincerity

Through its complex structure and storytelling mode, *The Author* pursues a profoundly provocative strategy which unsettles the relationship between stage and auditorium. Employing a strategic insincerity by both inciting and paralysing spectatorial agency, the play challenges the precarious dialectic created, for example, in Smith's *all that is solid*. Rather than establishing a productive form of exchange between on- and offstage, the spectators seem to end up completely entangled in the play's manipulations, and trapped in a participatory dilemma which apparently offers no productive way out of this experience of crisis. Foregrounding in this way the role of the spectators for the play as a whole, it is in the relations between performers and audiences that the political nexus of the play resides. For this purpose, various dramaturgical techniques are employed to raise awareness of the act of spectating in the play. Crucially, however, these strategies are employed not to assert, but rather to critically interrogate the possibility of spectatorial involvement and the potential of the theatre to provide an empowering experience of the performance for the audience, to establish a sincere exchange and, ultimately, a progressive appeal for critique and intervention.

This problematic treatment of the audience is initiated first and foremost through the exceptional stage design, which turns the auditorium itself into the stage. As the performance note indicates, the space is empty except for 'two banks of seating, facing each other, comfortably spaced apart but with no "stage" in between' (Crouch 2011a: 164). As an integral part of the audience, the performers act from within the crowd and, wearing their own clothes and adopting their real names, cannot at first sight be clearly distinguished from either the spectators or the fictional characters they supposedly embody, which – initially, at least – creates a playful atmosphere and an intimate sense of collectivity. In this minimalist, seemingly simplistic set-up, it is thus the audience who is in the limelight and whose leading role for the performance is thereby underscored. The centrality of the spectators is also acknowledged by Adrian, who repeatedly enquires whether 'everyone [is] all right' (Crouch 2011a: 165) and gently solicits their participation, notably by asking for audience members' names, which he will then use to address spectators individually, engaging them in a dialogue and fostering a 'pleasurable complicity' (Wallace 2012: 62). Throughout the play, questions like '[i]s this okay? Is it okay if I carry on? Do you want me to stop? Do you?' (Crouch 2011a: 179) or '[w]hat do you think? Can you see all right?' (Crouch 2011a: 171) will continue to structure the monologues, seemingly emphasizing the performers' efforts to establish a relaxing atmosphere and to facilitate a sincere encounter between actors and audience.

Problematically, though, while the spectators seem to be firmly integrated – verbally, imaginatively and physically – into the performance, the resulting sense of intimacy is radically exploited for manipulative purposes, as it serves precisely to undermine any appearance of sincerity in the performers' relationship with the spectators. Thus, the stage design creates a close proximity which neither allows for personal space – '[o]ur knees touching!' (Crouch 2011a: 166), as Adrian enthusiastically comments – nor for 'distance or theatrical illusion' (Freshwater 2011: 407). According to Wendy Hubbard's personal account, the play's refusal of mimetic representation and its abolition of the stage 'denies its audience the relief of a clear, settled focal point outside of our bodies. It refuses me the illusion of absenting myself into a detached, observational stance: I am palpably on show and amidst' (Hubbard 2013: 23). Indeed, while the play rejects representational illusion, 'the "optical machinery" of theatre … – far from being removed or overcome – is here employed precisely so that we may look at other people's reactions, and be looked at for our own' (Bottoms 2011: 454). As a result, it is the audience members and their engagement with the performance which is thereby turned into spectacle.

In this respect, the stage design can be described as 'a chaotic, multi-directional panopticon' (Hubbard 2013: 23) which creates a precarious form of 'mutual spectatorship' (Ridout 2009: 15). Such a constellation is also realized in Greig's *The Events*, in which the amateur choir functions as an onstage audience who directly faces the spectators, too, thereby establishing a crucial connection between non-professional singers and audience members as a way of investigating questions about the forms and functions of communities. It is in a decidedly more radical vein, however, that *The Author* creates a similar set-up by entirely removing the stage to focus attention exclusively on the spectators themselves. In this confrontational arrangement, each audience member is constantly under the scrutiny of the others' gazes. Exploiting this self-awareness, the play promotes a profoundly ambivalent experience between feelings of comfort and curiosity, on the one hand, and apprehensions of unease and menace, on the other. Thus, rather than the characters, their actions or the story they tell, it is the audience who is effectively turned into the object of enquiry. Estranging, in a post-Brechtian vein, theatrical conventions by abolishing the distinction between stage and auditorium, and thereby undermining spectators' expectations with regard to their own position in the play, *The Author* facilitates an unsettling and disturbing experience of the performance as a prerequisite for interrogating the act of spectatorship.

The fundamental, but highly paradoxical role attributed to the audience in *The Author* is further underscored by the actual opportunities the play makes available for the spectators to actively participate – either verbally or physically – in the performance. From the very beginning, audience members are not only directly addressed but also explicitly encouraged to contribute to the dialogue, both through the characters' constant but unobtrusive use of tag questions, which invite responses while putting the audience 'under no pressure to [answer]' (Crouch 2011a: 164), and through Adrian's more explicit requests for spectators' names. While this may initially create space for the spectators' individual contributions and may give them the impression of being on an equal footing with Adrian, he will go on to strategically use these names to elicit the spectators' approval of the increasingly disturbing quality of his account, for example when he refers to his wound following Vic's attack on him after a show at the stage door: 'There was a moment when they thought I'd lose an eye. … Sounds gruesome, doesn't it! But I'm really fine now. I really am! Don't you think, ___?' (Crouch 2011a: 180). This enforced, involuntary form of spectatorial consent is particularly provocative when, at the end of the play, Tim presupposes the audience's approval of his consumption of pornography: 'We've all done that, at the end of a long day. Haven't we? A couple of clicks' (Crouch 2011a: 201). What is crucial about this strategy is that even if the spectators were to raise their voice and express their disapproval, their intervention would not affect the script; none of their verbal contributions will change the predetermined course of the action. Thus, Goode explains that part of the acting strategy is that 'responses from the audience' – especially if uninvited – 'are, ideally, not returned with improvised text, but perhaps simply with eye-contact or, if appropriate, a smile. The audience is invited, in other words, to understand that their speaking is heard … but it won't initiate an exchange within the structure of the play, because the play-text is … essentially fixed' (2015: 241). In the course of the play, however, this interaction with the audience gradually fades out, thereby denying the spectators any further opportunity to speak up, and thus emphasizing the futility of any kind of verbal participation in the first place.

Hence, while the characters' casual conversations with the spectators, in particular the use of the collective pronoun 'we', may initially seem harmless and invite identification, their increasingly 'over-solicitous attention' (White 2013: 190) to the audience and the gradual revelation of their disturbing attitudes may not only raise doubts as to the sincerity of the play's interactive approach but may also be interpreted as a provocative attack on the audience's agency. This strategic insincerity with regard to the audience's participation is explicitly addressed by Vic, who recapitulates his treatment of the audience as an actor in the fictional play:

You have to give the audience a character, a relationship to you. … Something has to be at stake for the audience. … Enlisting is a good one. I'm enlisting you! Or they need seducing or pleasuring. Then the relationship between me and the audience is alive, is real, not rhetorical but active. Something is at stake. Tim said you should get them to a point

where they *almost* feel able to answer back. Or should out. So, I'm, let's say, 'provoking' you! Or maybe 'rousing', or 'stirring' or something!
Crouch (2011a: 170–1; my emphasis)

Vic's manipulative approach can be understood as a self-reflexive comment on the relationship between performers and spectators in *The Author*: it reflects the extent to which the play, while pretending to treat the audience with care and gentleness, capitalizes on the spectators' intuitive 'desire to "play along"' (Freshwater 2011: 408) and to identify with the characters. Their participation is, however, immediately corrupted, as their contributions are ignored, ultimately making them complicit with the characters and, by extension, with the fictional play's disconcerting content: it is precisely at the 'point where they almost' participate that their involvement is undermined and strategically exploited.

The extent to which the play manipulates the audience's presence and participation reaches its climax in the explicit suggestion to leave the theatre, which is presented as an ostensibly sincere possibility of getting involved in the performance. Thus, at the end of Adrian's opening sequence, '*[a]n audience member in the middle of a block gets up and leaves*' (Crouch 2011a: 168). This staged walkout serves as an example of one possible reaction to the play and encourages the spectators to follow suit – an invitation which audiences have also widely taken up (Crouch 2011c). Yet, while the play seems in this way to approve of walkouts as a reflection of how the performers supposedly care for the audience's well-being, this form of physical intervention is rendered highly problematic. By walking out, spectators decline the burden of responsibility imposed on them, 'turn[ing] [their] eyes away from the violence, harm and injustice committed against the Other, from the precariousness of human life' (Henke 2018: 88). As a result, the play's aesthetic and strategic framework collapses. In this respect, walkouts cannot be considered an option that facilitates a genuinely critical engagement with the play, its subject matter or its contentious aesthetics.

More importantly, the play itself co-opts the one physical form of participation it offers to its audiences, and exploits it for its own purposes. This manipulation is foreshadowed by what Adrian says right before the staged walkout, which creates a deeply ironic contrast: 'Look at us. Look at all our lonely, hopeful hearts!! Sitting here. Staring out! Hoping for something to happen. Waiting for someone to talk to us. Really talk' (Crouch 2011a: 168). Adrian's – and, by implication, certainly also the real audience's – impatience for the actual play to start is thus effectively ridiculed by the ensuing walkout, which does not only undercut Adrian's own attempts to converse with the audience but also hints at the futility of leaving the performance as a possibility of creating meaning. Indeed, rather than successfully expressing their criticism by walking out, spectators are involuntarily rendered complicit with the play's manipulative strategy, since this is precisely the action the play expects them to take in this situation: 'This apparently masochistic licensing of the audience to leave the show' represents an 'uninvited participation, but clearly it is of a peculiar kind, where what is uninvited is partly expected, and mostly tolerated' (White 2013: 191). In this respect, walking out may come to imply an embarrassment about and an unwillingness to confront the play's subject matter and may therefore to some extent be (mis)understood as an admission of guilt. Hence, each walkout is turned into 'a mini drama in the unfolding narrative of the event' (Crouch 2011c). As Hubbard describes her experience of leaving the theatre, 'I walk out of the performance only to find that in doing so I've played my part perfectly and added myself back into its drama' (2013: 25). Vice versa, this also has significant implications for those who stay: 'Suddenly, audience members were *choosing* to listen to the atrocities described by the performers, becoming complicit in the action of the play' (Love 2017: 49). What results from the play's deliberate triggering of walkouts is thus a profoundly provocative paradox. On the one hand, this strategy seems to suggest an investment in sincerity on the part of the play, reflecting how the performers apparently care for the audience's comfort by accommodating spectators' departures, and to offer audiences the possibility of demonstrating an emancipating gesture of critique and rejection. On the other hand, however, the play directly undermines these attempts to reassert spectatorial authority by recuperating the walkouts for its own dramaturgical and strategic purposes, which underscores the extent to which the spectators are inevitably made complicit with the play's mechanisms.

Through this manipulation of audience walkouts and, indeed, all other forms of spectatorial involvement proposed by the play, *The Author* establishes a profoundly insincere dynamic in the relationship between performers and spectators through which the audience's mere presence in the auditorium is exploited as a form of consent and complicity. Thus, what the play proposes under the guise of participation is in fact a 'scripted failure to intervene' (Frieze 2012: 13). Arresting the audience in a participatory dilemma, the play invites, as shown above, several different forms of involvement – ranging from imaginative visualization to more conventional verbal and physical forms of participation – only to trap the spectators in 'a position of apathy' (Henke 2018: 87). This awareness of the futility of their attempt to intervene directly serves to confront audience members with the question of how to respond adequately to a performance which, while entirely depending on spectatorial engagement, manipulates and undermines any kind of audience reaction. Closing down any genuine possibility for the spectators to intervene in the play and emancipate themselves from its strategic manipulation, *The Author* thus stages a failure of fundamental notions of equality, co-authorship and participation, and thereby offers a decidedly self-critical perspective on its own aesthetic design and principles. While seemingly relinquishing authorial control as a way of recognizing more explicitly the role of the audience members and their individual reactions, the play in fact creates an illusion of spectatorial agency, and paradoxically 'reassert[s]' the power of 'authorship' (Rebellato 2013a: 25), thereby reflecting the extent to which textual openness and indeterminacy must be understood as vitally dependent on authorial intentionality rather than spectatorial freedom.

While Dan Rebellato goes on to contend that these experiments with forms of authorial and spectatorial empowerment create an 'instability' which may render the texts 'politically more questioning and radical' (2013a: 27), it is highly doubtful to what extent *The Author* can in this way be characterized as ambivalent in the first place. In a decidedly more radical approach, Crouch's play leaves behind *all that is solid*'s precarious balance and instead practices a one-sided and provocative exploitation of insincerity as a strategic tool for escalating the relations between performers and audiences. As a result, the dynamics fostered by the dialectic of sincerity are no longer productive, but instead seem to be replaced by a paralysing experience of paradox, as spectators' often extreme and fierce reactions vividly illustrate. Indeed, the play's strategic insincerity has in many cases turned out to be too overwhelming for audience members. What has emerged as particularly demanding is the extent to which *The Author* deliberately estranges, in a post-Brechtian vein, theatrical conventions to radically challenge spectators' expectations. Thus, Crouch recalls that 'audience members have read newspapers and novels, built paper aeroplanes, performed Mexican waves, sung happy birthday to one of their own, recited poetry, slow hand-clapped, physically threatened actors, hummed out loud with fingers in their ears, muttered obscenities, shouted actors down, and thrown copies of the text at the playwright' (Crouch 2011c), which illustrates the difficulty spectators have often experienced when trying to relate to the play. More acutely, playgoers have also shown strong physical reactions to the performance, caused in particular by an increasing difficulty to distinguish between fiction and reality. This became clear during a test run of the show for Royal Court staff, as Crouch recalls: 'as we met up outside, blinking, shaking and weeping in the sunshine, it became clear that discussion would not be possible. None of the audience members felt able to talk' (Crouch qtd. in Rebellato 2013b: 139). In a similar vein, Hubbard reflects on her own experience of the show, which she had to leave after only twenty minutes because she was about to pass out (2013: 22). The deliberate confusion between fiction and reality and the manipulation of the spectators' participation in the performance may thus indeed overpower audiences, whose lack of orientation and experience of paradox may lead to a collapse of the play's complex strategies.

These examples demonstrate the potential for disruption and failure at the heart of *The Author*'s manipulative and provocative insincerity and raise the question of whether the play offers any interstice at all for intervening in and breaking this self-referential cycle, and thus of whether it provides any possibility of sincere empowerment and critique on the part of the spectators. Of course, as Cristina Delgado-García stresses, the 'theatricalization of fruitless resistance and participation' does not automatically imply that '*The Author* conceives of its audience as inherently powerless' (2017: 104). On the contrary, while certainly rendered ambivalent, the different structural, diegetic and epistemological layers underpinning the play remain distinct. In this sense, the play's emphasis on paralysis and manipulation can be understood as a means of drawing the spectators' attention to their own potential complicity, thereby creating an important opportunity for self-reflexivity. The experience of the failure of participation can therefore, in post-Brechtian fashion, raise awareness of wider questions of agency, authority and equality addressed by the play, suggesting not only that spectators need to critically review their involvement but also the necessity of assuming responsibility as witnesses of the performance. It is thus in the spirit of Adorno's concept of negative dialectics, which foregrounds the critical value of unresolvable contradictions and paradoxically derives a critical thrust from its diagnosis of the very impossibility of resistance through art, that an important, if tentative and profoundly ambivalent, progressive impetus may emerge out of the play's strategic insincerity and its provocation of the spectators' agency.

Crucially, however, it is then only *ex negativo*, out of the very failure of intervention that a political impetus may be created, and it is highly doubtful to what extent this form of negative critique can be successfully spurred. The play's post-Brechtian *Verfremdung* of theatre-making and spectatorship may – and indeed has, as shown above – turned out to be too challenging for audiences and may thus prove inefficient for reinvigorating the dialectical dynamic necessary for negotiating the unresolvable contradictions *The Author* presents to its spectators. The performance itself seems too intense and too affectively charged, the spectators are too intricately implicated in the show for any critical analysis to develop, as notably scholars' personal accounts have reflected. Indeed, while 'real meaningful engagement with the piece emerges only when critical reflection … is deployed', this 'intellectual form of closure' (Radosavljević 2013: 154) can only be achieved *after* the performance, *outside of* the theatre, once the fictional universe is left behind, and it is questionable whether a productive form of engagement can be built on such an unstable and disrupted relation between fiction and reality. Thus, to the extent that *The Author*'s strategically insincere experiment may spur paralysis and rejection rather than empowerment and emancipation, its emphasis on failure offers a decidedly sceptical perspective. In *The Author*, the dialectic of sincerity is brought to its limits, replacing genuine encounter and critical exchange with alienating experiences of provocation, manipulation and insincerity.

Conclusion

This chapter has offered a fresh perspective on Andy Smith and Tim Crouch's work as well as on the question of Brecht's legacy in contemporary British drama by interpreting the theatre-makers' use of metatheatricality as a device of post-Brechtian *Verfremdung*. Employing self-reflexivity as a means of dialectical interrogation, they foreground the role of the spectators as co-creators of the performance, and negotiate a new, critical and dialectical form of sincerity in the interaction with the audience. Based on a precarious oscillation between genuine dialogue and ironic destabilization, they probe the possibility of moving beyond postmodernist relativism towards a new form of engagement.

In this vein, Andy Smith's *all that is solid melts into air*, which focuses on the question of how to create a politically mobilizing piece of theatre, can be understood as an example of post-Brechtian meta-theatre in the tradition of Brecht's 'Messingkauf', as it crosses the boundaries between theatre and philosophy as well as theory and practice. Through a strategic naivety, *all that is solid* stages a metatheatrical *Verfremdung* which introduces a profound uncertainty, and foregrounds the role of the spectators for the play's investigations. While aiming for an intimate dialogue with the audience, *all that is solid* also offers a self-critical perspective on the possibility of spectatorial equality and participation. Through a careful balance between genuineness and insincerity, the play introduces an antagonistic form of spectatorship which may give rise to a more productive form of engagement based on an experience of Rancièrean dissensus and conflict.

Pushing at the boundaries of this approach, Crouch's *The Author* offers a decidedly more sceptical perspective on the possibility of re-establishing sincerity and, by extension, on the theatre's power to spur spectatorial emancipation. Employing a strategic insincerity as a means of provocation, the play deliberately manipulates the audience's involvement in the play. Based on the failure of notions of equality, participation and sincerity, *The Author*'s metatheatrical *Verfremdung* may overwhelm and thereby prevent, rather than encourage, a productive form of commitment on the part of the spectators. In this way, *The Author* does not only critically interrogate Smith and Crouch's negotiations of sincerity but also sheds light on the limits of dialectics as a productive method of contemporary political theatre.

4

Political Theatre between Dialectics and Absurdity: Caryl Churchill's Twenty-First-Century Plays

Given Caryl Churchill's enduring presence on the British stage ever since the 1960s, her work represents a particularly significant point of reference for tracing the development of political drama over the second half of the twentieth century into the new millennium. For the purpose of creating a politically progressive theatre, Churchill has, throughout her long career, fruitfully combined an interest in Brechtian methodology with her unique creative imagination, developing an original and highly experimental form of Brechtian-inspired aesthetics. Brecht's significance as a major source of inspiration for Churchill's dramaturgy and politics has been widely acknowledged to the extent that she has been declared 'one of Brecht's successors' (Reinelt 1996: 106) in Britain. As Janelle Reinelt shows with reference to *Top Girls* (1982), *Cloud 9* (1978), *Softcops* (1984), *Serious Money* (1987) and *Mad Forest* (1990), Churchill employs a distinctly Brechtian mode to create a 'socialist feminist aesthetic' (1996: 107) which has dominated her plays from the 1960s to the early 1990s. More specifically, Elin Diamond demonstrates the significance of gestus for Churchill's works, which stage a 'gestic feminist criticism' (1997: 54). However, as Elaine Aston compellingly argues, Churchill's dialectical aesthetic and her socialist agenda have become increasingly compromised at the turn of the millennium by profound social and political transformations, which is above all reflected in the plays' 'heightened concern' with the question of 'what form political theatre can take when ideological resistance to capitalism has all but disappeared' (2013: 145). Thus, Churchill's post-1990s works have been preoccupied with the question of the potential and limits of politically engaged playwriting, notably exhibiting an increasingly critical stance towards the value of Brechtian dialectics.

In this context, *This Is a Chair* (1997) marks 'a critical/political turning point' (Aston 2013: 145) in Churchill's playwriting, as it anticipates – along with the 1997 diptych *Blue Heart* – important stylistic and political developments which would become characteristic of Churchill's twenty-first-century oeuvre. At first sight, the play employs a conventional dialectical structure, as it contrasts the personal sphere that is the focus of the individual scenes with the public realm reflected in the respective scene titles, which hint at a broader sociopolitical context. Yet, rather than intimately linking private and political through this dichotomous framework, the play stages a fundamental disconnection both on the level of content and, most crucially, with regard to its form. Thus, through a 'deliberate estrangement of word and meaning' (Kritzer 2002: 60), the titles are seemingly random and unrelated to the episodes from everyday life depicted by the scenes, hence underscoring that the connections between private and public have been radically severed, and that these discrepancies can no longer be negotiated by the characters or, indeed, by the theatre. Suggesting the dysfunctionality of traditional dialectical mechanisms as epistemological and dramaturgical devices, Churchill's postmillennial plays build on *This Is a Chair*'s diagnosis by self-consciously pushing at the boundaries of a Brechtian-inspired mode of theatre-making, as I will argue. Given these radical shifts, therefore, a discussion of Churchill's twenty-first-century plays represents a suitable coda for this study, as these texts reflect the fundamental changes that Brecht's model has undergone in British playwriting over the past decades. Most significantly, Churchill offers radical ways of problematizing, challenging and moving beyond Brecht in these works, and thus provides a tentative outlook on the potential of the post-Brechtian method for future applications.

In contrast with the more explicitly socialist stance and dialectical aesthetic of her pre-1990s works, Churchill's plays since *This Is a Chair* have critically engaged with this legacy by developing an increasingly minimalist style which has often been compared to Samuel Beckett's drama (Angel-Perez 2006: 195; Angelaki 2017: 52; Aston 2015: 59). This apparent turn to the absurd has notably been considered indicative of a 'late style' emerging in Churchill's playwriting. Gordon McMullan has defined the concept of 'late style' 'as a period towards the end of the life in which there is a marked shift in style and mode that is typically characterised as … a form of life review … which also serves as a kind of prolepsis, a looking-forward to artistic developments yet to emerge in history' (2018: 61). In this spirit, director James Macdonald, for example, interprets Churchill's recent plays as 'quite typical of senior artists' who 'don't need to say as much' (qtd. in Trueman 2016a). By the same token, playwright Moira Buffini suggests that 'Churchill, who in the 70s and 80s was the daughter of Brecht, has become the daughter of Beckett' (2015). While Churchill's twenty-first-century work undeniably features central elements traditionally associated with 'late style' – for instance, a thematic preoccupation with old age and death, a more experimental and minimalist approach as well as a 'prophetic ability' (McMullan 2016: 38) – such observations problematically conflate the emergence of these specific aesthetic characteristics with the artist's age, thereby to some extent explaining away stylistic complexity with a mere reference to biological factors instead of offering an in-depth critical analysis. Countering these tendencies and closely examining the implications of these distinct developments, I will argue that the emergence of a 'late style' in Churchill's recent plays does not represent an inevitable biographical, but rather, as it were, an eminently political necessity. Far from straightforward or self-explanatory, therefore, Churchill's turn to a Beckettian style of playwriting must be read as an expression of the author's ongoing struggle with the forms and functions of political, more precisely dialectical, theatre today.

Yet, this juxtaposition between Brechtian and Beckettian tendencies in Churchill's plays may seem paradoxical and counter-intuitive, as these playwrights have usually been considered in dichotomously opposed terms. While Brecht is generally associated with engaged art, emphasizing the role of the collective as well as the possibility for change, Beckett's drama is thought to exemplify artistic autonomy and a focus on the individual, which seem to dismiss the theatre's progressive potential (Taxidou 2004: 194–5; Zapf 1988: 44). Without denying the apparent ideological, philosophical and dramaturgical differences between Beckett and Brecht, I would nevertheless suggest that such polarizing interpretations tend to overlook significant intersections between both dramatists' approaches that can be made fruitful for reimagining dialectical theatre for the twenty-first century, as Churchill's plays so impressively illustrate. In this vein, Hubert Zapf challenges the ostensible incompatibility of epic and absurdist modes when he presents the history of British drama since the late 1950s as a process of dialectical synthesis between Brechtian and Beckettian styles (1988: 51). Yet, what Zapf suggests underpins the development of British playwriting is an oscillation between what he considers as essentially two extreme poles – Brecht on the one hand and Beckett on the other. While this is a significant observation which has opened up a fresh perspective on political theatre in the twentieth century, it is, as I propose, more productive for a discussion of contemporary drama to transcend these very binaries in the first place. As I will demonstrate in this chapter with reference to Churchill's twenty-first-century plays, Beckett and Brecht's approaches must be understood not as mutually exclusive, but as themselves already intricately intertwined with each other, thereby paving the way for reconsidering the forms and functions of dialectics today.

That it is possible to bring Beckett and Brecht into conversation for the purpose of rethinking dialectical theatre is illustrated by Adorno's dialectical reading of Beckett, which represents an important point of reference for identifying the crucial intersections between Brechtian and Beckettian modes. Challenging Martin Esslin's influential category of 'the theatre of the absurd', Adorno approaches Beckett's work from the perspective of negative dialectics in his essay 'Trying to Understand *Endgame*'. Rejecting Esslin's 'critical practice of elucidation, positivisation and humanisation that sought to understand and accommodate Beckett' (Boxall 2003: 22), Adorno offers a Marxist reading which situates the plays within a capitalist context. For this purpose, he identifies negativity as a central thematic and aesthetic technique through which Beckett, within a fundamentally dialectical framework, 'expos[es] art to its limits, its failure and its negative possibility' (Gritzner 2015: 34). In Adornian theory, negativity is attributed a crucial significance as 'both the *source* and the *means* of critical thinking' (Belmonte 2002: 21). Encapsulating an experience of lack, indeterminacy and failure, it is conceptualized as the basis of a new form of dialectical potentiality. Thus, the plays foreground negative situations of 'infinite catastrophe' (Adorno 1982: 148), which Adorno understands as a reflection of the 'completed reification of the world' (1982: 122) through capitalism. This impression of negativity is also expressed on the level of meaning and dramatic form, which are radically undermined: 'If drama were to strive to survive meaning aesthetically, it would be reduced to inadequate content ... The explosion of metaphysical meaning, which alone guaranteed the unity of an aesthetic structure of meaning, makes it crumble away with a necessity and stringency which equals that of the transmitted canon of dramaturgical form' (1982: 120). In a paradoxical twist, Adorno therefore concludes that '[u]nderstanding it [*Endgame*] can mean nothing other than understanding its incomprehensibility, or concretely restructuring its meaning structure – that it has none' (1982: 120). Rather than resolving these paradoxes, the spectators' contradictory task is thus to preserve the plays' 'resistance to meaning, to ideology, and to interpretation ... within the act of interpretation itself' (Boxall 2003: 22). Crucially, it is precisely in this precarious nature of the reception process that the *politics* of negativity in terms of a potential for resistance and an attempt at protest are negotiated. As Peter Boxall explains, 'This does not mean that his work is politically redundant'; rather, it implies 'that Beckett's drama does not offer an existing discourse in which to couch such protest' (2003: 40; Kleinberg-Levin 2015: 88–90). This implicit political impulse – which can only be expressed negatively, as 'a voiceless reflection' (Boxall 2003: 40) – is crucial to Adorno's dialectical reading of *Endgame*.

Thus, Adorno's emphatically political approach to Beckett underscores the dialectical potential inherent in his plays, which seek to inspire resistance to capitalism through their implicit critique of conventional dialectical forms and mechanisms. This crystallizes in their use of negativity as a thematic and aesthetic tool for creating a progressive dialectical mode on the basis of an experience of paradox, ambivalence and unresolved tension. Bringing the interest in creating an oppositional aesthetic together with the desire to eschew reification and to remain autonomous – the central paradox the Adornian artwork aspires to – Adorno's reading can be said to initiate a productive dialogue between Brecht and Beckett which reveals significant intersections between both playwrights' methodologies. It is in this vein that Hans-Thies Lehmann argues that discussing Brecht in relation to Beckett – and vice versa – represents a powerful source for approaching contemporary theatre practice. Identifying 'a curious closeness between them', Lehmann suggests that they must precisely not be understood as 'an alternative – B or B', arguing instead for the need of creating 'a space open to Brecht as well as to Beckett' (2002: 47). Thus, approaching Brecht through Beckett can, on the one hand, open up new perspectives on Brecht's work, uncovering the extent to which his theatre, from his early (often considered more surrealist) plays to the epic parables, shares with Beckett's drama an emphasis on failure, abstraction, gesture and the question of meaning (Lehmann 2002: 44–6; Taxidou 2004: 200). On the other hand, considering Beckett's oeuvre from a Brechtian perspective may bring an essentially political, and indeed dialectical, dimension to the fore, as Adorno has shown (Mendelson 1977: 350; Bennett 2015: 17). Recognizing these manifold overlaps between Brecht and Beckett may thus contribute to fostering new understandings of dialectical thinking, and to identifying its ongoing value as an epistemological and aesthetic device in the contemporary moment.

Arguing for a post-Brechtian turn in Churchill's post-millennial theatre, I will show in the following that her recent plays can be situated at this crucial nexus between Beckett's theatre of negativity and Brechtian dialectical drama. Searching for a way of resisting the neoliberal status quo, Churchill does not only leave the more conventional dialectical style as well as the explicit commitment to Brecht's stagecraft which dominated earlier plays like *Top Girls* or *Cloud 9* behind, but her recent works also decidedly stand out both thematically and aesthetically from other examples of post-Brechtian political theatre discussed in this study. Thus, Churchill's plays stage an ostensibly paradoxical aesthetic in which Brechtian dialectical strategies are creatively combined with absurdist elements. Rather than simply undermining dialectical mechanisms as such, however, this juxtaposition creates an Adornian impression of negativity, which functions as a prerequisite for invigorating a critical impetus at the heart of the plays. To achieve this, the seemingly sharp contrast between apocalyptic landscapes and banal ordinariness at the heart of the plays collapses; they employ an elliptical and fragmentary language, and disrupt structural conventions by rejecting chronology, linearity and coherence to foster an unfamiliar experience on the part of the spectators. Through the resulting blanks and paradoxes, the texts challenge audiences' attempts to relate to and understand the plays and resist the possibility of constructing any straightforward political meaning. It is this (thematic, aesthetic and interpretive) negativity which serves to challenge paralysis and encourage critical thinking instead. At the same time, however, this complex arrangement also destabilizes and works against the plays' dialectical framework and thereby raises urgent questions as to the ultimate value, potential and limits of the (post-)Brechtian mode in the contemporary moment.

Dystopian Negativity: *Escaped Alone*

Dystopian Performatives

Escaped Alone premiered at the Royal Court Jerwood Theatre Downstairs in 2016. Reuniting overarching leitmotifs as well as defining formal features that have shaped Churchill's oeuvre since the 1960s, the play may, to some extent, be read as a reconsideration of the playwright's entire theatrical project. Its central subject matter – personal and global catastrophe and our entanglement in it – directly connects *Escaped Alone* to *Far Away* (2000); its exclusive focus on female characters is indicative of Churchill's powerful socialist-feminist agenda and points back to earlier plays such as *Top Girls* and *Cloud 9*; finally, its commitment to the representation of old age, with all women performers '*at least seventy*' (2016: 4) years old according to the stage directions, brings it into dialogue with *Here We Go* (2015). At the same time, however, *Escaped Alone* also breaks new thematic and aesthetic ground, and suggests a different direction in Churchill's work. Given its 'dystopian extremity' (Angelaki 2017: 22) and its experimental character, it radicalizes the style developed in earlier plays, notably by turning the depiction of apocalyptic negativity into an eminently formal concern. As Dan Rebellato suggests, '[i]t is as if Churchill wants to present chaos chaotically' (2017). As I will argue in the following, it is through this focus on catastrophe and extremely pessimistic visions of the future that *Escaped Alone* explores the consequences of both personal and theatrical (dis)engagement – key concerns not only in Churchill's playwriting but also in Brechtian theatre.

In this sense, rather than offering a nihilist, anti-utopian perspective on the future, *Escaped Alone*'s emphasis on the dystopian must be understood as integral to the play's political fabric. For this purpose, dystopia is employed on the level of both content and form as a post-Brechtian technique of *Verfremdung*. Challenging audiences to rationalize the apocalyptic, estranged scenarios depicted by the plays, and inciting the spectators to re-establish connections between the fictional dystopian worlds on stage and their own lived experience, dystopia fulfils eminent Brechtian functions of fostering analysis and critique. Rather than making the familiar strange to create analytical distance, however, Churchill seems to reverse the process in *Escaped Alone* by bringing the abstract, inconceivable and unrepresentable idea of catastrophe closer. This confrontational effect is notably created through the use of absurdist elements gradually infiltrating and undermining the play's language, character constellation and temporal structure to offer an increasingly surreal and strange impression of *Escaped Alone*'s fictional universe. Undermining, in this way, conventional forms of theatre-making and spectatorial interpretation, these absurdist devices give rise to an oscillation between the recognizable and the alienated through which any straightforward attribution of meaning is resisted, providing a potentially precarious experience of disorientation for the audience. It is through this interplay between confrontation and alienation, certainty and ambiguity, identification and distance that the play creates a profound impression of Adornian negativity, which serves precisely as a means of examining fundamental political and ethical questions from a dialectical vantage point.

As a powerful example of theatrical dystopia, *Escaped Alone* reflects 'the dominance of the dystopian mode' (Levitas and Sargisson 2003: 14) manifest in contemporary culture. While dystopia represents a central trend in the theatre, too, it has so far remained relatively underexplored – in particular from a Brechtian perspective. The increasing presence of dystopia in the collective imagination is often linked to a 'crisis of the utopian imagination' (Klaić 1991: 63) under the impression of postmodernist and neoliberal ideologies. Thus, Siân Adiseshiah explains that core utopian features have become 'appropriated by commercial discourses and the ideal state of happiness was re-categorized as the fetishization of commodity consumption in the Western capitalist imagination' (2009: 41). Crucially, however, the resulting turn to dystopia must not be understood as an anti-utopian expression of nihilism and resignation; rather, utopian and dystopian concepts are intricately intertwined. As Dragan Klaić argues, while dystopia is defined 'as an unexpected and aborted outcome of utopian strivings, a mismatched result of utopian efforts ..., it nevertheless implies utopia as a subverted or suppressed desire' (1991: 3). In a similar vein, Raffaella Baccolini and Tom Moylan use the term 'critical dystopia' to describe texts which 'negotiate the necessary pessimism of the generic dystopia with a militant or utopian stance that not only breaks through the hegemonic enclosure of the text's alternative world but also self-reflexively refuses the anti-utopian temptation that lingers in every dystopian account' (2003: 7). In this respect, Adorno foregrounds the dystopian mode as a source of dialectical negativity and thus as a means of resistance to capitalist ideology, attributing an eminently utopian potential to dystopia. As Adorno argues, '[o]nly by virtue of the absolute of collapse does art enunciate the unspeakable: utopia' (1997: 32). Rather than harmony, solution and synthesis, it is negativity, ambivalence and paradox which are conceptualized in Adorno's model as new sources for a radical – indeed utopian – form of dialectical art.

Escaped Alone illustrates how dystopian negativity can be employed as a means of fostering an implicit utopian impulse. For this purpose, the play juxtaposes and subsequently blends glimpses of the apocalypse with images of an ostensibly normal world. This strategy is initiated right at the beginning of the play. The setting, '*Sally's backyard*' on a '*[s]ummer afternoon*' (Churchill 2016: 4), is presented as an overwhelmingly idyllic space. The stage design chosen for the Royal Court production underscored this impression through its hyperrealist representation of the garden, which was combined with an impeccably, almost unnaturally perfect blue sky. In the garden, three women, Vi, Sally and Lena, are having tea and chatting together. The emphatic ordinariness of this situation is, however, immediately undermined when the women are joined by Mrs Jarrett in a seemingly playful moment of disruption – literally and metaphorically:

Mrs J I'm walking down the street and there's a door in the fence open and inside are three women I have seen before.
Vi   Don't look now but there's someone watching us.
Lena Is it that woman?
Sally Is that you, Mrs Jarrett?
Mrs J So I go in.

Churchill (2016: 5)

Presented in fairy-tale style, Mrs J's entry into the garden signals an intrusion and irruption – formally, narratively and on the level of character interaction – which undercuts any initial impression of innocence. Indeed, it is Mrs J who represents the key to an interpretation of the play through her paradoxical position between both inclusion and exclusion with regard to the other women and the particular impact her interventions have on the action. Her peculiar status in the fictional world is already signalled by the first lines of the text. Thus, while the three women seem to know Mrs J, she is unequivocally presented as an outsider, which particularly materializes in the image of Mrs J's position behind the fence. Vi is the first to be aware of and disturbed by Mrs J's arrival, and thereby confirms the impression that Mrs J represents an observer figure, almost a voyeur. This is underscored by

Lena, who reveals her reluctance to have Mrs J join their company, thereby evoking a sense of unease in Mrs J's presence. Hence, Mrs J's appearance on stage serves to destabilize any initial impression of harmony. The play's title, taken from the Book of Job, further underscores this process, since its evocation of imminent threat and discomfort – embodied in the person of Mrs J – contrasts with, looms over and gradually infiltrates the seeming idyll of the garden.

The specific moments of interruption initiated by Mrs J and, more importantly, the profound implications they have for the play's dialectical mechanisms can be described with reference to Jill Dolan as *dys*topian performatives. In her influential study *Utopia in Performance: Finding Hope at the Theatre* (2005), Dolan investigates the theatre's potential to reflect and convey a '[belief] in the possibility of a better future' (2005: 3) by triggering '[u]topian performatives', which she defines as 'small but profound moments in which performance calls the attention of the audience in a way that lifts everyone slightly above the present, into a hopeful feeling of what the world might be like' (2005: 5). In Dolan's understanding, utopian performatives may provoke analysis, critique and transformation on the basis of a profoundly affective experience. To the extent that they facilitate a fresh perspective on reality and, more precisely, on social relations, they can be brought into fruitful dialogue with Brecht's notion of gestus, as Dolan insightfully argues:

> In some ways, utopian performatives are the received moment of gestus, when those well-delineated, moving pictures of social relations become not only intellectually clear but felt and lived by spectators as well as actors. Utopian performatives persuade us that beyond this 'now' of material oppression and unequal power relations lives a future that might be different, one whose potential we can feel as we're seared by the promise of a present that gestures towards a better later. (2005: 7)

As a form of Brechtian gestus, utopian performatives thus make it possible, in an eminently dialectical vein, to take into account and analyse the wider social context which determines the action of the play as well as the relations between stage and audience, thereby also bridging the gap between theatre and reality with an impulse for change and intervention.

Crucially, while Dolan's disarming optimism may seem overly idealistic, she also hints at the potential of dystopian theatre to develop a progressive impetus: 'spectators might draw a utopian performative from even the most dystopian theatrical universe' (2005: 8). It is this power of the dystopian mode to incite critical analysis based on a dialectical engagement with social reality which *Escaped Alone* exploits through its use of what I propose to describe as dystopian performatives. Determining the play on the level of content and form, most explicitly through the figure of Mrs J, dystopian performatives are employed in *Escaped Alone* as a means of post-Brechtian *Verfremdung* on the level of structure, language, character constellation and (dramatic) time. In this spirit, they blur the boundaries between the familiar and the unfamiliar, the recognizable and the estranged as well as diagnoses of dystopian catastrophe and utopian hope. In this sense, the play seems to be based on a rigid dialectic: distinctions between idyllic Eden and dystopian hell, between present and future, between the fictional here-and-now and the apocalyptic there-and-then as well as, formally, between dialogue and monologue, and epic and dramatic modes supposedly structure the play. Yet, these binaries are in fact increasingly rendered insignificant. Bringing these apocalyptic visions uncomfortably close through its complex use of *Verfremdung*, the play not only raises the question of if and how we can intervene and, indeed, 'escape' these scenarios but also what functions (dialectical) theatre can fulfil and which difference(s) it can or does make in the face of these catastrophic prognoses.

Confronting (Dis)Engagement

At the centre of the play's *dramatis personae*, Mrs J emerges as a key character for *Escaped Alone*'s dialectical framework because of the various functions she fulfils for both the action on stage and the relationship with the audience. The play's strategic use of dystopian negativity hinges above all on her interventions, which unsettle the conventional dramatic frame of the play. More precisely, her role can be understood as an agent of dystopian *Verfremdung*, which is particularly evident in her ambivalent double function as both character and narrator in the play. While Mrs J is involved in the dialogue with the other women, she also serves as a commentator. This is most explicit when, at the end of seven of the eight scenes – the final one being the exception – she appears as a messenger, turning to the audience to deliver her accounts of an apocalyptic future. These reports suggest that she has previously experienced and survived catastrophic events from which she appears to have 'escaped alone', thereby reinforcing the urgency of her appearance and emphasizing the precarious state of the world to which she has returned. Interrupting the dramatic mode of the women's conversation, Mrs J's reports can to some extent be considered epic in a conventional Brechtian sense. This disruption is reinforced by a spatial shift from the garden to an indeterminate, dark space. In the original stage production, this level of mediation was also visualized through the projection of two red frames. Hence, Aston suggests that *Escaped Alone*'s use of '[r]eportage; the breaking of the fourth (garden) wall ...; and a monologic delivery that calls for a non-emotional style of acting ... evince[s] a reprise of Brechtian estrangement' (2018: 308). Yet, this interpretation overlooks that the actual impact of these epic techniques is in fact not so much to adapt as to challenge Brechtian stagecraft. Thus, Mrs J's interventions serve above all to bring the future closer, and to initiate an experiential confrontation with – rather than, in a more traditional Brechtian vein, an analytical distancing from – the images of chaos and destruction which are conjured up. The explicit visualization of the play's narrative frame in the Royal Court's production can therefore be understood as a metatheatrical, indeed ironic comment not only on Mrs J's complex position as narrator and character but also on Brecht's attempts to break the fourth wall.

Practising a fundamental reversal of *Verfremdung*, the play thus establishes an uncomfortable proximity with Mrs J's dystopian visions, which, crucially, hinges on a blurring of the different spatial, temporal and experiential dimensions evoked by the text: garden and apocalypse, present and future, ordinariness and catastrophe and, by extension, stage and auditorium begin to overlap. This is reflected on the level of dialogue, too. Even though Mrs J's dystopian accounts seem to be neatly set off from the women's conversation, she consciously interrupts them mid-sentence, which shows the degree to which the boundaries between these supposedly separate realms are gradually dissolved. In the Royal Court production, this effect also materialized on the level of sound, as alarming noises, such as sirens, accompanied the transitions between the two spaces. As a result, 'the contrast between the bucolic garden scenes and these scenes of atrocity' is rendered more and more unstable, resulting in 'a continuum of experience' (Harvie 2018: 342) for both the characters and the spectators. Undermining the binary distinctions supposedly structuring the play and thereby spurring its fundamental ambivalence, Mrs J's narrative interventions raise important questions regarding the connection between these instants of dystopia and the retreat in the garden, between monologue and dialogue, between Mrs J and the other women – and, by implication, between stage and auditorium.

Crucially, the dystopian quality of Mrs J's monologues is not only reflected on the level of content but also has a palpable effect on the linguistic features of the text, as they acquire an increasingly erratic, random and absurd quality (Hartl 2018a: 351–3). According to Rebellato, it is here that the disruptive force of dystopian negativity inscribes itself: 'What the apocalyptic disrupts is precisely the assuredness of language, the unity of meaning, the clarity of expression' (2017). In this respect, Mrs J's disturbing descriptions, which are reminiscent of *Far Away*'s final part, create a profound impression of ambivalence for the audience:

> The wind developed by property developers started as breezes on cheeks and soon turned heads inside out. The army fired nets to catch flying cars but most spun by with dozens clinging and shrieking, dropping off slowly. Buildings migrated from London to Lahore, Kyoto to Kansas City, and survivors were interned for having no travel documents. Some in the whirlwind went higher and higher, the airsick families taking selfies in case they could ever share them. Shanty towns were cleared. Pets rained from the sky. A kitten became famous.
>
> Churchill (2016: 28)

Even though Mrs J's monologues are replete with illogical images, they are also uncannily interspersed with more familiar elements. Indeed, through these absurd, paradoxical juxtapositions, the play voices a powerful satirical critique of our contemporary practices on both a private and a political level; they create a shocking moment of recognition which arises from the parallels suggested by the play between the surrealist, dystopian scenes supposedly 'far away' and the contemporary catastrophes that have already set in, for example, the refugee crisis to which Mrs J. refers. In this respect, the surrealist quality of the monologues does not offer 'unreal' visions disconnected from either the women's or the spectators' experience, 'but rather, an augmented version of the real' (Boll 2013: 56), which serves as a means of bringing the apocalypse closer through a post-Brechtian use of *Verfremdung*. Crucially, this reversal hinges above all on a profound affective ambivalence, which the text articulates by creating a 'two-toned effect' (Harvie 2018: 342), as Mrs J's narration 'veers from humor to horror' (Trueman 2016b), thereby fostering an emotionally disorientating experience for the audience.

Significantly, these absurdist mechanisms underpinning Mrs J's monologues also impact on the women's dialogue. Initially, their conversation seems harmless and innocent, revolving around the ordinary and the everyday, sharing memories of the past, and telling their personal stories. Reminiscent of Beckettian drama, the dialogue is rendered in elliptical, unrelated fragments. While this may suggest a high degree of familiarity and harmony between the women – they are, for example, able to complete each other's thoughts, and to understand each other without having to spell out their ideas – the banality and superficial simplicity of these conversations are deceptive. Thus, the many blanks in the text increasingly suggest a growing impression of confusion and unease, creating a sense of Pinteresque menace through the play's distinct silences and gaps. Indeed, already in the first scene, a certain degree of anxiety shines through the seemingly playful and ordinary conversation when the women suddenly switch topic, from animatedly talking about their relatives to hinting at their struggles finding guidance in a deeply disorientating world:

Vi   I can't really follow
Sally I can't even add up
Lena they don't add up any more
Vi   particles and waves I can manage but after that
Churchill (2016: 7)

These personal anxieties and feelings of paranoia gradually infiltrate the women's conversation and, to some extent, reflect a growing impact of Mrs J's dystopian visions on this private sphere. It is, above all, the condition of the world beyond the garden – the public sphere – that represents an increasingly difficult challenge for them, as women, and as aging women, to cope with.

In this sense, the garden is far from representing a paradisiacal retreat for the characters. On the contrary, as Mrs J's dystopian visions and the women's dialogue increasingly intersect, 'the home as a place of relative safety is rendered uncanny' (Aston 2018: 307). In this respect, the play offers an implicit, but fundamental critique of Vi, Lena and Sally's passive endurance and retreat, which clearly distinguishes them from Mrs J. While their 'tea-drinking' is presented 'as a passively marked palliative to the worst kinds of events life can throw at us – a soothing away of catastrophic happenings' (Aston 2018: 307), the play simultaneously suggests, as shown above, that this protection is but a fallacy and, more to the point, that the disengagement the women practise through their retreat into the garden fails as a gesture of emancipation and self-assertion. By contrast, whereas the three women represent stasis, inaction, self-centredness and detachment from the public sphere, Mrs J's spatial and temporal mobility and her experience of the world beyond the boundaries of the garden suggest a certain degree of agency and commitment. Indeed, as Vicky Angelaki argues, '[i]n a group of characters involved in their own personal narratives, she is the only sensitized citizen who imagines herself a participant and not a detached observer. Therefore, Mrs Jarrett does not indulge in the narrative of the self, but vocalizes the narrative of society' (2017: 25). It is thus through the complex relationships between Mrs J and the other women that the play's fundamental political investment emerges as a plea for reconnecting the personal and the political instead of searching for remedy in the private sphere alone.

The critique of, and frustration with, political disengagement crystallizes in particular in Mrs J's final monologue, which disrupts the conversation in the middle of the final scene, and sharply contrasts both with her apocalyptic visions and with the other women's speeches. In an intensely emotional moment, Mrs J repeats with increasing vehemence the words 'terrible rage' twenty-five times. It is in Mrs J's outburst of indignation – the source of which is never defined – that the play's call for active engagement, resistance and conflict can be located. Her monologue constitutes 'an act of ferocious political despair', reflected on the level of language in 'an apocalyptic breakdown of linguistic invention' (Rebellato 2017). Besides evoking a strongly affective form of commitment, this eruption thus also represents 'beyond a confession, a political statement, an indictment, even a chant' (Angelaki 2017: 24). In this respect, it is problematic to assume, as Jen Harvie does, that the women's community can 'provide a powerful sense of comfort in the face of those atrocities' (2018: 342). It is also in this optimistic vein that the women's song in scene 6 tends to be considered a symbol of harmony and thus, as Aston suggests, as a '[v]isceral and upbeat' (2018: 309) antidote to the overwhelming impression of dystopia at the heart of the play. However, these interpretations overlook that this song is not external to but, crucially, intimately embedded into the play's dystopian structure. This is underscored by the fact that another of Mrs J's dystopian reports directly follows this incident (Churchill 2016: 29). In this way, Mrs J's apocalyptic visions can be seen to directly impact on the women's retreat in the garden on the level of both content and form, which suggests that the play to some extent problematizes the women's apparent disengagement. *Escaped Alone*'s dystopian performatives must hence be understood as a confrontational call for action – rather than for passive endurance – to rewrite the script of the future conjured up by Mrs J's dystopian visions.

Crucially, this turn to engagement is implicit in the text itself. While the object of the play's inquiry and critique, the three women nevertheless display a certain self-awareness in their monologues, in which they are given the chance to openly talk about their preoccupations and fears. In a moment of introspection and 'confession' – perhaps above all to themselves and to the audience rather than to each other – they enter into an extended stream of consciousness in which they reflect on their lives from a critical distance, thereby briefly opening up to, and considering their individual stories in terms of, a broader political context. Indeed, through retro- and introspection, the women are able to consider themselves and their lives in tentatively social rather than purely solipsistic terms, which is, for example, reflected in Vi and Lena's difficulties of establishing relationships with friends, colleagues or family (Churchill 2016: 32, 40–1). In these instances, the women implicitly reassert the political relevance of their personal experiences. As Aston argues, the monologues draw attention to the fact that 'personal anxieties often eschew the larger, social, catastrophic pictures' and thereby '[register] the psycho-social breakdown between the personal and the political ... intensifying under neoliberal capitalism' (2018: 307). Hence, the women's engagement with their own histories seems to offer an opportunity for critical reflection – on the fictional level of the play, but also as a model for the audience to follow, thereby reaching out beyond the stage and the theatre to the spectators. Left with an affective experience of the play's dystopian negativity as orchestrated by Mrs J, it is through an interrogation into the spectators' own lives, their attitudes and their behaviour that a genuine political engagement might re-emerge.

Historicizing the Future

Escaped Alone's use of dystopian *Verfremdung* does not only establish a spatial proximity with catastrophe, as the boundaries between the dark, indeterminate space of Mrs J's visionary monologues, on the one hand, and the women's retreat in the garden, on the other, increasingly dissolve, but also has a considerable impact on the experience of (dramatic) time – both thematically and aesthetically speaking. The play is preoccupied with time as a central category determining individual and collective identities, and reflects how conventional understandings of temporality have been put under pressure by recent sociopolitical and economic developments through its dystopian framework. Thus, postmodernist relativism is often thought to have fostered an impression of 'globalised timelessness' (Harvie 2018: 344), suggesting that we live in 'a fetishized super-now' (Harvie 2018: 344) in which an exclusive focus on the immediate present risks undermining our sense of historical interconnectedness, as well as the geographically and temporally wider responsibilities this entails. In this context, time has most notably been turned into an important economic factor. Elizabeth Freeman employs the term 'chrononormativity' to describe how '[m]anipulations of time convert historically specific regimes of asymmetrical power into seemingly ordinary bodily tempos and routines, which in turn organize the value and meaning of time' (Freeman 2010: 3). This chrononormative management serves to impose specific time patterns with the aim of fulfilling economic purposes. Encompassing everything, from individuals to populations to state apparatuses, chrononormative regimes adjust time according to certain schemes to reinforce not only commonly accepted patterns of identity and social conduct but also of consumption and economically beneficial behaviour (Freeman 2010: 4). Through its dystopian theme and aesthetic,

Escaped Alone exposes these processes, and, even more significantly, offers an alternative experience of time for both characters and spectators.

On the level of content, *Escaped Alone* reflects the difficulty of coming to terms with these developments, notably through its focus on old age. Countering, in a Rancièrean vein, common exclusions of issues related to ageing from social and political debates, the play foregrounds the women's experiences and stages above all their increasing lack of orientation:

> **Lena** things do speed up
> **Sally** everything does
> **Mrs J** you get used to it
> **Sally** so that can be good but when it's your whole life speeding up
> **Lena** don't start on that
>
> Churchill (2016: 21)

Struggling to accommodate this impression of overwhelming acceleration and to understand its implications for everyday life, the women acknowledge the challenges they experience as a result. In this respect, time performs vital functions for their identities. Yet, the significance of the women's relationship to time for developing a stable sense of themselves is in fact only suggested *ex negativo*, precisely by denying the characters any meaningful engagement with time through an experience of a lack of chronology, temporal coherence and teleology. This is reflected by their preoccupation with memory, which, however, no longer provides them with a reliable sense of the past:

> **Vi** there must be quite a few things I missed
> **Sally** not really, it all goes by, I can't remember those years specially
> **Vi** remember what was happening where I was of course
> **Sally** yes of course
> **Vi** though it gets to be a blur because it's all a bit the same
>
> Churchill (2016: 11)

Crucially, rather than merely indicative of the challenges of old age in general, I would suggest that the play presents the women's difficulties to establish a coherent sense of time as a direct consequence of their passivity. In this respect, Mrs J again stands out from the rest of the group. As an embodiment of the future, her prophetic return to share her wisdom and to warn the women – and, by extension, the spectators – can be read as a sign of her mobility, agency and commitment to the wider public sphere. Thus, she is not struggling with the same challenges as Vi, Lena and Sally, who have sought refuge in the garden and have thereby deliberately disconnected themselves from their surroundings. Their retreat, however, does ultimately not protect them from the impact of the outside world. While they are unaware of Mrs J's dystopian visions, the news of impending catastrophe nevertheless increasingly affects their conversations, as their anxieties and growing confusion illustrate their fundamental vulnerability, underscoring the futility of their withdrawal from any form of commitment.

It is this emphasis on engagement and agency embodied by Mrs J which is at the heart of Churchill's reassertion of time as a central factor for political commitment in *Escaped Alone*, illustrated not only by the play's thematic preoccupations with apocalyptic visions but also through its formal treatment of time. Challenging normative understandings of time, and laying bare their implications on a social, political and economic level, *Escaped Alone* foregrounds in particular the temporal dimension of the future. While seemingly clear-cut distinctions may determine the play's form on the surface, an unequivocal separation is increasingly undermined through Mrs J's interventions, as she literally crosses the boundaries between the different temporal and spatial frames. As part of her various dramaturgical functions, Mrs J spurs a 'temporal fluidity' (Angelaki 2017: 24) which effectively blurs past, present and future. This indeterminacy is above all reflected in *Escaped Alone*'s playful, experimental and idiosyncratic treatment of dramatic time. Thus, paradoxically, the stage directions indicate that the eight scenes take place on '*[a] number of afternoons but the action is continuous*' (Churchill 2016: 4), underscoring not only the extent to which conventional conceptualizations of time are undermined in the play but also mirroring the inevitable acceleration towards apocalypse underpinning the action. While defined by a clear *telos* – catastrophe – the play disrupts chronology and rejects linearity. Characterized by ellipses, fragments and gaps, it estranges any normative experience of temporality: time is interrupted, accelerated or slowed down in the different scenes. As a result, in *Escaped Alone*, 'one time is simultaneously many' (Harvie 2018: 344). While the play is thus obsessed with temporality both on a thematic and on a formal level, it is characterized by a profound ambivalence which transcends any common categorizations to expose the complexity of time in the present moment.

Foregrounding in this way the temporal dimension of dystopia, the play facilitates an unconventional experience of time which serves above all to estrange the present, while offering a different perspective on the contemporary moment from the perspective of the future. Trish Reid usefully connects this to the idea of *Verfremdung* when she writes that 'the strange temporality inherent in the dramaturgy of unwelcome futures, and the schism that separates the audience from those futures, become the means by which we understand the horrors of the present' (2019: 75). In this sense, *Escaped Alone*'s experiments with dystopian temporality initiate a form of historicization, a key technique in Brechtian theatre which aims to raise awareness of the fundamentally relative and dynamic nature of historical developments. Crucially the mechanism underpinning Brechtian historicization is again reversed in *Escaped Alone*. Rather than reconsidering the present through the past, Churchill's play is invested in speculatively historicizing the future. It looks forward rather than back and employs confrontation rather than distanciation as a prerequisite for inspiring a different perspective on actions, attitudes and behaviours in the present moment; it considers the present *as history*. Hence, the play's creative use of dramatic time 'slows and alienates the present' in order to challenge 'aspects of dailiness that are so familiar they become chrononormative and neglected' (Harvie 2018: 344). In this respect, Churchill's post-Brechtian historicization contributes to creating an opportunity for a new 'distribution of the sensible' in Rancière's sense of the term by forcing both the characters and the audience not only to confront the future consequences of their lack of engagement but also, and most crucially, to re-establish a connection between present and future, private and political, local and global, and thus to reassert responsibility as a prerequisite for effecting change in the present – for the sake of a 'better' future. With this Brechtian emphasis on the possibility of change and intervention, *Escaped Alone*'s dystopian confusion of time thus underpins a process of speculation from which a post-Brechtian call for critique based on ambivalence and experience may emerge.

Dialectic at a Standstill

On the level of character constellation, language, space and time, *Escaped Alone*'s dystopian performatives evoke conventional dichotomies – between here and there, now and then, paradise and apocalypse – which, however, increasingly blur and collapse under the impact of the play's use of absurdist stylistic devices. As a result, the dynamic movement shaping these supposedly binary structures is suspended, preventing any productive dialectical exchange between the contradictions exposed by the play. This raises the question of whether the apocalyptic scenarios envisioned by Mrs J are inevitable, and whether anything at all can be done to change the course of events. This impression culminates in the play's abrupt ending, when, shortly after her outburst of 'terrible rage', Mrs J suddenly gets up to leave the garden in a surprisingly anti-climactic gesture: 'And then I said thanks for the tea and I went home' (Churchill 2016: 42; Hartl 2018a: 355). Through this unexpected move, the various temporal, spatial and narrative frames upheld by Mrs J's central position merge into one and meaningful distinctions become suspended. In the original stage production, this idea of suspension was visualized, as the different settings – the garden and the dark void with its red frames – were blended into one incoherent image at the end of the performance. Through its sheer lack of explanation and coherence, this final moment provides an experience of perplexity which immediately confronts the spectators with the play's negativity. *Escaped Alone* offers no explanations for why the action is suddenly disrupted and ended mid-sentence, why Mrs J leaves the other women or where she is going, passing these questions on to the audience and asking them to determine the relationship between the different temporal and spatial dimensions as well as their own position with regard to the play.

Significantly, this mechanism of suspension can be brought into a fruitful dialogue with Walter Benjamin's concept of standstill. As a central thought figure in his approach to Brechtian epic theatre, Benjamin employs the metaphor of the standstill to describe the dialectical principle underpinning Brecht's theatre model. For this purpose, Benjamin foregrounds the temporal dimension of the dialectical dynamic and proposes a negative understanding which notably challenges 'the received paradigm of the dialectic as an inevitable process of progressive change' (Carney 2005: 48). Thus, what characterizes Brechtian dialectics (according to Benjamin) is a focus on temporal disruption, rather than on progress and development. This shift in emphasis is encapsulated in the notion of standstill and is realized through a form of gestus, which serves to interrupt actions and processes:

> the dialectic which epic theatre sets out to present is not dependent on a sequence of scenes in time; rather, it declares itself in those gestural elements that form the basis of each sequence in time. ... The thing that is revealed as though by lightning in the 'condition' represented on the stage – as a copy of human gestures, actions and words – is an immanently dialectical attitude. The conditions which epic theatre reveals is the dialectic at a standstill. (Benjamin 1998: 12)

Hence, according to Benjamin, Brecht's plays portray fragmented, isolated conditions which are revealed through gestic instances of standstill. Crucially, however, the form of interruption created through gestus does not simply mark a moment of ultimate paralysis; rather, it is 'from the outset qualified as a type of non-static stillness' (Ruprecht 2015: 26), oscillating between standstill, on the one hand, and movement, flow and change, on the other. Sean Carney explains that '[t]he dialectic is a contradiction between stasis and dynamism that is phenomenologically manifested in the arrested gesture of the epic theatre. The gestures of the epic theatre stage the contradiction of the dialectic at a standstill. ... The gesture of the epic theatre is a timeless moment in which the stream of life crests and hangs frozen in space' (2005: 49). It is this tension between forward movement and paralysis which Benjamin identifies as the key to Brecht's dialectical drama.

Crucially, Adorno makes use of Benjamin's concept for his interpretation of Beckett's plays, describing their negative dialectic in terms of the notion of standstill. The paradox between progress and stasis inherent in this idea is particularly explicit, even literal, in *Waiting for Godot* (1953), in which Vladimir's concluding 'let's go' is answered by the characters' silent immobility at the end of the play: '*They do not move*' (Beckett 1965: 94). Thus, Beckett refuses any form of dialectical dynamic, as the ongoing back and forth between dialectical contradictions is radically brought to a halt here – literally, that is, spatially and temporally, as well as metaphorically. What prevails at the end is a profound sense of paralysis, which collapses dialectical distinctions, renders them ambivalent and thus dysfunctional and thereby obstructs any further exchange. Rather than representing an instance of ultimate resignation, however, this essentially negative moment is preliminary to the extent that it is charged with 'maximum ambiguity and tension' (Kleinberg-Levin 2015: 87), as the final scene mirrors the beginning of the play, reflecting the play's essentially circular structure. According to Adorno, '[n]o spectator and no philosopher can say if the play will not begin anew. The dialectic swings to a standstill' (1982: 145). It is from this emphasis on ambivalence that Adorno derives an indefinite potentiality and openness through which the negative and suspended dialectic can be reactivated. Immobility, paralysis and collapse are thereby paradoxically reconfigured as a radically empowering experience.

These ideas can be fruitfully applied to Churchill's *Escaped Alone*, which stages a literal moment of dialectical standstill at the end. Through a Benjaminian and Adornian lens, the profound negativity created by *Escaped Alone*'s abrupt ending can be conceptualized as a utopian moment of potentiality. Thus, the heightened indeterminacy crystallizing in the suspension and intensity of this moment – juxtaposing Mrs J's enraged outburst with her sudden, anti-climactic departure from the scene – can be understood as an implicit appeal to the audience, challenging spectators to look for answers, indeed, following the women's model of introspection, to look to themselves to renegotiate their relationship with the world in the face of catastrophe, and to develop an understanding of their place in, and of their responsibility for, history. Hence, it is through *Escaped Alone*'s temporal negativity that the dialectic can be said to be reactivated in the relationship between stage and audience. Reinforcing the play's unresolved tensions and contradictions and denying any resolution, *Escaped Alone* implicitly turns to the audience, challenging spectators to engage productively with the absurdities, incoherences and indeterminacies they are confronted with. Crucially, this reactivation of the play's critical impulse is fuelled by an affective reaction on the part of the spectators. As Carney explains, Benjamin's notion of standstill describes not a passive form of paralysis, but an active 'moment of collision' between different temporalities which creates a fundamental 'dialectical shock, where the future asserts itself in the present' (2005: 58): 'The damming of the stream of real life', as Benjamin writes, 'the moment when its flow comes to a standstill, makes itself felt as reflux: this reflux is astonishment' (1998: 13). The crux of Brechtian epic theatre is therefore, in Benjamin's understanding, 'the ability to connect dissimilars in such a way as to "shock" people into new recognitions and understandings' (Mitchell 1998: xiii). This emphasis on affect as a significant factor in the process of dialectical interpretation can be made fruitful for *Escaped Alone*. Rather than producing what Darko Suvin has identified as 'cognitive estrangement' (1979: 4), the play's use of dystopia initiates an affective process of *Verfremdung*, which underscores the importance of individual audience members for bringing the play's dialectic from standstill back into motion. In this sense, Reid also argues for an interpretation of dystopia as a structure of feeling rather than of cognition (2019: 77). The decidedly visceral dimension at the heart of Churchill's recent plays has been increasingly recognized as a crucial factor in her work (Luckhurst 2014: 143). Whereas R. Darren Gobert interprets this shift as a sign of Churchill's eschewal of 'Brechtian-styled dialectics in favour of a visceral-critical "sensing" of the divorce between the personal and political, and of capitalism's relentless "progress"' (2014: 212), I argue that, on the contrary, this turn to the affective must be understood within, and as a decisive part of, the plays' dialectical framework. Thus, the play's reassertion of the dialectical mechanism as a progressive form of analysis and critique is expressed on the basis of emotional, rather than exclusively intellectual, engagement. What underpins *Escaped Alone*'s reinvigoration of dialectical drama is thus, as Aston explains with reference to Brecht, an 'A-affect', which she defines as 'a technique of affectively realised distanciation [which] might serve as a means to reawaken critical perceptions blunted or anesthetised by the ideological and economic forces of neoliberalism' (2018: 302). Hence, it is first and foremost through the spectators' emotional reactions to the play that a progressive impulse, through which critical reflection and intervention are incited, may emerge.

Again, this shift from a rational to a more experiential and hence more individual form of interpretation hinges above all on the play's use of absurdist devices, which spur an impression of intellectual confusion and disorientation on the part of the spectators. The blanks created by the play's paradoxes and ellipses thus serve to reactivate the dialogue between stage and auditorium by undermining conventional patterns of analysis, and by creating space for a more individual process of reception. As Bennett argues, 'the response to the contradictions presented onstage in an absurd play cannot be merely an *objective intellectual* response' (2015: 118); instead, 'because it is a *subjective emotional* response, the audience feels personally part of the world that does not make sense and must resolve their own emotions; however, in order to resolve those emotions, it is necessary to have a subsequent *subjective intellectual* response' (2015: 118). Hence, the play's turn to the absurd underscores its dystopian strategy, which serves to undermine any structural, spatial or temporal clarity and orientation, bringing the future closer, and confronting the spectators with a radical diagnosis of catastrophe through a post-Brechtian form of *Verfremdung*. By inviting us to imagine the unimaginable, the play's dystopian dialectical strategy represents an Adornian 'attempt to imagine the end of totality' (Rebellato 2017). While the play foregrounds the spectators' subjective responses, its emphasis on disorientation and ambivalence creates a precarious, self-conscious and decidedly negative aesthetic which certainly pushes at the boundaries of dialectical theatre and dialectical thinking as such. Yet, it is precisely by situating the dialectic in a liminal space on the threshold between dynamism and suspension, between remobilizing critical thought and rejecting its possibility that, in an Adornian spirit, its radical potential for the twenty-first century may re-emerge.

Deconstructing the Dialectic: *Here We Go*

Death as Thematic and Aesthetic Metaphor

Here We Go premiered at the National Theatre in 2015 and can be considered one of the most unusual and radical examples of contemporary (political) drama in Britain. As such, it represents a thought-provoking coda to this study to the extent that it pushes at the boundaries of political theatre in general, and powerfully raises the question of the ongoing relevance of Brecht's legacy in the twenty-first century in particular. Carrying forward her experiments with minimalism, Churchill proposes a play stripped off its most basic ingredients, gradually reducing the text to a bare minimum on the level of character, dialogue and (temporal) structure. Described as 'cryptic' (Rebellato 2015), the play explores, in a Beckettian vein, temporality, death and finitude through a non-chronological triptych structure which offers three different, not necessarily interconnected perspectives on death. While scene 1, 'Here We Go', stages a reunion during a funeral party, scene 2, 'After', enters surrealist terrain with its monologue from and on the afterlife, before scene 3, 'Getting There', returns to a more realist setting, showing the monotonous but inexorable rhythm of the life of an old person, whose days seem to consist solely of getting dressed and undressed with the help of a carer – an action that is repeated in complete silence ad infinitum, or, indeed, until death. Focusing on such intimate moments, *Here We Go* is, at first sight, neither obviously sociopolitically committed nor explicitly (post-) Brechtian in approach, and has therefore been described as Churchill's 'least political play' (Rebellato 2015), in particular in comparison with her other, more immediately engaged works. Concerned with the first and last of all possible contradictions, life versus death, *Here We Go*'s thematic focus seems to render the very idea of change irrelevant, and questions of political engagement must seem obsolete in light of the inevitable finality of life with which the play confronts its spectators. This self-conscious emphasis on death also serves as a metaphor of the play's wider concerns, as *Here We Go* can be understood to question the ultimate value of social commitment as well as the role of – and, more precisely, its own role as – a politically engaged work of art.

While its focus on death may seem to suggest the futility of any form of commitment during one's lifetime, it is important to stress that *Here We Go* in fact eschews such straightforward conclusions. Instead, death is conceptualized as a highly ambivalent concept, and the play exploits this indeterminacy both thematically and aesthetically to explore questions of politics and engagement in the context of the theatre. This is evident in the evocative, but profoundly ambiguous title. The adverb 'here' is unspecific to the extent that it is unclear which (fictional or real) space – the characters' *hic*, the theatre's auditorium or an unspecified place external to both – it refers to. If 'here' is taken to be synonymous with death, which seems plausible in the context of the play, the title can be understood to ask what implications this inevitable approach of death has for the life that precedes it. In this respect, ideas of dynamism and progress as connoted by the verb 'go' draw attention to what lies in-between 'here' and 'there' and, more precisely, to the potential directions, motivations and aspirations which shape this path. Thus, the title paradoxically invokes notions of both movement and paralysis, and it is through this ambivalence that *Here We Go* attempts to raise awareness of fundamental questions regarding the relationship between life and death. Crucially, its focus on 'we' suggests that this is precisely not a solipsistic concern; it is a matter of collective rather than individual, of social rather than personal interest. It is in the idea that death binds us all together and in the resulting emphasis on the public rather than private sphere that a political dimension may be seen to emerge from the play's concerns.

Reflecting the indeterminate quality of the title, Churchill's use of language similarly foregrounds the ambiguous and paradoxical nature of the concept of death, which is strategically exploited by the play. Thematically preoccupied with dying, *Here We Go* is 'about the impossible' as it attempts to represent the essentially 'unrepresentable' (Middeke 2017: 226) and experientially inaccessible. The challenges of addressing and staging death are above all palpable in the dialogue, as words fail to establish any coherent sense. Hence, the play seems to suggest that death 'can only be understood in its absence' (Rebellato 2015). Consequently, language is 'fractured and ambiguous' (Rebellato 2015) and thereby prevents, in Beckettian style, any meaningful communication. This is particularly evident in scene 1, which consists of an incoherent discussion revolving around the characters' incomplete and inconclusive memories of the deceased person whose life they have assembled to mourn. Crucially, neither the number of actors to deliver the lines nor the number of characters to be included in this section are predetermined by the author, which serves to underscore the fundamental openness of the text. Rather than offering a logically structured conversation, the first scene presents a polyphone ensemble in which different speakers and voices become indistinguishable from each other:

> We miss him
> of course
> everyone
> but his closest
> because friendship was
> wider range of acquaintance than anyone I've ever
> gift
> closeness
> listened
> and so witty I remember him saying
> listened and understood
> always seemed
>
> Churchill (2015: 11)

Incapable of developing a meaningful narrative and mirroring the difficulty, if not impossibility, of coming to terms with death, the characters oscillate incoherently between reminiscences of the dead person's life, on the one hand, and their own preoccupations, on the other. Under these conditions, all that is left is a set of fragmentary, abstract and stereotypical recollections which can no longer provide them with a stable sense of identity. This impression is reinforced in scene 2, in which all 'the character can actually say about something s/he cannot know in the first place is mostly made up of clichés' (Middeke 2017: 227). In a '*[v]ery fast*' (Churchill 2015: 23) soliloquy, the character delivers a fantastical, mythical and indeed absurd reflection on death to the spectators:

> surely I must be in for something more Nordic
> Thor with a thunderbolt
> Valhalla or is that just for war heroes yes there they are sitting around the table drunk and roaring not my idea of fun
> and for illness or old age here's a blue black giantess come to take me somewhere bleaker maybe a cold beach with a wind I once went swimming I'd rather a warm Greek white stones can I have that and is that Charon in the boat I can get in wobble sit down and over the dark river we go
> Churchill (2015: 25–6)

Speaking to the audience from the realm of the dead, the character tries 'to fill the void with language' (Rebellato 2015). Yet, just like the elliptical dialogue of scene 1, this eloquence fails to provide any meaningful representation of, or reflection on death, and denies the character a clearly defined identity.

Hence, rather than in the words themselves, actual meaning seems to reside in what is not said. The text is characterized by blanks, which acquire a significant role in the process of interpretation, as they not only symbolize the inexpressibility of death but also create (a literal) space for reflection for the spectators. Thus, the play's excess of language is in sharp contrast to, and increasingly replaced with, an acute silence. The ellipses shaping the dialogue in scene 1 illustrate this gradual erasure of language. This was also underscored in the original stage production to the extent that '[t]he linguistic silences [made] themselves felt in actual silence' (Rebellato 2015). In an even more radical gesture, silence is absolute in scene 3, which is completely non-verbal and thereby privileges, in postdramatic spirit, other dimensions of theatrical signification, for example, the corporeal rather than the written text (or spoken word), as sources of meaning. In the end, however, neither words nor their absence can be said to enhance understanding. In this respect, the complex and absurd interplay between language and silence in *Here We Go* reflects the characters' unsuccessful attempts to come to terms with the experience of death and, crucially, the play's failure to offer a genuine representation of it. Paradoxically, death is both an omnipresent preoccupation and a radical absence in the play. As *présence absente* or *absence présente*, it cannot be explicitly staged, but constantly looms over the dialogue; it fails to be represented, but its unrepresentability is always problematized and challenged.

On the level of content and language, then, the central dialectical contradiction at the heart of the play collapses, undermining the distinction between life and death, and creating a profound impression of ambivalence. Through a strategic suspension of categories, *Here We Go* rejects binary structures and any guiding sense of orientation to present a complex, paradoxical and open form. This dissolution raises fundamental questions in the context of both Churchill's oeuvre and the overarching argument of this study: can such a framework be understood as dialectical at all, and if so, what critical impetus may emerge from the distinct absence of structure and contradiction, as well as from the emphasis on solipsism and finality? From an Adornian perspective, death, in particular as it is represented in Beckett's works, constitutes the essence of negativity. Rather than as a sign of nihilism, Adorno conceptualizes it as a central metaphor for the plays' dialectical potential (1982: 150). Yet, is such a utopian impulse still palpable in a play which refuses any distinctions, and which seems to eschew any immediate social relevance? On the one hand, the play employs death as a thematic and aesthetic strategy for examining life from both individual and collective perspectives, and offers an experience of estrangement in the spirit of Brecht's *Verfremdung*. Yet, through its emphasis on the inescapability of death, what it seems to foreground is ultimately the futility of any form of engagement, provocatively asking not only if social and political commitment can make any difference but also interrogating the role of the engaged artwork under these conditions. Probing whether and how a Brechtian methodology can be applied to these mechanisms with a specific focus on *Here We Go*'s characters and temporal structure, the remainder of this chapter will critically examine the political potential of this play which radically pushes at the boundaries of conventional theatre-making.

Spectral *Verfremdung*

Given its fundamental experiential and representational inaccessibility, *Here We Go* attempts to approach death by creating a profound sense of ambivalence, depicting 'living as dying' or, vice versa, 'a dying indistinguishable from life' (Robson 2019: 19–20). This effect is particularly palpable on the level of characters, where Churchill employs a strategic spectrality to realize this sense of in-betweenness. Ghost figures have been a recurrent feature in many of Churchill's plays, where they have fulfilled eminent political functions. As Alice Rayner astutely observes, they 'are theatrical devices that give theatrical reality to the economic, political and social conditions that are Churchill's primary concerns' (1998: 206). While earlier works emphasized the supernatural dimension of spectrality, Rachel Clements has demonstrated that the spectres haunting Churchill's plays have increasingly acquired distinctly human traits in her twenty-first-century works (2014: 78). This tendency can also be observed in *Here We Go*, where the characters are all recognizable human beings – yet with unequivocal ghostly qualities. Scene 3, for example, appears at first sight to offer a conventional approach; the two characters appear to be very much alive through their repetitive actions, which depict the familiar constellation of a carer helping an old or ill person to dress and undress. However, the absence of language, and thus the lack of information or contextualisation, can be seen to create an effect of spectrality, as the scene foregrounds the gradual approach of death. This sense of liminality between life and death is reinforced by the first scene. While it sets up a seemingly realistic frame by staging the all-too-familiar and stereotypically formulaic chit-chat of a funeral party, this impression of familiarity and conventionality is soon destabilized, as the fragmentary and elliptical quality of the dialogue undermines any attempt to make out individual characters. This is further exacerbated by deliberate interruptions of the conversation through direct addresses, with which the figures regularly turn to the audience. The choice of speeches and the specific moments of their insertion into the dialogue are not prescribed by the author, hence reinforcing the indeterminacy and contingency of the text. As the stage directions indicate, the speeches '*are to be inserted at random during the dialogue. There are ten – use as many as you need for each character to have one*' (Churchill 2015: 11). In these monologues, the characters step out of the dramatic frame to report the moment and cause of their own death. These accounts are all the more striking because of their detached, matter-of-fact, at times almost cynical quality. For example, a character may say: 'I die the next day. I'm knocked over by a motorbike crossing a road in North London. I think I can get over while the light's red but I'm looking for cars. I'm dead before the ambulance comes and it comes very quickly' (Churchill 2015: 21). Crucially, the temporal and causal relations between these monologic sections and the dialogue are never specified. In their role as participants of the funeral party, the characters are portrayed as living beings – in stark contrast to the deceased person they have gathered to commemorate. Yet, their speeches invalidate such straightforward interpretations, suggesting instead that the figures we encounter on stage are dead, too, and thus speak to us from a spectral position.

Hence, the characters inhabit a decidedly liminal space in which conventional distinctions have been suspended. This ambivalent ontological status has a profound impact on the relationship between stage and auditorium, challenging any process of identification and any meaning that is attributed to the play in the process of interpretation. This effect is particularly evident in scene 2, which is set in a 'purgatory-like in-between space' (Middeke 2017: 227). Introducing a profound indeterminacy with regard to the character's ontological status, 'After' creates a deeply confusing experience for the audience, as the speaker directly addresses the spectators from the realm of the dead, and thereby implicates them in the account. In the fast-paced monologue spoken from the afterlife, the deceased person turns to the auditorium to reveal a fundamental sense of disorientation: 'Falling falling down the tunnel down the tunnel a tunnel a light a train a tube train aaah coming to kill me / but I'm already dead is that right and ah here I am arrived somewhere and hello is that grandpa?' (Churchill 2015: 23). Uncertain about 'what's happened to me what's going to happen' (Churchill 2015: 24), the character oscillates between fantastical images of death and personal recollections. Crucially, the soliloquy suggests an increasing self-awareness:

> I was comfortable comfortable in my life chicken and a warm bed
> and how much good did I very little because I was always loving someone or organising something or looking at trees or having a quiet sit-down with the paper and I'm sorry I'm sorry …
> going back and having another life my own life over again like that movie and do it better of course because most of the time I hardly noticed it going by and I used to look back and think how careless I was when I was young I never noticed and by then I was middle-aged and later I'd look back and think *then* I never noticed.
>
> Churchill (2015: 25–6)

In this instant, the scene seems to culminate in a confession, as the speaker 'emanates a sense that more could have been achieved with a life in which security of comfort simply did not provide an urgent enough incentive. The life had been well-lived, but more could have been done with it' (Angelaki 2017: 51). Angelaki identifies a critical impetus in the character's acknowledgement which is implicitly directed at the audience members, and challenges them to reflect on their lives and responsibilities while it is not yet too late. As Angelaki argues, the monologue can therefore be understood as a 'call to action' which is indicative of 'the astuteness of the play's politics' (2017: 51). Yet, the values reflected in the soliloquy – consumption, individual happiness and comfort – do not only suggest a certain self-centredness but are, for that reason, also unmistakably neoliberal in nature. In the context of the play's wider concerns, the genuineness and authenticity of this posthumous recognition is doubtful. Given that the character's life is already over at this stage, this realization comes too late for any changes to be effected. Seen in this light, the character's monologue seems entirely self-righteous, an attempt to deflect from an anxiety over missed chances, and a sense of unfulfillment, and thus ultimately a justification of a solipsistic life rather than an honest acknowledgement of regret. Instead of offering an authentic call for engagement addressed to the audience, this scene seems to be set in a realm in which notions of change, intervention and commitment may have become meaningless.

To some extent, then, spectrality as it is employed by Churchill on the level of characters can be attributed distinct dialectical and therefore Brechtian – even post-Brechtian – qualities. Challenging surface appearances and blurring the boundaries between the visible and the invisible, the living and the dead, the real and the supernatural (and/or fictional), spectrality is an unsettling device which disrupts, in a Rancièrean vein, normative forms of perception, and facilitates fresh perspectives to inspire awareness and critique. While it may evoke dichotomous structures, it serves to destabilize and transcend these binaries in a post-Brechtian vein. However, even though spectrality may fulfil central dialectical functions, *Here We Go*'s thematic emphasis on finality, solipsism and futility and its profound formal indeterminacy seem to deliberately work against any dialectical framework or appeal to the audience, as illustrated notably in the second scene. While remnants of a (post-)Brechtian form of *Verfremdung* and a preoccupation with dialectical concerns – most significantly change and agency and the mechanisms by which they can be achieved – are identifiable, the play's impetus towards the spectators is ambiguous at best. It is only *ex negativo*, out of the text's lack of clarity and engagement that such an appeal can be deduced, and given the monologue's distinct sense of self-righteousness, the play ultimately seems too removed from any concrete purpose beyond the level of the individual, and beyond the fundamental ontological contradiction between life and death. In its self-conscious rejection of dialectical concepts and structures, the play may therefore offer an example of where the limits of Brechtian methodologies might be located – as a means of theatre-making, as a technique of interpretation and as a device for critical analysis.

Ghostly Repetitions

Spectrality is not only realized literally through the use of ghost figures, but its effects also manifest themselves on a temporal level, as conventional experiences of time based on notions of chronology, difference, progress and change are radically challenged. As both subject matter and formal strategy, spectral temporality represents a rich field of experimentation in *Here We Go*, where boundaries between past, present and future as well as life and death are dissolved and replaced by an impression of simultaneity and disorientation. For this purpose, *Here We Go* dissolves time as a meaningful, structuring and guiding dramatic category altogether by employing strategies which can be described with the help of Lehmann's notion of temporal 'distortion' (Lehmann 2006: 156), which he defines as a distinct feature of the postdramatic mode. This is above all mirrored in the anti-chronological structure, which underscores the fundamental ambiguity between life and death at the heart of the play. Thus, the three scenes are not explicitly interconnected and the perspectives on death they offer move illogically from the moment after death as depicted in scenes 1 and 2 'back' to the period leading up to it in scene 3. The resulting lack of orientation is reinforced by the various temporal experiments within the individual scenes. Whereas the increasing pauses and silences in 'Here We Go' suggest that time gradually slows down, the deceased person's '*[v]ery fast*' (Churchill 2015: 23) monologue in scene 2 offers a contrasting experience of acceleration. This is also reflected by the sheer amount of words and lack of punctuation in this section, which sharply contrasts with the incomplete fragments and gaps shaping the dialogue of the preceding scene, and suggests a high degree of emotional intensity. No longer functioning as a source of orientation, meaning and identity, neither for the characters nor for the spectators, time thus acquires a spectral quality in *Here We Go* to the extent that it destabilizes normative temporal categories and distinctions, and instead offers an uncanny experience of disjunction.

Of particular interest with regard to the spectral quality of the play's treatment of time is the last scene, 'Getting There', which stages the characters' repetitive movements of getting dressed and undressed. Because of its non-verbal 'looping movement of repetitive acts', it has been described as 'a piece of performance art or Minimal Art rather than a stage play' (Middeke 2017: 228). Crucially, as a fundamental mechanism of theatre-making and performance, repetition also depends on spectral principles of return and doubling. While Churchill's recent plays, for example *Heart's Desire* (1997) or *Ding Dong the Wicked* (2012), prolifically employ repetition as a distinct dramaturgical device that challenges theatrical conventions and audience habits, *Here We Go* nevertheless differs from its predecessors to the extent that its manipulation of time radically challenges the spectators' capacity for endurance and attention. The stage directions are unspecific, indicating that the action is to be repeated '*for as long as the scene lasts*' (Churchill 2015: 29).

The number of repetitions – and thus the actual length of the scene – is a production choice. In the National Theatre's version, it lasted about twenty minutes – making up almost half of the overall duration of the piece, probing spectators' patience by confronting them with a seemingly endless iteration of the same movements, which continued even as the lights faded out. This emphasis on repetitiveness is reminiscent of 'the absurdly cyclical and recursive movements of (empty) repetition in Beckett's work' (Middeke 2017: 229), where they are employed to suggest deterioration rather than improvement. In a similarly pessimistic vein, *Here We Go*'s final scene stages the inexorable process of approaching death, which is also captured by its title, 'Getting There', and its present-participle, progressive structure, suggesting that the old person is gradually approaching the threshold to death over the course of the action.

Crucially, through this postdramatic 'time distortion' based on repetition and duration, *Here We Go* creates an immersive, direct experience of time which tests the spectators' patience and challenges their relation to the play. Hence, the third scene has been described as 'painful' (Middeke 2017: 229), 'remorseless' and 'unbearable' (Taylor 2015). Aleks Sierz's account illustrates the profoundly unsettling impact the play may have on audience members:

> At first, in this section, everyone is intensely quiet. I can hear the tick of my companion's wrist watch. But watching an old man is uncomfortable. There are more and more coughs, people fidget, a few walk out in exasperation. Many just hate the intensity of this 20-minute section. Some switch off and look at their phones. Some are enraged – on the way out they give vent. (2015a)

Similarly, Mark Robson describes a 'groan' in the audience in reaction to the realization that 'this repeated moment could potentially go on forever' (2019: 19). These recollections reflect the strongly affective dimension the play acquires during the last scene, with spectators' reactions ranging from embarrassment and denial to rage and incomprehension. In this respect, what seems most provocative about 'Getting There' is the experience of ageing and of the approaching end of life spectators are forced to undergo and confront.

At the same time as it inevitably immerses spectators into the scene, however, *Here We Go*'s use of repetition also acquires an important self-reflexive dimension, through which it draws attention to the experience of time itself. Creating a '[c]onsciously noticeable duration', repetition 'turn[s] time as such into an object of the aesthetic experience', providing, in Rancièrean spirit, 'an experience of time that deviates from habit', which 'provokes its explicit perception, permitting it to move from something taken for granted as a mere accompaniment to the rank of a theme' (Lehmann 2006: 156). In this respect, the play's distortion of time can be said to function as a device of *Verfremdung* to the extent that it raises awareness and may thereby foster critique. Crucially, this also extends to the mode of theatrical representation and the act of spectating themselves. As Lehmann explains, this self-reflexive awareness is particularly facilitated by the extent to which aesthetic repetition paradoxically creates an impression of difference rather than similarity – an effect which was reinforced by the National Theatre's production, which introduced slight, but noticeable changes into the repetitive movements to foreground those aspects that distinguished the repeated gestures from each other. Thus, Lehmann writes that 'we always see something different in what we have seen before. Therefore, repetition is also capable of producing a new attention punctuated by the memory of the preceding events, *an attending to the little differences*'; crucially, this 'turns the stage into the arena of reflection on the spectators' act of seeing' (2006: 157). Confronted with a seemingly endless form of iteration, the spectators' attention gradually shifts from the action performed on stage to the phenomenon of repetition itself, as well as to their own relation to, and role in, the performance. By focussing on the 'act of seeing' as such, repetition may facilitate a self-conscious interrogation of the processes of spectating and interpreting, suggesting that any attempt to make visible and known – on stage and beyond – always simultaneously involves a gesture of exclusion, invisibility and suppression.

In this respect, *Here We Go*'s aesthetic of repetition is not a purely self-referential exercise; rather, it is in the space of difference that the scene's political dimension can be seen to open up. Thus, the repetitiveness and insistent silence of this part serve to focus attention exclusively on the interactions between the characters, which acquire a profoundly gestic quality in the Brechtian sense of the term. Connecting the action on stage with the social conditions outside of the theatre, this arrangement encourages critical engagement with the play and raises awareness of its wider relevance regarding, for example, issues of ageing, intergenerational relations in society, and the value and purpose of life in the face of death. However, while the play's temporal distortion can, in this sense, be understood as a form of post-Brechtian *Verfremdung* which estranges conventional temporal dramaturgies and experiences of time in order to encourage critical reflection, *Here We Go* may just as well exasperate spectators, as audience reactions have demonstrated. Particularly the opacity of the final scene and its seemingly meaningless repetitive aesthetic can alienate audiences to the extent that it prevents any productive engagement with the performance. Moreover, the scene's silent repetitions serve to create a form which 'is in itself the thing it demonstrates' (Luckhurst 2014: 139). In this respect, the characters' movements first and foremost represent 'structural reflections of the insight that, in the end, we are nothing but time, temporality, and finitude' (Middeke 2017: 229). Hence, what the scene forces the spectators to confront is ultimately their own transience through an experience of the relentless passing of time. Foregrounding finality, the play's focus is not on change and agency, but on the absurdity of life, which must end in death for each and every one of us. Thus, while a Brechtian appeal to the audience is definitely more readily identifiable in 'Getting There' than in the previous scenes, the play's political fabric remains profoundly ambivalent.

Deconstructing the Dialectic

As the earlier sections have demonstrated, *Here We Go* employs spectrality as a central aesthetic and philosophical device to offer a representation of the inaccessible and inexpressible experience of death by introducing a profound ambivalence which collapses the paradigmatic contradiction between life and death. Consequently, the figures are characterized by a radically liminal ontological status on the threshold between life and death and, in a similar vein, temporal distinctions between past, present and future as well as conventional chronologies from living to dying can no longer be upheld. Through this approach, *Here We Go* creates a profound sense of disorientation for the audience, which is further reinforced by the extent to which the play's strategic spectral indeterminacy destabilizes dialectical structures, as well as principles of synthesization and change. In this respect, *Here We Go*'s strategy can be described as deconstructive in Jacques Derrida's sense of the term, which may offer a valuable lens for considering more closely the play's aesthetic mechanisms and political fabric, as I propose by way of conclusion.

Significantly, the spectre represents a central metaphor in Derridean theory, as it encapsulates not only the philosopher's poststructuralist critique but also its political and ethical implications. Most notably, Derrida employs the notion of spectrality to describe power relations within hegemonic systems (Clements 2014: 67). To the extent that any form of hegemony depends on processes of exclusion to impose itself in the first place, it automatically acquires a spectral quality: the voices, forms and ideas which need to be suppressed are still implicitly there. This paradoxical constellation harbours a distinct subversive potential. While spectrality serves to establish and maintain power, it can also function as a critical force because the invisible and hidden may, in a Rancièrean vein, reappear on the surface at any moment. In *Spectres of Marx* (1994), Derrida applies this fundamental insight to an analysis of Marxist ideology. In a typically deconstructive gesture, the idea of the spectre serves seemingly conflicting functions. On the one hand, it harks back to Karl Marx and Friedrich Engels's *The Communist Manifesto* (1848), which opens with the proclamation that '[a] specter is haunting Europe – the specter of Communism' (1964: 55), and thereby establishes a certain continuity between these philosophical traditions. On the other hand, however, it also encapsulates Derrida's critique of central Marxist principles, particularly the insistence on dichotomous structures, clear teleology and absolute stances integral to dialectical materialism. By blurring distinctions and replacing them with a profound sense of ambivalence, Derridean deconstruction destabilizes this rigid system with the help of the spectral. Given this paradox, rather than rejecting Marxism *tout court*, Derrida interrogates its fundamental tenets and is thus indebted to the very tradition it seeks to transcend: 'Deconstruction has never had any sense of interest, in my view at least, except as a radicalization, which is to say also *in the tradition* of a certain Marxism, in a certain *spirit of Marxism*. … But a radicalization is always indebted to the very thing it radicalizes' (Derrida 1994: 92). In this respect, Derrida's deconstruction of Marx also always involves a return to, and of, 'the spectres of Marx', and is thus also defined by its engagement with dialectical materialism.

In this vein, critics have more recently offered reinterpretations of Derrida's theory from a dialectical perspective, focusing more specifically on the complex intersections that can be established between Hegelian dialectics and Derrida's critique via Marxist and Adornian theory. Notably, what reunites dialectical philosophy from Hegel to the Frankfurt School with Derrida's approach is the notion of negativity (Belmonte 2002: 18–21). Thus, Derrida's assessment of the dialectical tradition from Hegel to Adorno can be understood as 'a continuation and radicalisation of Adorno's project, with *différance* as the central notion that embodies his negativity' (Grebe 2010: 96). Applying the notion of negativity to his deconstructive reading of Marx, Derrida proposes the concept of spectrality as a tool for transcending the binaries and concepts of origin and presence which underpin the conventional dialectical framework, thereby confronting Marx's legacy with 'the uncertainty, heterogeneity, multiplicity, and indeterminacy that characterize language and Being' (del Pilar Blanco and Peeren 2013: 9) in poststructuralism. As a result, Derrida imagines 'another scholar' who is 'capable, beyond the opposition between presence and non-presence, actuality and inactuality, life and non-life, of thinking the possibility of the specter, the specter as possibility' (Derrida 1994: 12). Yet, while deconstruction remains paradoxically implicated in the very framework it aims to deconstruct, it is important to acknowledge that it does not represent 'a new form of dialectic' (Belmonte 2002: 48) either. The fundamental difference between both thought systems emerges most notably in the specific purpose they attribute to negativity as a strategic epistemological device. Whereas, within a deconstructive framework, negativity 'no longer works ...; it plays' and is 'set free from the strictures of any governing economy' (Belmonte 2002: 49), dialectics foregrounds structure and form as significant sources of meaning and intention. This does not imply, however, that deconstruction rejects political significance altogether. It offers a structural approach which differs from dialectics, not through a refusal of agency and intervention, but through the mechanism by which change can be envisioned and brought about, as it attempts to leave the dialectical framework and its principles behind.

As I argue, these distinctions can be made productive for a critical consideration of *Here We Go*'s dramaturgical and political fabric. As shown in the above discussions of language, characters and dramatic time, *Here We Go*'s strategies are deconstructive to the extent that they serve to undermine the dialectical structure that the play's emphasis on spectrality as well as on the contradiction between life and death may implicitly evoke. Thus, as Andrew Jeffrey Weinstock writes, 'the ghost functions as the paradigmatic deconstructive gesture' (2004: 4). Yet, rather than offering a new understanding of the dialectic through this critical approach to conventional forms, the play seems, in Derridean spirit, to demonstrate its boundaries. While remnants of dialectical principles and concepts which have shaped Churchill's entire career are identifiable, and while a Brechtian methodology – notably ideas of *Verfremdung* and gestus – can be applied to an analysis of the play, they can no longer be synthesized within a single framework. Instead, *Here We Go* ultimately leaves these mechanisms behind. Its negativity serves more directly to confront spectators with the only truth of life – the inevitability of death – than to voice a concrete appeal to change and intervention, privileging the individual over the collective sphere. Even though this negativity is not to be confused with nihilism and a rejection of political and ethical meaning altogether, it does leave dialectics as an epistemological and dramaturgical device behind to offer a fundamentally paradoxical, absurd, pluralist and indeterminate representation and experience of liminality as a means of engaging spectators with the action on stage. Reflecting the critical, self-reflexive approach to Brecht's dialectical legacy which this book has traced in post-1990s British playwriting, Churchill's twenty-first-century plays therefore offer a decidedly more tentative outlook on the future of the post-Brechtian mode, which seems to lie in ambivalence, negativity and self-reflexivity and thus, as *Here We Go* suggests, radically 'on the threshold'.

Conclusion

This chapter has demonstrated that Caryl Churchill's dramatic oeuvre offers an important perspective on the continuity and significance of Brecht's legacy in contemporary British playwriting. Departing from the more explicit socialist and dialectical aesthetic of her earlier plays, Churchill's twenty-first-century works are indicative of a turn towards a decidedly more sceptical post-Brechtian mode. Characteristically, these texts can be situated at the nexus between Beckettian and Brechtian styles of theatre-making, which are creatively combined to resist any straightforward (and thus ultimately simplistic) attribution of meaning, to underscore the unresolved nature of the contradictions they present, and to spur an impression of disorientation on the part of both characters and audiences as a prerequisite for critique and engagement. Through a paradoxical juxtaposition of absurdist and dialectical strategies, the plays create an Adornian impression of negativity as a central dialectical tool for interrogating the potential and limits of political theatre today.

For this purpose, *Escaped Alone* employs dystopian performatives to stage a post-Brechtian form of *Verfremdung* which reverses the process of estrangement by bringing catastrophe closer to create a confrontational effect for the spectators. Blurring different spatial, temporal and experiential dimensions, the text establishes an uncomfortable proximity with the play's dystopian visions of an apocalyptic future as a means of inspiring critique. This technique is notably based on a post-Brechtian form of historicization which collapses temporal distinctions and thereby suspends the dialectical dynamic. Facilitating both intellectual and affective responses, this essentially negative dialectic is situated in a liminal space between dynamism and paralysis from which, in an Adornian spirit, a radical potentiality may emerge.

In contrast, *Here We Go* moves beyond earlier experiments to push at the boundaries of Brechtian-inspired forms of theatre-making. Collapsing the central contradiction at the heart of the play between life and death on the level of both content and form, it offers a fundamentally estranged perspective on the value of engagement in light of the inevitability of death. Employing spectrality on the level of characters and dramatic time, the play creates a profound impression of ambivalence in an indefinite realm on the threshold to death, in which notions of change, intervention and commitment seem to have become meaningless. Emphasizing finality, solipsism and futility, *Here We Go* deconstructs, in a Derridean sense of the term, the play's implicit dialectical framework, leaving dialectics as an epistemological and aesthetic device behind, and offering an experience of negativity that can no longer be reconciled by the spectators.

Conclusion

Preoccupied throughout his career with imagining – or, perhaps more accurately, with trying to actively shape – his legacy for future generations, Brecht was particularly explicit about his expectations with regard to his obituary, which he discussed with a Protestant cleric: 'Don't write that you admire me! Write that I was an uncomfortable person, and that I intend to remain so after my death. Even then there are certain possibilities' (Brecht qtd. in Esslin 1971: 204). In this spirit, Brecht has indeed continued to be an 'uncomfortable' presence in contemporary culture, provoking and stimulating artists, philosophers and audiences in Germany and beyond. As this book has shown, Brecht's impact has been particularly long-lasting and pervasive in Britain, where his work has continued to provide an important, albeit contentious, source of inspiration for playwrights and theatre practitioners in the twenty-first century.

As a theatrical and political provocateur, Brecht designed his projects with the intention of resisting and challenging the status quo, reflecting his stubborn insistence on the possibility of change and intervention against all the odds, as well as his strong belief in the theatre as the medium *par excellence* for achieving these aims by empowering spectators to analyse, voice critique and transform reality. While Brecht's works have inarguably remained acutely relevant as thought-provoking parables for our times, the 'discomfort' they trigger today emerges most notably from their philosophical and political core, which is defined by Brecht's engagement with dialectics as an epistemological device for critical analysis, and as a fundamental aesthetic paradigm in the context of his theatre model. Adopting a specific perspective on social reality as unstable and therefore changeable by foregrounding the conflicts and oppositions under the surface, dialectics offers a radical and progressive framework which Brecht applied to his theatre practice. With the aim of staging this dialectical worldview, the characteristic dramaturgy of epic theatre is designed to expose the contradictions underlying social relations, and to encourage dialectical thinking in the audience as a prerequisite for critique, commitment and, ultimately, transformation.

In order to understand the role, forms and functions of this distinctly Brechtian approach to theatre-making at the turn of the millennium, this book has argued that it is essential to take into account this dialectical dimension underpinning Brecht's methodology, and has offered a critical examination of its potential and limits from a contemporary vantage point. For this purpose, this study has notably focused on the increasingly intricate dynamics that can be observed in the relationship between politics and aesthetics in the present moment, and has investigated their implications for Brechtian theatre. In dialogue with Adorno and Rancière's theories, I have adopted a philosophical perspective to highlight that, while fundamental tenets of dialectical thought – in particular concepts of absoluteness, clarity, teleology and synthesis – seem to require revision today, the characteristic dialectical insistence on notions of agency, change and contradiction, as well as on a dynamic understanding of social reality, continues to provide a powerful and stimulating framework for analysis and critique – despite, or precisely because of the anti-dialectical impact of neoliberal and postmodernist philosophies which ostensibly paralyse attempts at resistance and political commitment.

As a constitutive part of this search for a redefinition of the nexus between politics and aesthetics, contemporary British drama has productively engaged with the Brechtian model, critically examining its functions and creatively reimagining dialectical theatre for the purposes of the contemporary moment. Thus, drawing on a wide range of examples, this study has shown how the plays interrogate the value of dialectics as a radical dramaturgical and analytical device in the present moment, while working actively towards shaping new Brechtian-inspired forms that are capable of engaging with, and responding to, the paradoxes of the twenty-first-century context. This is above all reflected in a decidedly more critical approach to Brecht's theory and practice, as the plays stage a failure of conventional dialectical forms, evident for example in their rejection of binary structures, of the belief in resolution as well as of ideas of mastery and knowledge, while creatively rethinking the potentiality of dialectical analysis on the basis of contradiction, negativity and ambivalence. Most notably, this indicates a clear shift in the history of Brecht's reception in Britain, as the turn to a 'post-Brechtian' mode of playwriting and performance, which this study has identified in the late 1990s, can be described in terms of a negotiation and interrogation – rather than straightforward application – of Brecht's legacy as well as a self-reflexive enquiry into the forms and functions of political drama more broadly.

This criticism – both of social reality and, most crucially, of established forms of theatre-making – is above all expressed through a heightened aesthetic hybridity, with which the plays explore the radical potential of the theatre today. The case studies have demonstrated how post-Brechtian dramaturgies draw on a variety of theatrical styles to create mobilizing pieces of theatre, thereby productively interacting with and shaping the energetic and aesthetically diverse field of contemporary playwriting in Britain. In this vein, I have suggested with reference to the work of Mark Ravenhill that the emergence of 'in-yer-face' theatre in the late 1990s can be understood as an innovative approach to Brecht's model. This observation has not only shed a fresh light on the controversial question of the 'in-yer-face' sensibility's political fabric but has also challenged common understandings of Brecht's conceptualization of theatre and spectatorship. Thus, I have argued that the specific use of provocation and shock within the post-Brechtian mode serves to diagnose a crisis of conventional dialectical mechanisms, which is reflected most explicitly in a strategic manipulation of dialectical categories in public discourse. At the same time, these visceral tools serve the purpose of initiating a new form of theatre based on 'dialectical emotions' rather than reason, thereby revaluing individual experience and affective engagement as significant motors of dialectical critique. In this sense, the post-Brechtian paradigm gives rise to a more experiential form of spectatorship on the basis of an impression of ambivalence and uncertainty. As a result, the audience is, in the spirit of Rancière's concept of 'emancipation', attributed a more central role as part of the dialectical negotiations on stage and in-between theatre and reality, which foregrounds the significance of both affective and intellectual forms of engagement – a shift which is pertinent to all examples discussed in this book.

As I have illustrated with regard to Caryl Churchill's twenty-first-century plays, the post-Brechtian mode also fruitfully interacts with the theatre of the absurd. While Brecht and Beckett are widely understood as representatives of dichotomously opposed styles in theatre history, I have offered a different perspective by showing how important intersections between Brechtian and Beckettian modes can be identified with the help of Adorno's notion of negativity. These seemingly paradoxical juxtapositions between dialectical and absurd devices are employed by Churchill to navigate the politics of her plays and to critically engage with established forms of theatre-making, thereby also pushing at the boundaries of the texts' dialectical framework. In this vein, a distinct development can be identified in her oeuvre, as her plays have radically shifted from a more explicitly socialist-feminist aesthetic clearly inspired by Brecht, which dominated her works up until the 1980s, to a decidedly more obscure, cryptic and politically ambiguous style at the turn of the millennium. Yet, as I have shown, rather than offering a nihilist outlook on the radical potential of the theatre, these twenty-first-century plays in fact re-function, in an Adornian vein, strategies of the absurd as dialectical tools to give expression to the struggle for a new form of theatre which can respond to the political and social conditions of the contemporary moment. Through a reversal of Brechtian principles of *Verfremdung* and historicization, they create a confrontational and disorientating aesthetic which not only underscores the central role of the audience in the process of dialectical interpretation but also interrogates the forms and functions of the theatre as a medium of critique.

This emphasis on spectatorship is also evident in David Greig's dramatic works, which combine different theatrical styles to create a post-Brechtian aesthetic based on the audience's imaginative engagement with the paradoxes presented on stage. For this purpose, Greig employs strategies which Brecht himself drew on for developing his theatre theory and practice, most notably the use of music and the integration of amateurs, to heighten the plays' emphasis on the imagination as well as on the audience's contributions to the performances. This participatory approach is particularly pertinent to Brecht's *Lehrstücke*, which invite spectatorial involvement and empathetic identification and thereby blur the boundaries not only between stage and auditorium but also between conventional and non-professional actors. Significantly, these experiments with participation and amateurism as a means of implicating the audience are representative of wider trends in contemporary British drama, where participatory and immersive forms have proliferated, erasing distinctions between fiction and reality, and redefining the relationship between stage and audience to produce a radical and progressive piece of theatre.

The limits of these developments towards spectatorial agency, control and responsibility are particularly brought into focus by the work of theatre-makers Andy Smith and Tim Crouch, whose plays can be said to offer a self-reflexive perspective on these tendencies within a dialectical framework. Directly implicating the spectators into their metatheatrical explorations by casting them as co-producers and co-authors of the performances, their shows specifically test forms of sincerity and insincerity in the relationship between stage and auditorium – notions which have recently gained increasing importance as a means of negotiating a (re)turn to engagement in the (post-)postmodernist moment. Establishing a precarious balance between sincere and genuine interaction with the audience, on the one hand, and an ironic undermining of any productive kind of exchange, on the other, Smith and Crouch's theatre problematizes the potential of a dialectical mode based on ambivalence, self-reflexivity and spectatorial experience.

Creatively interacting with a variety of trends and styles, the post-Brechtian mode is therefore defined by a distinct hybridity which facilitates experimentation with the forms and functions of Brechtian dialectics on the contemporary British stage. Significantly, the ambivalence which results from these creative reimaginings shapes the plays' treatment of thematic concerns, their aesthetic characteristics as well as the audience's experience of the performances, and can thus be understood as offering above all a critical perspective on the progressive potential of Brecht's model in the twenty-first century. Hence, emphasizing notions of negativity, failure and indeterminacy, the post-Brechtian must be situated on the threshold between potentiality and failure. Yet, as this study has shown, it is precisely this precarious position which opens up a considerable creative and radical potential. Indeed, the current sociopolitical, economic and cultural situation would – unfortunately – still be instantly recognizable to Brecht and will therefore in all likelihood continue to provide a fertile ground for Brechtian-inspired dialectical theatre, paving the way for ever more daring experiments with Brecht's method which will keep pushing at the boundaries of drama and politics in an effort to unsettle the theatrical and political status quo. In this respect, the history of the 'special relationship' between Brecht and Britain looks to a bright future, which is why this study on post-Brechtian theatre in post-1990s British drama must necessarily be considered unfinished. Of course, this unfinished quality constitutes a central element of Brecht's own aesthetic theory and practice, which are always open to critique, development and creative adjustments, and it is in this sense that Brechtian dialectics will continue to offer a contentious source of inspiration and a critical means for renewal and engagement for playwrights and theatre-makers in Britain and beyond.

Therefore, it is only apt that, by way of conclusion, this survey (re)turns to Brecht himself to draw attention to the significance of indeterminacy as a mobilizing impulse at the heart of Brechtian theatre itself, and to emphatically stress the fundamental optimism inscribed into his project against all the odds – perhaps the most significant lesson we can learn from Brecht in a time of a seemingly never-ending escalation of political, social, economic and environmental crises. It is thus with an emphasis on the necessity to keep thinking with, through, about and certainly also against and beyond Brecht that this study closes with a reference to the ironic, but all the more assertive address to the audience in the epilogue to *The Good Person of Szechwan*. While fully aware of the impossibility of ultimately achieving denouement and closure, The Player nevertheless calls on the spectators to take on the responsibility to continue to engage with theatre in an insistence on the possibility of change – an appeal which could not be timelier: 'Ladies and gentlemen, don't feel let down: / We know this ending makes some people frown. / … Indeed it is a curious way of coping: / To close the play, leaving the issue open. / … Ladies and gentlemen, in you we trust: / There must be happy endings, must, must, must!' (Brecht 1998: 111).

Bibliography

Actors Touring Company (n.d.), 'The Events by David Greig: Choir Pack', PDF.
Adiseshiah, S. (2009), *Churchill's Socialism: Political Resistance in the Plays of Caryl Churchill*, Newcastle upon Tyne: Cambridge Scholars.
Adiseshiah, S. (2016), 'Spectatorship and the New (Critical) Sincerity: The Case of Forced Entertainment's *Tommorow's Parties*', *Journal of Contemporary Drama in English* 4 (1): 180–95.
Adorno, T. W. (1973), *Negative Dialectics*, trans. E. B. Ashton, London: Routledge.
Adorno, T. W. (1977), 'Commitment', in T. Adorno et al., *Aesthetics and Politics: Debates between Ernst Bloch, Georg Lukács, Bertolt Brecht, Walter Benjamin, Theodor Adorno*, 177–95, London: Verso.
Adorno, T. W. (1982), 'Trying to Understand *Endgame*', *New German Critique* 26: 119–50.
Adorno, T. W. (1997), *Aesthetic Theory*, ed. G. Adorno and R. Tiedemann, trans. R. Hullot-Kentor, London: Continuum.
Adorno, T. W. (2008), *Lectures on Negative Dialectics: Fragments of a Lecture Course 1965/1966*, ed. R. Tiedemann, trans. R. Livingstone, Cambridge: Polity.
Aitchison, N. B. (1999), *Macbeth: Man and Myth*, Thrupp: Sutton.
Alker, S., and H. F. Nelson (2007), 'Macbeth, the Jacobean Scot, and the Politics of the Union', *Studies in English Literature, 1500–1900* 47 (2): 379–401.
Alston, A. (2016), *Beyond Immersive Theatre: Aesthetics, Politics and Productive Participation*, Basingstoke: Palgrave.
Anderson, B. (1991), *Imagined Communities: Reflections on the Origin and Spread of Nationalism*, rev. edn, London: Verso.
Angelaki, V. (2013), 'Whose Voice? Tim Crouch's *The Author* and Active Listening on the Contemporary Stage', *Sillages Critiques* 16: n.p. Available online: https://journals.openedition.org/sillagescritiques/2989 (accessed 15 February 2020).
Angelaki, V. (2017), *Social and Political Theatre in 21st-Century Britain: Staging Crisis*, London: Bloomsbury.
Angel-Perez, E. (2006), *Voyages au bout du possible: Les théâtres du traumatisme de Samuel Beckett à Sarah Kane*, Paris: Klincksieck.
Angel-Perez, E. (2013), 'Back to Verbal Theatre: Post-Post-Dramatic Theatres from Crimp to Crouch', *Etudes britanniques contemporaines* 45: n.p. Available online: https://journals.openedition.org/ebc/862 (accessed 15 February 2020).
Arendt, H. (2006), *Eichmann in Jerusalem: A Report on the Banality of Evil*, London: Penguin.

Aston, E. (2013), 'But Not That: Caryl Churchill's Political Shape Shifting at the Turn of the Millennium', *Modern Drama* 56 (2): 145–64.
Aston, E. (2015), 'Caryl Churchill's "Dark Ecology"', in C. Lavery and C. Finburgh (eds), *Rethinking the Theatre of the Absurd: Ecology, the Environment and the Greening of the Modern Stage*, 1–58, London: Bloomsbury.
Aston, E. (2018), 'Enter Stage Left: "Recognition," "Redistribution," and the A-Affect', *Contemporary Theatre Review* 28 (3): 299–309.
Auslander, P. (1987), 'Towards a Concept of the Political in Postmodern Theatre', *Theatre Journal* 39 (1): 20–34.
Baccolini, R., and T. Moylan (2003), 'Dystopia and Histories', in R. Baccolini and T. Moylan (eds), *Dark Horizons: Science Fiction and the Dystopian Imagination*, 1–12, London: Routledge.
Barnett, D. (2011), 'Toward a Definition of Post-Brechtian Performance: The Example of *In the Jungle of the Cities* at the Berliner Ensemble, 1971', *Modern Drama* 54 (3): 333–56.
Barnett, D. (2013a), 'Brecht as Great Shakespearean: A Lifelong Connection', in R. Morse (ed.), *Hugo, Pasternak, Brecht, Césaire*, vol. 14 of *Great Shakespeareans*, 113–54, London: Bloomsbury.
Barnett, D. (2013b), 'Performing Dialectics in an Age of Uncertainty, or: Why Post-Brechtian ≠ Postdramatic', in K. Jürs-Munby, J. Carroll and S. Giles (eds), *Postdramatic Theatre and the Political: International Perspectives on Contemporary Performance*, 47–66, London: Bloomsbury.
Barnett, D. (2015), *Brecht in Practice: Theatre, Theory and Performance*, London: Bloomsbury.
Barnett, D. (2016), 'Dialectics and the Brechtian Tradition', *Performance Research* 21 (3): 6–15.
Barnett, D. (2017), 'The Possibilities of Contemporary Dialectical Theatre: The Example of Representing Neonazism in Germany', *Contemporary Theatre Review* 27 (2): 245–62.
Beckett, S. (1965), *Waiting for Godot*, London: Faber and Faber.
Beckett, S. (1969), *Endgame*, London: Faber and Faber.
Belmonte, N. (2002), 'Evolving Negativity: From Hegel to Derrida', *Philosophy & Social Criticism* 28 (1): 18–58.
Belsey, C. (2008), *Shakespeare in Theory and Practice*, Edinburgh: Edinburgh University Press.
Benjamin, W. (1998), *Understanding Brecht*, trans. Anna Bostock, London: Verso.
Bennett, M. Y. (2015), *The Cambridge Introduction to Theatre and Literature of the Absurd*, Cambridge: Cambridge University Press.
Berlant, L. (2011), *Cruel Optimism*, Durham, NC: Duke University Press.
Bhabha, H. K. (1990), *Nation and Narration*, London: Routledge.
Bharucha, R. (2014), *Terror and Performance*, London: Routledge.

Billington, M. (2013), 'Bertolt Brecht: Irresistible Force or Forgotten Chapter in Theatrical History?', *Guardian*, 18 September. Available online: https://www.theguardian.com/stage/2013/sep/18/bertolt-brecht-arturo-ui-revival (accessed 13 February 2020).
Bishop, C. (2004), 'Antagonism and Relational Aesthetics', *October* 110: 51–79.
Boll, J. (2013), *The New War Plays: From Kane to Harris*, Basingstoke: Palgrave.
Botham, P. (2014), 'From Tribe to Chorus: David Greig's *The Events*', *TCG Circle*. Available online: http://www.tcgcircle.org/2014/07/from-tribe-to-chorus-david-greigs-the-events/ (accessed 14 May 2016).
Bottici, C. (2011), 'From Imagination to the Imaginary and Beyond: Towards a Theory of Imaginal Politics', in C. Bottici and B. Challand (eds), *The Politics of Imagination*, 16–37, Abingdon: Birkbeck Law Press.
Bottoms, S. (2011), 'Materialising the Audience: Tim Crouch's Sight Specifics in *ENGLAND* and *The Author*', *Contemporary Theatre Review* 21 (4): 445–63.
Boxall, P. (2003), *Samuel Beckett: Waiting for Godot, Endgame*, Basingstoke: Palgrave.
Brantley, B. (2015), 'In *The Events*, a Shooting Leaves a Survivor in Purgatory', *New York Times*, 12 February. Available online: https://www.nytimes.com/2015/02/13/theater/review-in-the-events-a-shooting-leaves-a-survivor-in-purgatory.html (accessed 2 February 2020).
Brecht, B. (1977), 'Against Georg Lukács', in T. Adorno et al., *Aesthetics and Politics: Debates between Ernst Bloch, Georg Lukács, Bertolt Brecht, Walter Benjamin, Theodor Adorno*, 68–85, London: Verso.
Brecht, B. (1978), *Die Lehrstücke*, ed. B. K. Tragelehn, Leipzig: Reclam.
Brecht, B. (1992), *Schriften 1*, vol. 21 of *Werke: Große kommentierte Berliner und Frankfurter Ausgabe*, ed. W. Hecht et al., Frankfurt/M.: Suhrkamp.
Brecht, B. (1993), *Schriften 2*, vol. 22.1 of *Werke: Große kommentierte Berliner und Frankfurter Ausgabe*, ed. W. Hecht et al., Frankfurt/M.: Suhrkamp.
Brecht, B. (1997), *The Mother*, in B. Brecht, *Collected Plays: Three*, ed. J. Willett, 93–151, London: Bloomsbury.
Brecht, B. (1998), *The Good Person of Szechwan*, in B. Brecht, *Collected Plays: Six*, ed. J. Willett and R. Manheim, 1–111, London: Bloomsbury.
Brecht, B. (2001), *Fear and Misery of the Third Reich*, in B. Brecht, *Collected Plays: Four*, ed. T. Kuhn and J. Willett, trans. J. Willett, 115–206, London: Bloomsbury.
Brecht, B. (2015a), *Brecht on Theatre*, 3rd rev. edn, ed. M. Silberman, S. Giles and T. Kuhn, London: Bloomsbury.
Brecht, B. (2015b), 'Messingkauf, or Buying Brass', in T. Kuhn, S. Giles and M. Silberman (eds), *Brecht on Performance*, 1–141, London: Bloomsbury.
Brecht, B. (2019), 'Freedom and Democracy', in T. Kuhn and D. Constantine (eds and trans), *The Collected Poems of Bertolt Brecht*, 935–40, New York: Liveright.
Brown, I. (2016), *History as Theatrical Metaphor: History, Myth and National Identities in Modern Scottish Drama*, Basingstoke: Palgrave.

Brown, W. (2017), 'What Exactly Is Neoliberalism?', *Void Network*, 4 April. Available online: http://voidnetwork.gr/2017/04/04/exactly-neoliberalism-talk-wendy-brown/ (accessed 13 February 2020).

Buck-Morss, S. (1977), *The Origin of Negative Dialectics: Theodor W. Adorno, Walter Benjamin, and the Frankfurt Institute*, New York: Free Press.

Buffini, M. (2015), 'Caryl Churchill: The Playwright's Finest Hours', *Guardian*, 29 June. Available online: https://www.theguardian.com/stage/2015/jun/29/caryl-churchill-the-playwrights-finest-hours (accessed 4 February 2020).

Butler, J. (2011), 'Hannah Arendt's Challenge to Adolf Eichmann', *Guardian*, 29 August. Available online: https://www.theguardian.com/commentisfree/2011/aug/29/hannah-arendt-adolf-eichmann-banality-of-evil (accessed 8 February 2020).

Calico, J. H. (2008), *Brecht at the Opera*, Berkeley: University of California Press.

Capitani, M. E. (2016), 'Appropriating *Macbeth* in the Contact Zone: The Politics of Place, Space, and Liminality in David Greig's *Dunsinane*', *Anglistica AION* 20 (2): 17–29.

Carney, S. (2005), *Brecht and Critical Theory: Dialectics and Contemporary Aesthetics*, London: Routledge.

Carney, S. (2013), *The Politics and Poetics of Contemporary English Tragedy*, Toronto: University of Toronto Press.

Churchill, C. (2008), *This Is a Chair*, in C. Churchill, *Plays: 4*, 37–58, London: Nick Hern Books.

Churchill, C. (2015), *Here We Go*, London: Nick Hern Books.

Churchill, C. (2016), *Escaped Alone*, London: Nick Hern Books.

Clements, R. (2014), 'Apprehending the Spectral: Hauntology and Precarity in Caryl Churchill's Plays', in M. Luckhurst and E. Morin (eds), *Theatre and Ghosts: Materiality, Performance and Modernity*, 65–81, Basingstoke: Palgrave.

Clohesy, A. M. (2013), *Politics of Empathy: Ethics, Solidarity, Recognition*, London: Routledge.

Crouch, T. (2011a), *The Author*, in T. Crouch, *Plays One*, 161–203, London: Oberon.

Crouch, T. (2011b), '*The Author*: Response and Responsibility', *Contemporary Theatre Review* 21 (4): 416–22.

Crouch, T. (2011c), 'Death of *The Author*: How Did My Play Fare in LA?', *Guardian*, 7 March. Available online: https://www.theguardian.com/stage/2011/mar/07/tim-crouch-the-author-la-tour (accessed 11 February 2020).

Crouch, T. (2016), 'Standing with the Audience', *Coup de théâtre* 30: 175–89.

Cummings, L. B. (2016), *Empathy as Dialogue in Theatre and Performance*, Basingstoke: Palgrave.

Dahl, M. K. (1992), 'State Terror and Dramatic Countermeasures', in J. Orr and D. Klaić (eds), *Terrorism and Modern Drama*, 109–22, Edinburgh: Edinburgh University Press.

Defraeye, P. (2004), 'In-Yer-Face Theatre? Reflections on Provocation and Provoked Audiences in Contemporary Theatre', in H.-U. Mohr and K. Mächler (eds), *Extending the Code: New Forms of Dramatic and Theatrical Expressions*, 79–97, Trier: WVT.

del Pilar Blanco, M., and E. Peeren (2013), 'Introduction', in M. del Pilar Blanco and E. Peeren (eds), *The Spectralities Reader: Ghosts and Haunting in Contemporary Cultural Theory*, 1–28, London: Bloomsbury.

Delgado-García, C. (2014), 'Dematerialised Political and Theatrical Legacies: Rethinking the Roots and Influences of Tim Crouch's Work', *Platform: Journal of Theatre and Performing Arts* 8 (1): 69–85.

Delgado-García, C. (2015), *Rethinking Character in Contemporary British Theatre: Aesthetics, Politics, Subjectivity*, Berlin: De Gruyter.

Delgado-García, C. (2017), '"We're All in This Together": Reality, Vulnerability and Democratic Representation in Tim Crouch's *The Author*', in M. Aragay and M. Middeke (eds), *Of Precariousness: Vulnerabilities, Responsibilities, Communities in 21st-Century British Drama and Theatre*, 91–107, Berlin: De Gruyter.

Derrida, J. (1994), *Specters of Marx: The State of the Debt, the Work of Mourning, and the New International*, trans. P. Kamuf, London: Routledge.

Desmet, C. (2014), 'Recognizing Shakespeare, Rethinking Fidelity: A Rhetoric and Ethics of Appropriation', in A. Huang and E. Rivlin (eds), *Shakespeare and the Ethics of Appropriation*, 41–57, Basingstoke: Palgrave.

Desmet, C., N. Loper and J. Casey (2017), 'Introduction', in C. Desmet, N. Loper and J. Casey (eds), *Shakespeare/Not Shakespeare*, 1–22, Basingstoke: Palgrave.

de Waal, A. (2017a), 'Expel, Exploit, Exfoliate: Taking on Terror in Mark Ravenhill's *Shoot/Get Treasure/Repeat* (2007)', in K. Frank and C. Lusin (eds), *Finance, Terror, and Science on Stage: Current Public Concerns in 21st-Century British Drama*, 59–78, Tübingen: Narr.

de Waal, A. (2017b), *Theatre on Terror: Subject Positions in British Drama*, Berlin: de Gruyter.

Diamond, E. (1997), *Unmaking Mimesis: Essays on Feminism and Theater*, New York: Routledge.

Dicecco, N. (2017), 'Aura of Againness: Performing Adaptation', in T. Leitch (ed.), *The Oxford Handbook of Adaptation Studies*, 607–21, Oxford: Oxford University Press.

Dolan, J. (2005), *Utopia in Performance: Finding Hope at the Theatre*, Ann Arbor: University of Michigan Press.

Ellis, J. (1982), 'The Literary Adaptation', *Screen* 23 (1): 3–5.

Esslin, M. (1971), *Brecht: The Man and His Work*, New York: Norton.

Esslin, M. (1973), *The Theatre of the Absurd*, rev. edn, Woodstock, NY: Overlook Press.

Finburgh, C. (2017), *Watching War on the Twenty-First Century Stage: Spectacles of Conflict*, London: Bloomsbury.

Fischer-Lichte, E. (2004), *History of European Drama and Theatre*, trans. J. Riley, London: Routledge.
Fragkou, M. (2018), *Ecologies of Precarity in Twenty-First-Century Theatre: Politics, Affect, Responsibility*, London: Bloomsbury.
Frank, M. C. (2017), *The Cultural Imaginary of Terrorism in Public Discourse, Literature, and Film: Narrating Terror*, London: Routledge.
Freeman, E. (2010), *Time Binds: Queer Temporalities, Queer Histories*, Durham: Duke University Press.
Freshwater, H. (2011), '"You Say Something": Audience Participation and *The Author*', *Contemporary Theatre Review* 24 (1): 405–9.
Frieze, J. (2012), 'Actualizing a Spectator Like You: The Ethics of Intrusive-Hypothetical', *Performing Ethos* 3 (1): 7–22.
Funk, W. (2015), *The Literature of Reconstruction: Authentic Fiction in the New Millennium*, London: Bloomsbury.
Garde, U., and M. Mumford (2016), *Theatre of Real People: Diverse Encounters at Berlin's Hebbel am Ufer and Beyond*, London: Bloomsbury.
Garner, S. B. (1990), 'Post-Brechtian Anatomies: Weiss, Bond, and the Politics of Embodiment', *Theatre Journal* 42 (2): 145–64.
Giles, S. (2014), 'Introduction', in T. Kuhn, S. Giles and M. Silberman (eds), *Brecht on Performance: Messingkauf and Modelbooks*, 1–9, London: Bloomsbury.
Giroux, H. A. (2013), 'The Disimagination Machine and the Pathologies of Power', *symploke* 21 (1–2): 257–69.
Gobert, R. D. (2014), *The Theatre of Caryl Churchill*, London: Bloomsbury.
Goode, C. (2015), *The Forest and the Field: Changing Theatre in a Changing World*, London: Oberon.
Gottlieb, V. (2003), 'Theatre Today – The "New Realism"', *Contemporary Theatre Review* 13 (1): 5–14.
Gray, R. (2013), 'Director's Note', in D. Greig, *The Events*, xi, London: Faber and Faber.
Grebe, E. (2010), 'Negativity, Difference and Critique: The Ethical Moment in Complexity', in P. Cilliers and R. Preiser (eds), *Complexity, Difference and Identity*, 95–111, Dordrecht: Springer.
Greig, D. (1999), *The Speculator*, London: Methuen.
Greig, D. (2007), 'Rough Theatre', in G. Saunders and R. D'Monté (eds), *Cool Britannia? British Political Drama in the 1990s*, 208–21, Basingstoke: Palgrave.
Greig, D. (2010), *Dunsinane*, London: Faber and Faber.
Greig, D. (2013a), *The Events*, London: Faber and Faber.
Greig, D. (2013b), 'Why the Debate on Scottish Independence Might Be More Interesting Than You Think?', *Bella Caledonia*, 4 August. Available online: https://bellacaledonia.wordpress.com/2013/08/04/why-the-debate-on-scottish-independence-might-be-more-interesting-than-you-think/ (accessed 1 February 2020).

Greig, D. (2014), *The Events*, rev. edn, London: Faber and Faber.
Greig, D. (2016), 'Collaborating with Audiences', *Journal of Contemporary Drama in English* 4 (1): 243–54.
Gritzner, K. (2015), *Adorno and Modern Theatre: The Drama of the Damaged Self in Bond, Rudkin, Barker and Kane*, Basingstoke: Palgrave.
Grochala, S. (2017), *The Contemporary Political Play: Rethinking Dramaturgical Structure*, London: Bloomsbury.
Gruber, W. (2010), *Offstage Space, Narrative, and the Theatre of the Imagination*, Basingstoke: Palgrave.
Hartl, A. (2018a), '"Finstere Zeiten": Post-brechtsche Dialektik im Werk von Caryl Churchill', in J. Hillesheim (ed.), *Bertolt Brecht: Zwischen Tradition und Moderne*, 337–57, Würzburg: Königshausen & Neumann.
Hartl, A. (2018b), 'Recycling Brecht in Britain: David Greig's *The Events* as Post-Brechtian *Lehrstück*', in T. Kuhn, D. Barnett and T. F. Rippey (eds), *Recycling Brecht*, 152–69, Rochester, NY: Camden.
Harvey, D. (2005), *A Brief History of Neoliberalism*, Oxford: Oxford University Press.
Harvie, J. (2005), *Staging the UK*, Manchester: Manchester University Press.
Harvie, J. (2018), 'Boom! Adversarial Ageism, Chrononormativity, and the Anthropocene', *Contemporary Theatre Review* 28 (3): 332–44.
Heinemann, M. (1994), 'How Brecht Read Shakespeare', in J. Dollimore and A. Sinfield (eds), *Political Shakespeare: Essays in Cultural Materialism*, 2nd edn, 226–54, Manchester: Manchester University Press.
Henke, C. (2018), 'Precarious Virtuality in Participatory Theatre: Tim Crouch's *The Author*', in M. Aragay and M. Middeke (eds), *Representations of the Precarious in Contemporary British Theatre*, 77–90, Berlin: De Gruyter.
Hodges, A. (2011), *The 'War on Terror' Narrative: Discourses and Intertextuality in the Construction and Contestation of Sociopolitical Reality*, Oxford: Oxford University Press.
Hodges, A., and C. Nilep (2007), 'Introduction: Discourse, War and Terrorism', in A. Hodges and C. Nilep (eds), *Discourse, War and Terrorism*, 3–17, Amsterdam: John Benjamins.
Holdsworth, N. (2010), *Theatre and Nation*, Basingstoke: Palgrave.
Holdsworth, N. (2013), 'David Greig', in D. Rebellato (ed.), *Modern British Playwriting: 2000–2009 – Voices, Documents, New Interpretations*, 169–89, London: Bloomsbury.
Huang, A., and E. Rivlin (2014), 'Shakespeare and the Ethics of Appropriation', in A. Huang and E. Rivlin (eds), *Shakespeare and the Ethics of Appropriation*, 1–20, Basingstoke: Palgrave.
Hubbard, W. (2013), 'Falling Faint: On Syncopated Spectatorship and *The Author*', *Performance Research* 18 (4): 22–9.
Hughes, J. (2011), *Performance in a Time of Terror: Critical Mimesis and the Age of Uncertainty*, Manchester: Manchester University Press.

Hutcheon, L. (1988), *A Poetics of Postmodernism: History, Theory, Fiction*, London: Routledge.
Hutcheon, L. (2013), *A Theory of Adaptation*, 2nd edn, London: Routledge.
Illouz, E. (2007), *Cold Intimacies: The Making of Emotional Capitalism*, Cambridge: Polity.
Jackson, R. (2005), *Writing the War on Terrorism: Language, Politics and Counter-Terrorism*, Manchester: Manchester University Press.
Jameson, F. (1991), *Postmodernism, or, the Cultural Logic of Late Capitalism*, Durham: Duke University Press.
Jameson, F. (2008), 'Persistencies of the Dialectic: Three Sites', in B. Ollman and T. Smith (eds), *Dialectics for the New Century*, 118–31, Basingstoke: Palgrave.
Juergensmeyer, M. (2017), *Terror in the Mind of God: The Global Rise of Religious Violence*, 4th edn, Oakland: University of California Press.
Kalb, J. (1998). *The Theater of Heiner Müller*, Cambridge: Cambridge University Press.
Katz, C. (2007), 'Banal Terrorism: Spatial Fetishism and Everyday Insecurity', in D. Gregory and A. Pred (eds), *Violent Geographies: Fear, Terror, and Political Violence*, 349–61, London: Routledge.
Kearney, R. (1998), *Poetics of Imagining: Modern to Post-Modern*, Edinburgh: Edinburgh University Press.
Kelly, A. (2010), 'David Foster Wallace and the New Sincerity in American Fiction', in D. Hering (ed.), *Consider David Foster Wallace: Critical Essays*, 131–46, Los Angeles: SSMG.
Kershaw, B. (1999), *The Radical in Performance: Between Brecht and Baudrillard*, London: Routledge.
Klaić, D. (1991), *The Plot of the Future: Utopia and Dystopia in Modern Drama*, Ann Arbor: University of Michigan Press.
Kleinberg-Levin, D. (2015), *Beckett's Words: The Promise of Happiness in a Time of Mourning*, London: Bloomsbury.
Krabiel, K.-D. (2001), 'Die Lehrstücke', in J. Knopf (ed.), *Brecht-Handbuch: Stücke*, vol. 1, 28–39, Stuttgart: Metzler.
Kritzer, A. H. (2002), 'Political Currents in Caryl Churchill's Plays at the Turn of the Millennium', in M. Maufort and F. Bellarsi (eds), *Crucible of Cultures: Anglophone Drama at the Dawn of a New Millennium*, 57–67, Brussels: Peter Lang.
Kritzer, A. H. (2008), *Political Theatre in Post-Thatcher Britain: New Writing – 1995–2005*, Basingstoke: Palgrave.
Laclau, E., and C. Mouffe (1985), *Hegemony and Socialist Strategy: Towards a Radical Democratic Politics*, London: Verso.
Lanier, D. (2014), 'Shakespearean Rhizomatics: Appropriation, Ethics, Value', in A. Huang and E. Rivlin (eds), *Shakespeare and the Ethics of Appropriation*, 21–40, Basingstoke: Palgrave.
Lavender, A. (2016), *Performance in the Twenty-First Century: Theatres of Engagement*, London: Routledge.

Lehmann, H.-T. (2002), 'B, B, and B. Fifteen Minutes to Comply', in A. Tatlow (ed.), *Where Extremes Meet: Rereading Brecht and Beckett*, 43–8, Madison: University of Wisconsin Press.

Lehmann, H.-T. (2006), *Postdramatic Theatre*, trans. K. Jürs-Munby, London: Routledge.

Lehmann, H.-T. (2012), *Das politische Schreiben: Essays zu Theatertexten*, Berlin: Theater der Zeit.

Levitas, R., and L. Sargisson (2003), 'Utopia in Dark Times: Optimism/ Pessimism and Utopia/Dystopia', in R. Baccolini and T. Moylan (eds), *Dark Horizons: Science Fiction and the Dystopian Imagination*, 13–27, London: Routledge.

Linneman, E. (2010), ' "A Mistaken Understanding": *Dunsinane* and New Writing at the RSC', *Borrowers and Lenders: The Journal of Shakespeare and Appropriation* 5 (1). Available online: http://www.borrowers.uga.edu/782405/show (accessed 1 February 2020).

Love, C. (2014), 'Stories about Stories', *Exeunt Magazine*, 30 June. Available online: http://exeuntmagazine.com/features/stories-about-stories/ (accessed 10 February 2020).

Love, C. (2017), *Tim Crouch's* An Oak Tree, London: Routledge.

Luckhurst, M. (2014), *Caryl Churchill*, London: Routledge.

Lyotard, J.-F. (1986), *The Postmodern Condition: A Report on Knowledge*, trans. G. Bennington and B. Massumi, Manchester: Manchester University Press.

Malpas, S. (2005), *The Postmodern*, London: Routledge.

Marx, K., and F. Engels (1964), *The Communist Manifesto*, ed. J. Katz, trans. S. Moore, New York: Pocket.

McConachie, B. (2012), 'Moving Spectators toward Progressive Politics by Combining Brechtian Theory with Cognitive Science', in M. Alrutz, J. Listengarten and M. Van Duyn Wood (eds), *Playing with Theory in Theatre Practice*, 148–60, Basingstoke: Palgrave.

McGinn, C. (2008), 'Mark Ravenhill's Iraq Plays Blog', *Time Out*, 7 April. Available online: https://www.timeout.com/london/theatre/mark-ravenhills-iraq-plays-blog-1 (accessed 8 February 2020).

McGlone, J. (n.d.), 'After the Dictator Falls: Tracing the Steps of Gruach', *Chicago Shakespeare Theater*. Available online: https://www.chicagoshakes.com/plays_and_events/dunsinane/dunsinan_after_the_dictator_falls (accessed 31 January 2020).

McMullan, G. (2016), 'The 'Strangeness' of George Oppen: Criticism, Modernity, and the Conditions of Late Style', in G. McMullan and S. Smiles (eds), *Late Style and Its Discontents: Essays in Art, Literature, and Music*, 31–47, Oxford: Oxford University Press.

McMullan, G. (2018), 'Constructing a Late Style for David Bowie: Old Age, Late-Life Creativity, Popular Culture', in D. Amigoni and G. McMullan (eds), *Creativity in Later Life: Beyond Late Style*, 61–76, London: Routledge.

Mendelson, E. (1977), 'The Caucasian Chalk Circle and Endgame', in M. Seidel and E. Mendelson (eds), Homer to Brecht: The European Epic and Dramatic Traditions, 336–52, New Haven, CT: Yale University Press.
Meštrović, S. G. (1997), Postemotional Society, London: Sage.
Middeke, M. (2017), 'The Inoperative Community and Death: Ontological Aspects of the Precarious in David Greig's The Events and Caryl Churchill's Here We Go', in M. Aragay and M. Middeke (eds), Of Precariousness: Vulnerabilities, Responsibilities, Communities in 21st-Century British Drama and Theatre, 217–33, Berlin: De Gruyter.
Mitchell, S. (1998), 'Introduction', in W. Benjamin, Understanding Brecht, trans. A. Bostock, vii–xix, London: Verso.
Monforte, E. (2007), 'Mark Ravenhill', in M. Aragay, H. Klein, E. Monforte and P. Zozaya (eds), British Theatre of the 1990s: Interviews with Directors, Playwrights, Critics and Academics, 91–104, Basingstoke: Palgrave.
Morin, E. (2011), '"Look Again": Indeterminacy and Contemporary British Drama', New Theatre Quarterly 27 (1): 71–85.
Müller, A., and C. Wallace (2011), 'Neutral Spaces & Transnational Encounters', in A. Müller and C. Wallace (eds), Cosmotopia: Transnational Identities in David Greig's Theatre, 1–13, Prague: Litteraria Pragensia.
Müller, K. P. (2002), 'Political Plays in England in the 1990s', in B. Reitz and M. Berninger (eds), British Drama of the 1990s, 15–36, Heidelberg: Winter.
Mumford, M. (2009), Bertolt Brecht, London: Routledge.
Myers, W. A. (2004), 'The Banality of Evil in an Age of Terrorism', in M. Sönser Breen (ed.), Truth, Reconciliation and Evil, 95–113, Amsterdam: Rodopi.
Nussbaum, M. (2001), Upheavals of Thought: The Intelligence of Emotions, Cambridge: Cambridge University Press.
Nuzzo, A. (2007), 'Dialectical Reason and Necessary Conflict: Understanding and the Nature of Terror', Cosmos and History: The Journal of Natural and Social Philosophy 3 (2–3): 291–307.
Ollman, B. (2008), 'Why Dialectics? Why Now?', in B. Ollman and T. Smith (eds), Dialectics for the New Century, 8–25, Basingstoke: Palgrave.
Ollman, B., and T. Smith (2008), 'Introduction', in B. Ollman and T. Smith (eds), Dialectics for the New Century, 1–7, Basingstoke: Palgrave.
Panagia, D. (2010), '"Partage du sensible": The Distribution of the Sensible', in J.-P. Deranty (ed.), Jacques Rancière: Key Concepts, 95–103, Durham: Acumen.
Panitch, L., and C. Leys (2001), The End of Parliamentary Socialism: From New Left to New Labour, 2nd edn, London: Verso.
Pattie, D. (2011), 'Scotland & Anywhere: The Theatre of David Greig', in A. Müller and C. Wallace (eds), Cosmotopia: Transnational Identities in David Greig's Theatre, 50–65, Prague: Litteraria Pragensia.
Pattie, D. (2016a), 'Dissolving into Scotland: National Identity in Dunsinane and The Strange Undoing of Prudencia Heart', Contemporary Theatre Review 26 (1): 19–30.

Pattie, D. (2016b), 'The Events: Immanence and the Audience', Journal of Contemporary Drama in English 4 (1): 49–60.
Pavis, P. (1998), Dictionary of the Theatre: Terms, Concepts, and Analysis, trans. C. Shantz, Toronto: University of Toronto Press.
Pavis, P. (2004), 'Ravenhill and Durringer, or the Entente Cordiale Misunderstood', trans. D. Bradby, Contemporary Theatre Review 14 (2): 4–16.
Pountain, D., and D. Robins (2000), Cool Rules: Anatomy of an Attitude, London: Reaktion.
Pratt, M. L. (1991), 'Arts of the Contact Zone', Profession: 33–40.
Price, V. E. (2018), '"Two Kingdoms … Compassed with One Sea": Reconstructing Kingdoms and Reclaiming Histories in David Greig's Dunsinane', International Journal of Scottish Theatre and Screen 5 (1): 19–32.
Puchner, M. (2002), Stage Fright: Modernism, Anti-Theatricality & Drama, Baltimore: Johns Hopkins University Press.
Puchner, M. (2010), The Drama of Ideas: Platonic Provocations in Theatre and Philosophy, Oxford: Oxford University Press.
Radosavljević, D. (2013), Theatre-Making: Interplay Between Text and Performance in the 21st Century, Basingstoke: Palgrave.
Rancière, J. (1999), Disagreement: Politics and Philosophy, trans. J. Rose, Minneapolis: University of Minnesota Press.
Rancière, J. (2004), The Politics of Aesthetics: The Distribution of the Sensible, ed. and trans. G. Rockhill, London: Bloomsbury.
Rancière, J. (2011), The Emancipated Spectator, trans. G. Elliott, London: Verso.
Ravenhill, M. (2001a), Shopping and Fucking, in M. Ravenhill, Plays: 1, 1–91, London: Bloomsbury.
Ravenhill, M. (2001b), Some Explicit Polaroids, in M. Ravenhill, Plays: 1, 227–314, London: Bloomsbury.
Ravenhill, M. (2008a), 'Don't Bash Brecht', Guardian, 26 May. Available online: https://www.theguardian.com/stage/theatreblog/2008/may/26/dontbashbrecht (accessed 7 February 2020).
Ravenhill, M. (2008b), 'My Near Death Period', Guardian, 26 March. Available online: https://www.theguardian.com/stage/2008/mar/26/theatre (accessed 8 February 2020).
Ravenhill, M. (2013), Shoot/Get Treasure/Repeat, in M. Ravenhill, Plays: 3, 1–253, London: Bloomsbury.
Ravenhill, M. (2015), 'Locating History on the Contemporary Stage', Journal of Contemporary Drama in English 3 (1): 156–73.
Ravenhill, M. (2016), 'Theatre and Democracy', Dramaturgs' Network, 23 October. Available online: https://www.dramaturgy.co.uk/copy-of-dramaturgy-papers-hanna-sla (accessed 7 February 2020).
Ray, G. (2010), 'Dialectical Realism and Radical Commitments: Brecht and Adorno on Representing Capitalism', Historical Materialism 18: 3–24.

Rayner, A. (1998), 'All Her Children: Caryl Churchill's Furious Ghosts', in S. Rabillard (ed.), *Essays on Caryl Churchill: Contemporary Representations*, 206–24, Winnipeg: Blizzard.
Rebellato, D. (2003), '"And I Will Reach Out My Hand with a Kind of Infinite Slowness and Say the Perfect Thing": The Utopian Theatre of Suspect Culture', *Contemporary Theatre Review* 13 (1): 61–80.
Rebellato, D. (2008), '"Because It Feels Fucking Amazing": Recent British Drama and Bodily Mutilation', in R. D'Monté and G. Saunders (eds), *Cool Britannia? British Political Drama in the 1990s*, 192–207, Basingstoke: Palgrave.
Rebellato, D. (2009), 'Introduction', in D. Greig, *Plays 1*, ix–xxiii, London: Methuen.
Rebellato, D. (2013a), 'Exit the Author', in V. Angelaki (ed.), *Contemporary British Theatre: Breaking New Ground*, 9–31, Basingstoke: Palgrave.
Rebellato, D. (2013b), 'Tim Crouch', in D. Rebellato (ed.), *Modern British Playwriting: 2000–2009 – Voices, Documents, New Interpretations*, 125–44, London: Bloomsbury.
Rebellato, D. (2013c), '*what happens to the hope at the end of the evening*', *Dan Rebellato*, 21 July. Available online: www.danrebellato.co.uk/spilledink/2013/7/15/what-happens-to-the-hope-at-the-end-of-the-evening (accessed 10 February 2020).
Rebellato, D. (2014), 'Two: Duologues and the Differend', in M. Aragay and E. Monforte (eds), *Ethical Speculations in Contemporary British Drama*, 79–95, Basingstoke: Palgrave.
Rebellato, D. (2015), 'Here We Go', *Dan Rebellato*, 2 December. Available online: http://www.danrebellato.co.uk/spilledink/2015/12/2/here-we-go (accessed 6 February 2020).
Rebellato, D. (2017), 'Of an Apocalyptic Tone Recently Adopted in Theatre: British Drama, Violence and Writing', *Sillages Critiques* 22. Available online: https://journals.openedition.org/sillagescritiques/4798 (accessed 18 February 2020).
Reid, T. (2013), *Theatre and Scotland*, Basingstoke: Palgrave.
Reid, T. (2019), 'The Dystopian Near-Future in Contemporary British Drama', *Journal of Contemporary Drama in English* 7 (1): 72–88.
Reinelt, J. (1996), *After Brecht: British Epic Theatre*, Ann Arbor: University of Michigan Press.
Revermann, M. (2013), 'Brechtian Chorality', in J. Billings, F. Budelmann and F. Macintosh (eds), *Choruses: Ancient and Modern*, 151–69, Oxford: Oxford University Press.
Ridout, N. (2009), *Theatre and Ethics*, Basingstoke: Palgrave.
Riedelsheimer, M. (2017), 'Vulnerability and the Community of the Precarious in David Greig's *The Events*', in M. Aragay and M. Middeke (eds), *Of Precariousness: Vulnerabilities, Responsibilities, Communities in 21st-Century British Drama and Theatre*, 203–16, Berlin: De Gruyter.
Robson, M. (2019), *Theatre and Death*, London: Red Globe Press.

Rodosthenous, G. (2015), 'Staring at the Forbidden: Legitimizing Voyeurism', in G. Rodosthenous (ed.), *Theatre as Voyeurism: The Pleasures of Watching*, 1–25, Basingstoke: Palgrave.

Rodríguez, V. (2019a), *David Greig's Holed Theatre: Globalization, Ethics and the Spectator*, Cham: Palgrave.

Rodríguez, V. (2019b), '"Who Would Disagree That in a World of Trump and Putin and Boris Johnson … Brecht Is Not the Theorist and Playwright of Our Times?": Bertolt Brecht's Influence on David Greig's Work', *Journal of Contemporary Drama in English* 7 (2): 242–58.

Rothe, M. (2018), 'Adorno's Brecht: The Other Origin of Negative Dialectics', in B. Best, W. Bonefeld and C. O'Kane (eds), *The SAGE Handbook of Frankfurt School Critical Theory*, 1038–54, Los Angeles: SAGE.

Ruprecht, L. (2015), 'Gesture, Interruption, Vibration: Rethinking Early Twentieth-Century Gestural Theory and Practice in Walter Benjamin, Rudolf von Laban, and Mary Wigman', *Dance Research Journal* 47 (2): 23–41.

Sakellaridou, E. (2014), '"Oh My God, Audience Participation!": Some Twenty-First-Century Reflections', *Comparative Drama* 48 (1 and 2): 13–38.

Sanders, J. (2006), *Adaptation and Appropriation*, London: Routledge.

Saunders, G. (2008), 'Introduction', in R. D'Monté and G. Saunders (eds), *Cool Britannia? British Political Drama in the 1990s*, 1–15, Basingstoke: Palgrave.

Saunders, G. (2017), *Elizabethan and Jacobean Reappropriation in Contemporary British Drama: 'Upstart Crows'*, Basingstoke: Palgrave.

Schulze, D. (2017), *Authenticity in Contemporary Theatre and Performance: Make It Real*, London: Bloomsbury.

Shakespeare, W. (2015), *Macbeth*, ed. S. Clark and P. Mason, London: Bloomsbury.

Sierz, A. (2001), *In-Yer-Face Theatre: British Drama Today*, London: Faber and Faber.

Sierz, A. (2004), '"To Recommend a Cure": Beyond Social Realism and In-Yer-Face Theatre', in H.-U. Mohr and K. Mächler (eds), *Extending the Code: New Forms of Dramatic and Theatrical Expression*, Trier: WVT.

Sierz, A. (2008), '"We All Need Stories": The Politics of In-Yer-Face Theatre', in R. D'Monté and G. Saunders (eds), *Cool Britannia? British Political Drama in the 1990s*, 23–37, Basingstoke: Palgrave.

Sierz, A. (2015a), 'Here We Go, National Theatre', *Aleks Sierz*, 19 December. Available online: http://www.sierz.co.uk/reviews/here-we-go-national-theatre/ (accessed 6 February 2020).

Sierz, A. (2015b), 'What Ever Happened to *In-Yer-Face* Theatre?', *Coup de théâtre* 26: 17–36.

Silberman, M., S. Giles and T. Kuhn (2015), 'General Introduction', in B. Brecht, *Brecht on Theatre*, 3rd rev. edn, M. Silberman, S. Giles and T. Kuhn (eds), 1–7, London: Bloomsbury.

Smith, A. (2011), 'Gentle Acts of Removal, Replacement and Reduction: Considering the Audience in Co-Directing the Work of Tim Crouch', *Contemporary Theatre Review* 21 (4): 410–15.
Smith, A. (2015a), 'Afterwards', in A. Smith, *The Preston Bill*, 88–92, London: Oberon.
Smith, A. (2015b), *all that is solid melts into air*, in A. Smith, *The Preston Bill*, 63–86, London: Oberon.
Smith, A. (2015c), 'What Can We Do?', in C. Svich (ed.), *Innovation in Five Acts: Strategies for Theatre and Performance*, 55–8, New York: Theatre Communications Group.
Smith, A. (2017), 'Being Patient with What We Don't Understand', *The Lark*, 14 April. Available online: https://www.larktheatre.org/blog/being-patient-what-we-dont-understand/ (accessed 10 February 2020).
Solga, K. (2016), *Theatre and Feminism*, Basingstoke: Palgrave.
Spencer, J. (2012), 'Terrorized by the War on Terror: Mark Ravenhill's *Shoot/Get Treasure/Repeat*', in J. Spencer (ed.), *Political and Protest Theatre after 9/11: Patriotic Dissent*, 63–78, New York: Routledge.
Stevens, L. (2016), *Anti-War Theatre after Brecht: Dialectical Aesthetics in the Twenty-First Century*, Basingstoke: Palgrave.
Stevenson, R. (2004), *The Last of England?*, vol. 12 of *The Oxford English Literary History*, Oxford: Oxford University Press.
Suvin, D. (1979), *Metamorphoses of Science Fiction: On the Poetics and History of a Literary Genre*, New Haven: Yale University Press.
Svich, C. (2003), 'Commerce and Morality in the Theatre of Mark Ravenhill', *Contemporary Theatre Review* 13 (1): 81–95.
Svich, C. (2011), 'Mark Ravenhill', in M. Middeke, P. P. Schnierer and A. Sierz (eds), *The Methuen Drama Guide to Contemporary British Playwrights*, 403–24, London: Bloomsbury.
Taxidou, O. (2004), *Tragedy, Modernity, and Mourning*, Edinburgh: Edinburgh University Press.
Taylor, D. (2009), 'War Play', *PMLA* 124 (5): 1886–95.
Taylor, P. (2015), 'This Is Unforgettable', *Independent*, 30 November. Available online: https://www.independent.co.uk/arts-entertainment/theatre-dance/reviews/here-we-go-national-theatre-review-this-is-unforgettable-a6754436.html (accessed 6 February 2020).
Thomaidis, K. (2018), 'Voice: Performance and Forensics', in E. Bryon (ed.), *Performing Interdisciplinarity: Working across Disciplinary Boundaries through an Active Aesthetics*, 219–36, Abingdon: Routledge.
Tiedemann, R. (2008), 'Editor's Foreword', in T. W. Adorno, *Lectures on Negative Dialectics: Fragments of a Course 1965/1966*, ed. R. Tiedemann, trans. R. Livingstone, xi–xix, Cambridge: Polity.
Tomlin, L. (2008), 'Beyond Cynicism: The Sceptical Imperative and (Future) Contemporary Performance', *Contemporary Theatre Review* 18 (3): 355–69.

Tomlin, L. (2013), *Acts and Apparitions: Discourses on the Real in Performance Practice and Theory, 1990–2010*, Manchester: Manchester University Press.
Tomlin, L. (2019), *Political Dramaturgies and Theatre Spectatorship: Provocations for Change*, London: Bloomsbury.
Trencsényi, K. (2015), *Dramaturgy in the Making: A User's Guide for Theatre Practitioners*, London: Bloomsbury.
Treneman, A. (2019), 'Total Immediate Collective Imminent Terrestrial Salvation Review – The End Is Nigh, But Who Cares?', *Times*, 8 August. Available online: https://www.thetimes.co.uk/article/total-immediate-collective-imminent-terrestrial-salvation-review-the-end-is-nigh-but-who-cares-ztsqc0nq8 (accessed 11 February 2020).
Trilling, L. (1972), *Sincerity and Authenticity*, Oxford: Oxford University Press.
Trueman, M. (2016a), 'James Macdonald on Caryl Churchill's "Escaped Alone": "I'm Drawn to Plays I Don't Know How to Do"', *Independent*, 18 January. Available online: https://www.independent.co.uk/arts-entertainment/theatre-dance/features/james-macdonald-on-caryl-churchills-escaped-alone-im-drawn-to-plays-i-dont-know-how-to-do-a6819916.html (accessed 4 February 2020).
Trueman, M. (2016b), 'Caryl Churchill's "Escaped Alone"', *Variety*, 29 January. Available online: https://variety.com/2016/legit/reviews/escaped-alone-review-caryl-churchill-1201692064/ (accessed 5 February 2020).
Urban, K. (2004), 'Towards a Theory of Cruel Britannia: Coolness, Cruelty, and the 'Nineties', *New Theatre Quarterly* 20 (4): 354–72.
Wallace, C. (2005), 'Responsibility and Postmodernity: Mark Ravenhill and 1990s British Drama', *Theory and Practice in English Studies* 4: 269–75.
Wallace, C. (2011), 'Unfinished Business – Allegories of Otherness in *Dunsinane*', in A. Müller and C. Wallace (eds), *Cosmotopia: Transnational Identities in David Greig's Theatre*, 196–213, Prague: Litteraria Pragensia.
Wallace, C. (2012), 'Uncertain Convictions and the Politics of Perception', in M. Berninger and B. Reitz (eds), *Ethical Debates in Contemporary Theatre and Drama*, 55–64, Trier: WVT.
Wallace, C. (2013), *The Theatre of David Greig*, London: Bloomsbury.
Wallace, C. (2016), 'Yes and No? Dissensus and David Greig's Recent Work', *Contemporary Theatre Review* 26 (1): 31–8.
Watson, A. (2014), 'Birnam Wood: Scotland, Nationalism, and Theatres of War', *Theatre History Studies* 33: 226–49.
Weinstock, J. A. (2004), 'The Spectral Turn', in J. A. Weinstock (ed.), *Spectral America: Phantoms and the National Imagination*, 3–17, Madison: University of Wisconsin Press.
Wessendorf, M. (2011), '"Fear and Misery" Post-9/11: Mark Ravenhill's *Shoot/Get Treasure/Repeat*', in M. Wessendorf and F. J. Weidauer (eds), *Brecht in/and Asia – Brecht in/und Asien*, 336–51, Madison: University of Wisconsin Press.

White, G. (2013), *Audience Participation in Theatre: Aesthetics of the Invitation*, Basingstoke: Palgrave.
Willett, J. (1990), 'Ups and Downs of British Brecht', in P. Kleber and C. Visser (eds), *Re-Interpreting Brecht: His Influence on Contemporary Drama and Film*, 76–89, Cambridge: Cambridge University Press.
Willett, J. (1997), 'Introduction', in B. Brecht, *Collected Plays: Three*, ed. J. Willett, ix–xvi, London: Bloomsbury.
Wood, M. (2018), 'A Future for the *Lehrstück*? Andre Veiel and Gesina Schmidt's *Der Kick* and the Recycling of Form', in T. Kuhn, D. Barnett and T. F. Rippey (eds), *Recycling Brecht*, 171–85, Rochester, NY: Camden House.
Woolf, B. (2013), 'Towards a Paradoxically Parallaxical Postdramatic Politics?', in K. Jürs-Munby, J. Carroll and S. Giles (eds), *Postdramatic Theatre and the Political: International Perspectives on Contemporary Performance*, 31–46, London: Bloomsbury.
Zapf, H. (1988), *Das Drama in der abstrakten Gesellschaft: Zur Theorie und Struktur des modernen englischen Dramas*, Tübingen: Niemeyer.
Zaroulia, M. (2016), '"I Am a Blankness out of Which Emerges Only Darkness": Impressions and Aporias of Multiculturalism in *The Events*', *Contemporary Theatre Review* 26 (1): 71–81.
Zulaika, J., and W. A. Douglass (1996), *Terror and Taboo: The Follies, Fables, and Faces of Terrorism*, New York: Routledge.

Index

absurd 26–8, 131–7, 141–2, 148,
  151–2, 155, 161, 163, 165–6, 169
  See also Beckett, Samuel;
    Esslin, Martin
adaptation 1, 9, 12, 20, 56, 70, 77–9,
  99, 109
  rhizomatic 77
  See also appropriation
Adiseshiah, Siân 103–4, 112, 137
Adorno, Theodor W./Adornian 14–16,
  18–20, 22, 26–7, 40, 64–6, 99,
  128, 133–5, 137–8, 150, 152, 156,
  164, 166, 168–9
  'Commitment' 15
  'Trying to Understand
    Endgame' 134
  See also dialectics/dialectical;
    negativity
amateur theatre/amateurism 26, 83,
  93–7, 99, 107, 123, 170
Anderson, Benedict 67
Angelaki, Vicky 120, 132, 136, 143–4,
  147, 158
apocalypse/apocalyptic 135–6, 138,
  140–4, 147–8, 166
appropriation 16, 27, 48, 51, 66–7, 70,
  74, 76–9, 81–2, 99
  See also adaptation
Arendt, Hannah 47–8, 64
Aston, Elaine 131–2, 141, 143–5, 151

banality of evil 47–8
  See also Arendt, Hannah
Barnett, David 4, 7–9, 13–4, 20–2,
  24–5, 32, 35, 69, 84–5, 87, 107–9
Baudrillard, Jean 19
Bauman, Zygmunt 105
Beckett, Samuel 27, 132–5, 142, 150,
  152, 154, 156, 161, 166, 169

Endgame 134
Waiting for Godot 150
  See also absurd
Benjamin, Walter 9–10, 51–2, 90,
  108, 149–51
  'The Storyteller' 108
Berlant, Lauren 34
Berliner Ensemble 3, 56
Bhabha, Homi K. 67
Billington, Michael 1
Blair, Tony 34
Bond, Edward 3, 26
bourgeoisie/bourgeois theatre
  35, 50, 84
Brecht, Bertolt
  *Fear and Misery of the Third
    Reich* 41
  'Freedom and Democracy' 50
  The Good Person of Szechwan
    31, 171
  'Messingkauf, or Buying Brass' 68,
    106–8, 129
  The Mother 6
  'In Praise of Dialectics' 6
  The Resistible Rise of Arturo Ui 31
Brenton, Howard 3
Butler, Judith 48

Carney, Sean 5, 12, 14–16, 38–40,
  149, 151
choir 83, 86, 88, 91–8, 123
chorus 44, 54–7, 59–60, 71, 92
chrononormativity/chrononormative
  145, 148
Churchill, Caryl 3, 26–8, 131–66, 169
  Blue Heart 131
  Cloud 9 131, 135–6
  Ding Dong the Wicked 160
  Escaped Alone 27, 136–52, 166

Far Away 136, 142
Heart's Desire 160
Here We Go 27, 136, 152–66
Mad Forest 131
Serious Money 131
Softcops 131
This Is a Chair 131–2
Top Girls 131, 135–6
contradiction 5–8, 10, 12, 14–16, 18, 20, 22–3, 27–8, 30, 32–5, 37, 46–7, 49–50, 61, 64, 73–5, 81–2, 91, 94, 98–9, 109, 113, 117–8, 128, 148–53, 156, 159, 163, 165–8
See also dialectics/dialectical
Cool Britannia 31–4, 39, 41, 61
counterterrorism
See terrorism
Crouch, Tim 26–7, 101–4, 117–130, 170
Adler & Gibb 102
The Author 101–2, 117–30
ENGLAND 101–2
Total Immediate Collective Imminent Terrestrial Salvation 101
what happens to the hope at the end of the evening 101 (*see also* Smith, Andy)
Cummings, Lindsay B. 10, 84, 90

deconstruction 164–5
dematerialised 101
See also Crouch, Tim; Smith, Andy
Derrida, Jacques 163–6
de Waal, Ariane 42–4, 47, 49, 55, 58, 60
dialectics/dialectical
anti-dialectical 12–14, 18, 22, 29, 34, 47–9, 58, 168
materialism 5, 13, 164
meta-dialectical 23, 32, 35–6, 40
negative 14–15, 18–19, 27, 64–5, 128, 134, 149–50, 152, 166

at a standstill 52, 148–51 (*see also* Benjamin, Walter)
Diamond, Elin 7, 10, 131
dissensus 17–8, 24, 27, 40, 49, 56, 61, 63, 65, 70, 78, 81, 83, 98, 115, 129
distribution of the sensible 17, 148
Dolan, Jill 139
dystopia/dystopian 136–48, 151–2, 166

emancipated spectatorship 24–5, 54, 93, 96–7, 169
empathy/empathetic 27, 80, 82–6, 90, 98–9, 170
Engels, Friedrich 105, 164
epic theatre 3–6, 9–10, 12, 15, 20, 26, 107, 133, 135, 140–1, 149–51, 167
Esslin, Martin 134, 167
See also absurd
experiential 25, 30, 32, 37, 41, 49–50, 53, 56–7, 96, 99, 108, 114, 141, 151, 154, 156, 166, 169

Fabel 108–9
Foucault, Michel 42, 49
Freeman, Elizabeth 145

gestus/gestic 10, 39, 50–2, 92, 131, 139, 149, 162, 165
gestic music 92–3
globalization 12, 27, 63–4, 82, 89, 98, 105
Goode, Chris 105, 121, 124
Greig, David 26, 63–99, 123, 170
Dunsinane 27, 66–82, 99
The Events 27, 82–99, 123
'Rough Theatre' 64, 66, 83, 93
The Speculator 63–4
Griffiths, Trevor 3
Gritzner, Karoline 15–16, 65, 134
Gupta, Tanika 1

Hare, David 3
Harris, Zinnie 26

Harrower, David 1
Harvie, Jen 67, 141–8
Hegel, Georg W. F. 5, 164
  See also dialectics/dialectical
historicization 35–6, 66, 77, 148,
  166, 170
meta-historicization 77
history play 63, 77
Hutcheon, Linda 74, 77–9

Illouz, Eva 38
imagination/imaginative 26–7, 56–7,
  63–99, 109, 113, 119, 122, 126,
  131, 137, 140, 170
insincerity 55, 117–130, 170
  See also sincerity
interruption 9–10, 19, 27, 33, 38,
  51–2, 90, 94, 139, 149, 157
intimacy 37, 71, 94, 103, 113–15, 122
in-yer-ear theatre 57
in-yer-face theatre 21, 26, 29–31,
  41, 169
irrationality/irrational 26, 65–6, 92, 99
  See also Adorno, Theodor W.

Jameson, Fredric 7, 12–3, 19

Kane, Sarah 29
Krabiel, Klaus-Dieter 92
Kritzer, Amelia Howe 1, 39, 132

Laclau, Ernesto
  See relational antagonism
Lanier, Douglas 77
late style 132–3
Lehmann, Hans-Thies 19, 85, 94, 112,
  135, 160, 162
Lehrstück 56, 82, 85–7, 92, 95–6, 99,
  107–8, 170
Lyotard, François 13

Marxism/Marxist 1, 4–5, 13, 60,
  105–6, 134, 164
Marx, Karl 5, 105

McGrath, John 3, 105
McMullan, Gordon 132
Meštrović, Stjepan G. 38
metatheatricality/metatheatrical 8, 23,
  27, 31, 49, 56–7, 60–1, 101–102,
  104, 108, 112–13, 118, 120–1,
  129, 141, 170
Middeke, Martin 83, 89, 94, 98, 154–5,
  158, 160–1, 163
mimesis/mimetic 101, 108, 119, 123
minimalism/minimalist 87, 101, 109,
  111, 119, 122, 132, 152
mise-en-abyme 104, 119
Mouffe, Chantal
  See relational antagonism

naivety (Brechtian) 101, 103, 107–8,
  110–13, 115–17, 119, 121, 129
National Theatre 152, 161–2
negative dialectics
  See *under* dialectics/dialectical
negativity 15–6, 28, 40–1, 49, 134–8,
  140–1, 145, 149–50, 156, 164–6,
  168–9, 171
Neilson, Anthony 29
neoliberalism 1, 12–13, 16, 38–9, 64,
  102, 151

parable/parabolic 31–2, 35–6, 40–1,
  44, 61, 135, 167
participation/participatory 11–12,
  47–8, 53–4, 56–8, 69, 76, 78, 85,
  91–2, 95–7, 99, 104, 108, 114–5,
  121–2, 124–9, 170
Pattie, David 72, 81, 91, 96–7
Pavis, Patrice 32, 39, 92
police (Rancièrean) 17–8, 33
political theatre 1–5, 14, 18–19, 23,
  27, 31, 35, 37, 40, 61, 66, 70,
  102–3, 106, 116, 130–1, 133, 135,
  152, 166
politics (Rancièrean) 16–19, 22, 168
post-Brechtian 1, 4, 14–5, 20–8,
  30–2, 36–7, 40, 42, 49, 52, 54,

58, 61, 64, 66, 68–70, 74, 77–9, 82, 87, 90 98–102, 104, 113, 117–18, 123, 127–9, 132, 135–6, 140, 142, 148, 152, 159, 162, 165–6, 168–71
postdramatic 21, 112, 155, 160–1
  See also Lehmann, Hans-Thies
postmodernism 1, 12–14, 18–20, 23, 27, 77, 102–3, 105, 129, 137, 145, 168, 170
Pratt, Mary Louise 67
Prebble, Lucy 26
provocation 26, 29–32, 40, 42, 50–6, 61, 84–5, 102, 104–5, 119, 121, 124–9, 156, 161, 169
Puchner, Martin 107

Rancière, Jacques 16–19, 22, 24–5, 33–4, 40, 54, 56–7, 65, 81, 96, 98, 129, 146, 148, 159, 161, 163, 168–9
Ravenhill, Mark 1, 26, 29–62, 169
  Shoot/Get Treasure/Repeat 26, 41–62
  Shopping and Fucking 31, 33
  Some Explicit Polaroids 26, 31–41, 61
realism 8–9, 32, 51, 119, 153
Rebellato, Dan 38, 40, 44, 64–5, 82, 111, 127, 136, 141, 144, 152–5
Reid, Trish 68, 75, 147, 151
Reinelt, Janelle 3–4, 26, 131
relational antagonism 115, 117
repetition 50–1, 97, 111, 159–62
Ridout, Nicholas 85, 95, 123
Royal Court Theatre 127, 136, 138, 141

Sanders, Julie 70
Saunders, Graham 29, 68, 70
self-reflexivity/self-reflexive 8, 10–11, 19, 23, 27, 31–2, 37, 40–1, 56–62, 70, 76–7, 87, 90, 95–6, 101–130, 135, 137, 161–2, 165, 168, 170
separation of the elements 10
Shakespeare, William 6

Macbeth 27, 66–81, 99
shock 29, 31, 40, 50–2, 56, 119, 151, 169
Sierz, Aleks 29–31, 161
sincerity 27, 60, 101–30, 170
  See also insincerity
Smith, Andy 26–7, 101–20, 122, 129–30, 170
  all that is solid melts into air 27, 104–22, 127, 129
  The Preston Bill 102
  Summit 102
  what happens to the hope at the end of the evening 101 (*see also* Crouch, Tim)
socialist feminism 131, 136, 169
  See also Churchill, Caryl
spectrality 156–7, 159, 163–6
Spencer, Jenny 50, 53, 56
Stephens, Simon 1
Stevens, Lara 5, 7–8, 13–21, 23–5, 42, 96
storytelling 68, 75–7, 108–13, 119–21

terrorism/counterterrorism 41–61, 89, 99
Thatcher, Margaret 1, 3, 33
Tomlin, Liz 13–14, 109, 112
Trilling, Lionel 103
tucker green, debbie 26

utopia/utopian 13, 65, 137–40, 150, 156

Verfremdung (making the familiar strange) 7–9, 27, 36, 51, 66–71, 73, 78–9, 90, 92, 99, 102, 107, 111, 118, 121, 127–9, 132, 136–7, 140–2, 145, 147, 151–2, 156, 159, 162, 165–6, 170
voyeurism 29, 53–4, 119

Wallace, Clare 29, 64–8, 75, 82, 87, 98, 122

Zaroulia, Marilena 83, 88–90, 98

www.ingramcontent.com/pod-product-compliance
Lightning Source LLC
Chambersburg PA
CBHW070638300426
44111CB00013B/2155